ARBOREAL

A COLLECTION OF NEW WOODLAND WRITING

EDITED BY
ADRIAN COOPER

Little Toller Books

Published by Little Toller Books in 2016
Lower Dairy, Toller Fratrum, Dorset

Typeset by Little Toller Books

Printed by TJ International, Cornwall, Padstow

All papers used by Little Toller Books are natural, recyclable products made from wood
grown in sustainable, well-managed forests

A catalogue record for this book is available from the British Library

ISBN 978-1-908213-41-9

01

Contents

Introduction SOUTH MEAD COPPICE *Adrian Cooper* 9

Inshriach INSHRIACH BOTHY *Kathleen Jamie* 17

Birdsong HANNAH'S WOOD *Jay Griffiths* 19

Another Look at Glennamong NEPHIN BEG *Seán Lysaght* 29

Hidden Places THE LINCOLNSHIRE WOLDS *Fiona Stafford* 37

Arborotopia NEW FOREST *Philip Hoare* 42

Chanterelles PANKHURST FOREST *Evie Wyld* 53

Why Woods Matter BADBY WOODS *Fiona Reynolds* 67

Forest of Eyes BURNHAM BEECHES *Paul Kingsnorth* 76

Speaking Wood CAE'N-Y-COED *David Nash* 81

Princess Forest COILLE NA BANA-PHRIONNSA *Alec Finlay* 87

Medieval Survivor CHALKNEY WOOD *Simon Leatherdale* 92

Don't Look Back PILES COPSE *Gabriel Hemery* 97

Thinning KINGSETTLE WOOD *Robin Walter* 106

The Ramsbury Elm RAMSBURY VILLAGE *Peter Marren* 116

Two Storms TEDWORTH SQUARE *William Boyd* 126

Sand Forest TENTSMUIR FOREST *Jim Crumley* 131

Wood Woes UP THE FOREST! *Sue Clifford* 139

Ash FARNLEY ESTATE *Simon Armitage* 153

Nine Oaks CURRIDGE VILLAGE *Adam Thorpe* 154

Trunk SPINNEY WOOD *Jackie Kay* 156

City, Trees, Water   AVON GORGE   *Helen Dunmore*   161

Return to Ruskin Land   WYRE FOREST   *Neil Sinden*   167

Heartwood   WINDSOR HILL WOOD   *Tobias Jones*   182

Cusop Dingle   DULAS BROOK   *Nina Lyon*   188

The Gypsy Stone   EPPING FOREST   *Will Ashon*   194

The Green Stuff   WANDLEBURY WOOD   *Ali Smith*   206

Forest Fear   WOOD OF CREE   *Sara Maitland*   212

Thwaite   ULPHA FELL   *Richard Skelton*   221

On the 7.46   SHREWSBURY TO CREWE   *Paul Evans*   225

Alison   WEST SUSSEX DOWNS   *Madeleine Bunting*   233

Yggdrasil in Shetland   LEA GARDENS   *Jen Hadfield*   237

What is a Tree?   STUMP CROSS   *Germaine Greer*   246

Laburnum Time   B13   *Zaffar Kunial*   256

The Common Dean   THE EDGE   *Alan Garner*   268

Searching for Natural Woodland   LADY PARK   *George Peterken*   277

Woodcock   WICKEN FEN   *Tim Dee*   287

Taking Root   MOONSHINE WOOD   *Piers Taylor*   294

Discovering the Spinney   SPINNEY WOOD   *Deb Wilenski*   303

Rackham's Treasure   MERTHEN WOOD   *Philip Marsden*   312

Still Lives   BERKHAMSTED COMMON   *Richard Mabey*   321

Notes on Contributors   329

In memory of
Oliver Rackham

Introduction

SOUTH MEAD COPPICE, DORSET

Adrian Cooper

I felt at odds queuing at the post office, back in the summer of 2013, holding a cardboard box with Oliver Rackham's walking boots inside. By the time it was my turn to plant the package on the counter – *First class, please, Cambridge, Corpus Christi College* – I wasn't sure whether the book we were developing together, what later became *The Ash Tree*, was quite working. He'd been visiting us to deliver photographs and to discuss the first draft, and after lunch, while the taxi bustled Oliver away to the train station in his sandals, I started to feel uncertain about his approach to a particular chapter on the cultural history of ash, which I'd hoped would explore the artists and writers who'd responded to the nature of the tree. That's when I noticed his boots were left behind in the office, and my thoughts turned to the miles of ground they'd covered (in Dorset, Cambridge, Crete, Texas), the man and books they'd supported.

The works I'd most enjoyed publishing, until then, were illustrated with engravings, line drawings, paintings or photographs which, to my mind, expressed the essence of the book. Yet, in the early drafts of *The Ash Tree*, I felt that my task was to coax Oliver towards John Constable's Hampstead sketches, David Nash's living-ash sculptures at Cae'n-y-Coed, or John Clare's 'hollow ash', Edward Thomas' Llwyn Onn ('Ash Grove'), and even Yggdrasil, the world tree, of *Poetic Edda*. There were plenty of photographs taken by Oliver himself over decades of research, hand-picked from his collection. But must *every* image in the book illustrate a point raised in the text?

Plucking up courage, I confronted him. His response was to email a table of: 'The more commonly-mentioned trees in the works of literary writers', which compared how many times different tree species – oak, pine, yew, willow, hazel, beech, elm, poplar, cedar, cypress, holly, birch, lime – were mentioned in literary works, first by Shakespeare (one ash tree) then Wordsworth (thirteen ash trees), Tennyson (nine ash trees) and Yeats (sixteen ash trees). While this was not quite what I had in mind, it was something to build on, and when *The Ash Tree* went to press a year later, most of the suggestions I'd lobbied for were included. But this was no victory of publisher's will or taste; in the finished book, the sections on 'literary ash' and 'ash in art' occupy only four pages, in which Oliver insists on reminding the reader: 'No painting, drawing or photograph of a big tree can be naturalistic.'

On the surface, this is an obvious thing to say – put to mind a mature ash, with those complexities of branch and leaf, every wooded angle rich with the stories of the local environment which nurtured its growth. So yes, trees are difficult to draw. A complete woodland, therefore, will never be seen, even with drones now able to map every tree. But as with the many things he wrote, the simplicity of the prose quietly went to work challenging my preconceptions, even my feelings of attachment to particular trees or woods, changing fundamentally the way I understood landscape.

Knowingly or not, Oliver was teaching me to think about woodlands as dynamic places, living societies that support other living societies of plants and mammals, birds and micro-organisms. Of course, this is not to say that we shouldn't appreciate trees and woods, forming our own bonds through walking, making art, poetry, music, new architecture or social projects. It does mean, however, that what we understand about trees and woods will never form a complete picture.

Trees, like all wildlife, are autonomous, outside of our understanding and control. We are certainly neighbours, but not always very good ones. Human intervention in any landscape, like the management of woodland, can enrich both human communities and wildlife habitats. But we don't have to look far from our own doorsteps to discover these interventions are driven by human needs, and do not absorb the nuance that Oliver argued for. Neither do we need to look very far back over our shoulder, into the past, to be reminded that almost half of the ancient woodland in the British Isles was either felled or poisoned between 1933 and 1983, the work of policymakers and landowners reacting to ideas and needs of the time. As is true of anything in nature, trees aren't just the subject-matter of poets and artists, nor just a utility for burning or building, and they do not grow for ecologists to write about and so publishers have paper to print on.

On the day of his death, 12 February 2015, those boots I'd posted to him in Cambridge came back to mind. I was no longer thinking about the ground they must have walked. Instead, I wondered whether anybody could possibly fill them.

This book seeded while I stood in that post office queue, and took delicate root in the weeks after his death. But it is not an attempt to fill Oliver's boots, and nor does it continue anything particular about his work or life. (I also doubt that he would have been pleased to know of such a book, written in tribute: his own voice was distinct and clear enough.) Yet the very first page of *Arboreal* bears his name because the book is driven by a hope that, without Oliver Rackham, there will continue to be people who speak out for trees and woods; interpreters of the natural world who remind us of the complexities and demand sensitivity when we do intervene, as we inevitably do, leaving our marks on the land.

This hope has been nourished into growth by the pioneering work that Sue Clifford and Angela King began with Common Ground's band of collaborators back in 1986 (I was a ten-year-old, not even a resident of the UK), when the project 'Trees, Woods and the Green Man' began to explore the natural and cultural value of trees, with pamphlets, plays, books, newspapers and art exhibitions. This is why a small selection of the work of those collaborators – Andy Goldsworthy's sculpture, James Ravilious' photography, David Nash's charcoal drawings, Kathleen Basford's Green Man archive – appear through the book, acting as unannounced clearings amongst the words. They also tell their own story, illustrating the rich and enduring purpose of Common Ground's work, which, over three decades, has consistently challenged the growing estrangement between people and nature with imagination and activism.

Today, there is certainly a story of estrangement to confront in our relationship with woodlands. A century ago, along with hedgerows and orchards, woods began drifting away from parish life, becoming less essential for heat, food and shelter. The arrival of cheap coal, imports of Scandinavian timber, and improved transport across the British Isles, followed by the felling and ploughing-up of ancient woods during the First World War, meant that by the 1920s a majority of small, deciduous woods were becoming redundant to community life. Woodland culture began to vanish – the coppice and underwood crafts, the charcoal-makers, bodgers, the wheelwrights, boat-builders and cloth-dyers, all of which have their techniques and traditions in pre-history.

Yet here, in the twenty-first century, this distance from our day-to-day lives can seem slight. Think back to October 2010: the Conservative Government announced a consultation to 'reform the public forestry estate', the 'Big Society' shift away from state ownership and 'a greater role for private and civil society partners'. The idea, a 'forest sell-off' as the *Guardian* and *The Telegraph* had it, met with a great upswell of rejection, an outcry so wide and resounding that just four months later the proposal was abandoned. A similar public reaction followed the Great Storm of 1987, when, after the apparent loss of 15 million trees overnight, the public mourning did not stop the fallen or tilted trees – assumed dangerous or dead – being chopped up rather then left alone to keep living.

This combination of estrangement and affection is curious. On the one hand, we are able to stop a government in its tracks when they 'sell off' something that we feel attached to. On the other, we have spent over a century spending less time being in the woods, and as a consequence surely think less about what they are for and what they mean.

The majority of us do not own woodlands nor earn our living by them, yet it seems that the trees and the woods still inhabit us. I have several in me. There are memory forests, imagined or barely remembered places, and there are others which are living and very much alive, like the beech woodland in the Chilterns with its ancient boundaries still visible as humps in the shade, and a swilly hole that even now I imagine will swallow me up. There is also a plantation of Sitka spruce, the first place I rented in rural England, where the quality of light never seemed to change, that veil of blue-browns, except on autumn mornings when sunlight smoked through the high branches, translated as halos of white on the needle floor, and when the snowdrops announced themselves as a little miracle resisting the monoculture. Today, there is South Mead, a sloping hazel coppice on our doorstep, unused for at least fifty years, now pocked with setts, dens and burrows. It's a narrow corridor where our children have discovered for themselves that time warps in woodland, becomes elasticated, lasting much longer than out in open ground. There are probably more woods, too, if I go further back to count places like the Nairobi Arboretum near my boyhood home, with its gangs of vervet monkeys that dismantled the suburban hush with claws on corrugated rooftops.

We may be able to move through woodland, or climb up the branches of a particular tree, but it is the woods and trees which move into us, become entangled in our memories, taking root in our language. This is why the stories in this collection are personal and located, most often in real, living woodlands named on maps, although some are metaphorical places, memory forests, even fictitious. My hope is that the variety of voices gathered here, the writers, woodland ecologists, architects, artists, foresters and teachers, all of whom have harvested their own experience in the woods, combine to speak with the complexity and nuance that Oliver Rackham would have appreciated.

I also hope this breadth argues that trees and woods need not be exclusive, and that we should be widening access to some of the 47 per cent of woodlands that, according to Forestry Commission, 'remain unmanaged or under-managed . . . in private ownership' (about 1.5 million hectares of the United Kingdom). This situation has improved since the creation of the Forestry Commission in 1919, when access to woods first started to widen. More recently, the promises of the Localism Act 2011 should also give communities the opportunity to buy 'assets of community value', making it possible for woodlands to be looked after by small groups of people or local organisations, rather than individual landowners or big companies.

There is still much to learn about how to improve access for all, but community woodlands and social forestry initiatives are now spreading across England, and have been longer-established in Scotland and Wales. These woodland groups vary from place to place, from wood to wood, but generally begin with people getting together to buy, lease or borrow woodland from local landowners, wildlife trusts or the Forestry Commission. And this wider variety of people, now able to access and manage local woods for themselves, has meant the growth of new ideas about woodland practice. Wildlife conservation, woodfuel and timber for joinery are all still good reasons to manage woods, but a shift in *who* manages them also means a shift in *what* woods are managed for. Community healthcare projects, apprenticeships, firewood allotments, artistic practice, architectural education and Forest Schools are appearing all over the UK, creating new community spaces which, with sensitive and meaningful management, are bringing woodlands closer to the everyday lives of more people.

Imagination will always be one of the most powerful tools we have to counter estrangement, in the relationships we have with each other and the natural world. But so too is proximity. If we have contact with woods, the trees inhabit us. This transformative power is essential, and will continue to be so, no matter where you come from in the British Isles, whether you are rich or poor, young or old, and so long as there are hedges, spinneys, groves, thickets, hursts, holts and copses growing into the earth and towards the sun. Trees and woods absorb our restless activities, capture our imagination, not to mention our carbon dioxide, and all the while grow and fall, shake off leaves and regrow them again, living autonomous lives as they soak into us, becoming valuable characters in the places we live, sustaining and enriching nearby life, becoming part of who we are.

Inshriach

INSHRIACH BOTHY, CAIRNGORM NATIONAL PARK

Kathleen Jamie

This clearing in the wildwood –
        just as good as anywhere.

Frost-breath rises
        from the heathery floor.

A woodpecker drums
        that just flew between two birches.

Spangles on birch-twigs
        as the sun breaks through.

Through ancient pinewood
        the gleam of snow mountains.

Below the pines, a river
        winding from the snow.

With its glance, a breeze favours
        this pine-branch, not that.

Now that pine-bough wafts,
        though not now this.

From wraiths of juniper
        wren-song sparkles.

Fungus hooves harden
        on fallen trunks.

Heaving a pine-needle
        one ant, like a penitent.

Two cock chaffinches
        tussle in mid-air.

From a bed of moss, leaf-litter,
                    wintery heather

I gaze up through the branches
                    of my guardian birch.

The white clouds pass
                    way beyond the tree tops

making me a child again,
                    responsible for nought.

Night, the trees stand dark
                    as though switched off at the mains.

Badgers, in the small hours
                    topple our empty bottles.

May Day brings a lambing storm:
                    snow on the forest floor;

The stone out-staring the sky
                    blinks slowly white, then thaws.

Birdsong

HANNAH'S WOOD, HEART OF WALES

Jay Griffiths

I am thirsty for this music. I lean nearer. The tiny twig of a tail juts up – the wren stops. I freeze. He sings again. It is as if my listening is stretching out through my fingers to hear more nearly this mini-Paganini, the chanterelle of birds to me, the sweetest, highest string of the violin. (Its vocal range is one of the highest-pitched of birds, singing up to one full octave above the top note of a piano keyboard.)

My ears, though, are perplexed by him. I cannot hear fast enough to keep up, so the last notes of his cadence fall silent before I have properly heard the first, and by the time I deeply hear his song, he has already finished. If starlight is emitted light years ago, and we may only see it after a star has ceased to shine, so I seem to hear this bird only after it has ceased to sing, its song emitted just sound-seconds ago but always uncatchable.

It is both fleet and fleeting, fast and evanescent. Quick and quickening, it touches the quick of the spirit, in the acuteness of time. It quickens the woodlands with liveliness, as to be quick also means to be alive, germinating its seedling songs in the leaves, inseminating the air.

Dawn in the woods. A little riff-raff of sparrows chitter in the hedge. Blue tits and great tits chip in a divertimento in hemidemisemiquavers. The crow's croak cauls around the dark branch. A robin fills its little red sail with wind and sails into the day. All keel, no anchor. (Not solely a metaphor, that: a bird's flight muscles are attached to what is called a keel bone.)

As soon as I hear it, I want to describe it, as if once I have breathed in birdsong, I must transpose it into a human key and breathe it out in language. This imitation seems to be a perennial human desire, from childhood stories with the owl's *to-whit, to-whoo*, or John Clare's transliteration of a nightingale's song, 'Chew-chew chew-chew … jug jug jug', as if to set a filigree net of little letters to catch a song without breaking its wings. It is sweetly futile: the ineffable may be indicated but not reproduced, but still we try and birdsong seems to turn us all into diligent but endlessly frustrated secretaries to St Francis, missing his knowledge that the only way to speak with birds is simply to laugh (aloud: silently) and to let the birdsong blow across his strings.

John Bevis' book *Aaaaw to Zzzzd: The Words of Birds*, a compendium of the notation of bird sounds, dedicates itself humorously and eagerly to the acknowledged impossibility of the task, but ever willing to give it a try. *But-but* is a bullfinch, *chack chack* a fieldfare, *zzzzd* is the lazuli bunting and *aaaa* is a jay, not to be confused (clearly!) with the *aaaaw* of the black skimmer. Mnemonics also mimic the songs, such as the yellowhammer's 'a little bit of bread and no *cheese*' or the wood pigeon's 'take *two* cows, taffy,' or the great tit's '*tea*cher, *tea*cher.'

Onomatopoeic naming evokes birdsong on the instant, as the cuckoo calls its name in its two-note pan pipe, or the owl (*ule* in Old English, *ulula* in Latin) softly cries its way through all the nights of the world: owl, howl and ululation are all thought to be from a Proto Indo-European root, *u(wa)l*, created in imitation of the owl. The chiffchaff chatters its way to day unless it hears the sinister mew of the kite keening its onomatopoeic name overhead, while the stonechat does what its name tells, making the sound of two stones clacking against each other. The hoarse cries of the crow (*crawe* in Old English) or rook (*hroc* in Old English) or raven (*hræfn* in Old English) speak their own names. The ornithologist-poet Don McKay captures the latter in metaphor, describing the call of a raven as 'doorbell / crossed with oboe.'

The words peep, pipe and pibroch are onomatopoeic, from Old English *pipian*, to play on a pipe, which derives from Latin *pipare*, 'to peep, chirp' of imitative origin, because the word itself derives ultimately from the peeps of birds. (Sardinian has *pibiare*, retaining a form closer to Latin than Italian does, and Sardinian children, chicks nestled in bed, are told: '*Como muda, mancu unu pibiu.*' 'Now be quiet, not even a peep.')

Many collective nouns for birds paint a sound picture: a murmuration of starlings; a bellowing of bullfinches (that's not kind, now, is it? nor true); a dole of turtledoves; a clattering of choughs or jackdaws; a gaggle of geese; a storytelling of crows; a tittering or a tidings of magpies; a quarrel of sparrows; a clamour of rooks; a party or a scold of jays. (That's unfair too: they're too much like Sid James to be cross.)

Whether it is whistled, written, copied, or played, birdsong seems compulsively mimicable – in visual form too, and there are artists who have tried to draw birdsong, or use computer-generated images for it. Seeing birdsong written on a musical score is like concrete poetry, a graphic score, a fizzy dizzicato pizzicato of acciaccatura – that species of grace notes theoretically timeless.

Every dawn they sing up the sun in a *vivace* creation. Woodpecker braggadocio on the castanets of a chestnut tree. Four finches fiddling fugues in F sharp for a fiddlehead fern. Urchin sparrows flicking cheeps as a fox trots past on a dawn errand (*get* that pheasant, *get* that pheasant).

If I offered my notation, birds seem to sing the names of composers (particularly Russian) – Stra*viiin*ski, Stra*viiin*ski, or *Tcha*íkovski, *Tcha*íkovski, *Tcha*í! Sometimes chirping *Ti*pp*ett, Ti*pp*ett, Ti*pp*ett then calling low and sweet *Keeats, Keeats, Keeats*. This is my *scherzo giocoso*, undisprovable glee to my ears, and meanwhile the madrigal widens to a crescendo of coloratura as each bird becomes the maestro of its own cadenza into full morning.

Musicians and composers have an elective affinity with birdsong. Human music has entwined with birds since the earliest records of culture: the world's oldest recognisable musical instrument is a flute made of a hollow bird's bone, from a Griffon vulture. The cellist Beatrice Harrison famously performed with a nightingale and the duet was broadcast on BBC from 1924 until 1942 when it was interrupted by the drone of aircraft on the 'Thousand Bomber' raid.

'In my hours of gloom,' Olivier Messiaen wrote, 'when I am suddenly aware of my own futility ... what is left for me but to seek out the true, lost face of music somewhere off in the forest, in the fields, in the mountains or on the seashore, among the birds.' Vivaldi composed his flute concerto *Il Gardellino*, the 'Goldfinch', in 1702. Or so they say. But when you listen to that flute solo you know, of course, the bird composed it first. When Beethoven composed part of his *Pastoral Symphony*, he said 'The yellowhammers up there, the quails, nightingales and cuckoos around about, composed with me.' Mozart had a pet starling, and when it died, the composer held a full funeral for it, which has a certain sad prolepsis for a genius who would himself have a pauper's funeral. Vaughan Williams' *The Lark Ascending*, that sheer saturation of joy, was inspired by George Meredith's poem of the same name, which was inspired, of course, by the bird itself. Respighi's *Pines of Rome* requires a recording of a nightingale, and Magnus Robb's piece *Sprosser: Hallucinations of Purity* (1998) uses percussion to imitate the rhythms of the thrush nightingale, the Sprosser.

'Birds instructed man,' wrote Lucretius, 'and taught him songs before his art began.'

There is a case, some linguists say, for arguing that we sang before we spoke, that the emotional content of our language, in pitch, timbre, musicality, came before the lexical part. Shigeru Miyagawa, a linguist at Massachusetts Institute of Technology, suggests that, between 50,000 and 80,000 years ago, humans merged the expressive songs of birds with the information-bearing communications of other primates to create the unique music of human language.

Was it their grace notes which sang at the very source of our language? Is it possible? Is that part of the reason for my keen and keening listening, as if I am not just learning to hear but dimly remembering how we first learnt to speak? As if humanity's compulsive imitation of birds is because we are collectively unable to forget that we may have learnt language from the birds?

I am drinking the wren's silver laughter, thirsty for its liquid song. I'm not alone: 'One moment just to drink the sound / Her music made', writes John Clare of the nightingale, a beak, rather than a beakerful of the warm South. George Meredith pictures the skylark's song as a jet of water soaring 'With fountain ardor, fountain play', this carefree –

spilling – overflow as if the bird's song in its pure liquidity dissolves all the dry distinctions of joy and light, the listener and the singer, in an aural alchemy.

I listen soundlessly. I breathe in for this wren, but then I am rapt in beauty and each note reminds me of the jewels I had in my hand as a child when I pretended that drops of water were diamonds and I was surrounded by priceless treasure. Our best applause: first silence, then song.

In Western myth, the figure behind every poet and musician is Orpheus, singer in the woodlands, whose music is so sweetly compelling that the trees uproot themselves to come closer to him, the stones hop nearer like birds while the birds become as stones, transfixed. According to Ovid, the shrieking maenads who tore Orpheus apart killed the birds first, and as his spirit vanished down the wind 'the birds, lamenting, cried for you, Orpheus.' As if Ovid heard what so many people do, a melancholy in birdsong, longing for the very soul of music.

It seems we humans sing most like birds when we sing most in our Orphic keys of music and poetry, as if to be a poet is to be part bird, and poets have long made the comparison resonant. Shelley's skylark is

> Like a Poet hidden
> In the light of thought.

To me, the skylark high in the sky is the cloudless psyche at noon, and yet it has a tension of pleasure which can feel bittersweet. The speck of a bird, a punctuation of pure joy, pierces the sky and my heart. Birdsong, like poetry, tends towards poignancy, sharp, quick and deep: the beak is a flint which strikes the heart of feeling, so Robert Burns hears in the woodlark 'nocht but love and sorrow join'd'. The nightingale, its nocturne a solo sung in the dark, rhymes with the twilit knowing of poetry's shadow vision and Keats tends the night of both nightingale and poetry. The word 'nightingale' means 'night singer', for 'gale' is from Old English *galan*, to sing, which also gives us *galdor*: song, spell or enchantment; the song of the nightingale releases the song of the poet. To me, every blackbird is John Donne, singing a tender confluence of beauty without knowing whether he sings for the female or for the divine.

Why do they do it? The obvious deadening answers lie at my feet like litter. Courting. Mating. Territory. Machines for survival. Mechanical embodiments of genetic compulsion. Oh, I know these things are all true, I know it well. I have watched a woodpecker almost sheepish with horniness until, in order to broadcast his message louder, he became a metalpecker, clinging to a telegraph pole, rattling the metal strut with its beak, and I thought he would get a terrible headache as he tried to drum up a mate from thin air: roll up, roll up, can't hold on much longer. Drrrrrrrrrum úp. (Pause.) Drrrrrrrrrum úp. (Pause.) Drrrrrrrrrum úp. (Please?)

But here's the thing. Birds are known to sing beyond what is necessary to find, impress and keep a mate, beyond what is necessary to get and hold their territory. They sing well after the chicks have flown the nest, long into autumn, so late and so well. And this is the gap to watch, the opening which begs that the question is asked again, and willingly, why?

The gap between need and achieve that lets the beauty in. The eager profusion, the unmeasured abundance. You can't miss them, the ones which tickle the leaves of the woodlands for joy, tinkling the *ivresseries*, the ones which can't stop themselves, whose songs run rings of bright sound around themselves like otters chasing their own tails at a noon tide high as – ha! not kites, please god, not if you're a small bird in the woods, a wren hushed in quick quiet.

The musician, philosopher and writer David Rothenberg, author of the beautiful book *Why Birds Sing*, argues that as well as the obvious reasons, birds sing for joy. As a musician himself, he feels a camaraderie, an understanding that birds as much as humans are musicians and they sing for the sheer pleasure of performance, far over and above their need. 'Music is a songbird's utmost desire, an endless yearning to sing.'

Rothenberg plays music with birds, a gift between players, an exchange of beauty. Gift culture takes many forms and in my garden, it is strawberries. I give the blackbirds strawberries: they give me song. I think this is a good exchange. Joseph Addison gave his blackbirds cherries for the same reason.

Hans Christian Andersen explores the nature of gift in *The Nightingale* where the bird works within gift culture, singing free in the woods, responsive to wishes, seeing tears as true treasure. The ethic of the gift is dramatised: it cannot be bought; should not be sold; must not be caged, or held, meanly, in a tight fist. The emperor is sent an artificial nightingale, covered with diamonds, rubies and sapphires and when it was wound up, it would sing. The court decides the birds should sing a competitive duet and while the real nightingale sang its own song, 'the artificial bird sang only waltzes'. Yes, I thought, reading that: I have never heard a waltzing bird. The real nightingale is scorned, despised and banished, but only she can save the life of the emperor when he is ill, and only if she is allowed to sing for him as a gift.

The wren is watching me. I breathe out as quietly as I can. His tiny eyes are a brilliant, liquid black – he blinks. He is the smallest bird I see in these woods, but his song is the loudest and this is why, open-heartedly, simply, gratefully, admiringly, I love him. He dazzles my ears. There is courage here, cocky, proud, brave and beautiful. This is undaunted gift; how much sheer magnificence can you pack into one tiny wren?

Other songs nearby include the nuthatch – *do it*, *do it* – and the *yip yip yip* of the great spotted woodpecker, with the chiffchaff chafing at the *bit bit bit*. Together, they are getting the dew giggling and creating a pointillist painting in sound. Their calls are so familiar to me in the woodlands where I live that they are my belonging – and it was the wood pigeon which signed the title deeds of my heart's home, as a child. Chaffinches have dialects: the male chaffinch sings a variation on a shared theme, depending on geography. A Kentish chaffinch is different from a Welsh one, while chaffinch song in Scotland can alter from valley to valley. They co-create their landscapes.

A blue tit banks sharply to perch, an arpeggio in motion. A blackbird glides a glissando stream. A buzzard swoops an octave between hillsides. A pied flycatcher hops a staccato twig. To imagine one's landscapes without their soundtrack of birdsong is a bitter desolation, a fearful silent spring: air without birdsong is like a garden without flowers;

nights without dreams; language without metaphor. Our woodlands would be, year-round, 'Bare ruin'd choirs, where late the sweet birds sang,' as Shakespeare wrote.

'If you want a red rose you must build it out of music by moonlight, and stain it with your own heart's blood,' wrote Oscar Wilde in 'The Nightingale and the Rose': the nightingale must sing with its breast against a thorn. This, poets know as well as birds, is the willing though poignant sacrifice. But can you price the sacrifice, or measure this cost?

Could you weigh a nightingale's song? The very question delights me: there is something joyously pure in its superfluity of curiosity; this is science for science's sake. And someone has indeed tried to do so. Robert Thomas of Bristol University measured nightingales before singing, at dusk, and after singing, at dawn. The individuals which sang more lost more weight: it costs them dearly to sing.

It is not the weight which fascinates, of course, but the lightness of the birds themselves which is part of their appeal, their weightless flight contrasted with our flightless weight: the light lift of a bird, yet full of such weight of emotional message.

The flight makes visible the gap of yearning, the leaning longing which humans feel for their song. The feathers are the nearest tangible thing to their near-immateriality of music, the blue note of the song dropped on the path, and the mind has feathers which, unfurled, can sing our thoughts soaringly. In a beautiful rhyme of pragma and poetry, a bird-feather quill is a pen for the plumage of the writer, and in myth the god of writers, Hermes or Mercury, is feather-capped with wings at his heels. Feathers are to the air what individual private thought is to public meaning, and a word is like a secret feather of a hermeneutic language, placed carefully, winged to fly, free.

Each word is freighted with its meaning and fretted too with its etymology which draws lines, fret-marks scored to the word's biography, as a bird's feathers can have fret-marks, showing for the rest of the bird's life its history of stress or hunger.

I hate the idea that I am making this wren fret. While it sings, I know it is okay, and if it peeps its alarm call, I will step away. Even as I want to be nearer to it, I know I do not ever want to catch it, hold it or cage it. So much do I love birds and their elemental freedom that injured or caged birds, birds kept indoors, trapped or killed, can disturb me to the point of panic. 'He who binds to himself a joy / Does the wingéd life destroy' in Blake's words.

I have, of course, tried to get close to birdsong by listening to it online, to the great perturbation of my cats. (When it is running at actual speed, they go glittery as predators and pounce on my computer; when it is slowed right down so that a nightingale sounds like a humpback whale, they become fear-warped like prey and hide under the bed. Sorry.) When I heard wren-song slowed down nine times, my ear could finally catch up, and weigh the song's beauty recalibrated to human scales. In a glorious duet of bird and human voices, Marcus Coates first recorded birdsong then slowed it down up to sixteen times, and asked different humans to take different bird voices: their singing was then played at bird-speed, so the humans sound like the chirping birds.

The gifts of birdsong are given even in our inattention, and sometimes in the woods I have become aware that I have been lost in myself and have not been listening. Then, letting their windfall song wash over me again, I feel as if they had been pouring out a blessing, playing softly on, pedalling the priceless whether I noticed them or not. And what am I to the wren, after all, whose audience is other.

Angels are usually pictured winged like birds, flying to deliver their messages. The word 'angel' comes from the Greek word for messenger. Birds, meanwhile, have long been thought to be messengers, whether it is the casual remark, 'A little bird told me', or birds in folk tales offering wisdom or advice, and the birds' manifold messenger-role in myth.

There is a leitmotiv of longing when we humans hear birdsong, whether it is science's longing to measure, record and question; art's longing to translate the music; or the human spirit keening for all that quickens the soul. The same tangent of longing is there, yearning for the beyond. Hearing the song without seeing it, seeing the bird without touching it, the quest, not the destination.

The skylark circling higher and higher in the air becomes an invisible source of song always beyond, and a line of Browning is in my mind:

Ah, but a man's reach should exceed his grasp,
Or what's a heaven for?

What the senses can actually grasp is overtaken by the yearning to reach beyond them. Height beyond sight. Pitch beyond hearing. The song beyond the reasons. Reason not the need, Shakespeare wrote, as if only humans yearned for The Beyond. Birds, we know, sing beyond needfulness, and to the human mind they are the angels of abundance, creating and reflecting joy.

Birdsong seems to happen on the horizon of the human mind, just beyond the extent of our senses. Immanent but untranslatable – the dash — ! — the glimpse, the hint, the ellipsis. All birdsong is always partially eclipsed to us, as if it is always leaning towards the leading note, the seventh keening for the tonic, as a skylark, self-leading, rises higher and higher, to the high-octane octave — yet — always — leggerissimo, as lightly as possible, where light is both weight and sound, both brightness and joy, and the octave is reached only at a point of silence created by the very quintessence of its own music.

'Till lost on his aërial rings / In light,' writes Meredith.

Till lost in light. The quality of the silence after Mahler's *Ninth Symphony*, the silence into which we pour our hushed applause of the heart. Between sound and silence. Between earth and sky. Between visible and invisible. Between literal and metaphoric. Between seeing and dreaming. Between sight and insight. Shelley and Keats alike between waking and sleeping, as the skylark flies higher, sings its furthest reach yet, 'Until we hardly see, we feel that it is there', writes Shelley. I am drawn out of myself into its ecstasy of sound, and I have become the tangent of my yearning. Between all categories, this, before memory and beyond longing, both the nostalgic possibility and the charisma of loss at once, a synaesthesia of the soul.

Coda. It is evening now and serene. In the low trees a blackbird is serenading the world, distilling the day to a rhapsody of gold and candle-song.

Another Look at Glennamong

NEPHIN BEG, NORTH MAYO

Seán Lysaght

Glennamong is set in the heavily glaciated country around Clew Bay, between two long ridges of the Nephin Beg range. You approach it from Newport, across undulating, boulder-strewn ground which looks as though the ice had melted just a few, and not thousands, of years ago. The glacial legacy is nowhere more pronounced than here, with a drumlin landscape tilting into the sea, giving you hundreds of islands in the eastern part of the bay, one for every day of the year, according to tradition. When you turn off the coast road to go north, your route twists among the narrow tongues of lakes that have been formed between the moraines and drumlins of old glacial deposits.

Lough Feeagh, to the north of Newport, is the largest of these, a four-kilometre-long corridor of strangely inert water. The road runs along the eastern shore of the lake, heading for the start of the old Bangor trail, which connected the Clew Bay area to the vast moorlands of north Mayo before new roads were built on either side of the Nephin Beg mountains. In the old days, the herders and walkers bound for the Bangor trail kept going north, past the northern extremity of Lough Feeagh, and today this is still the preferred road for sign-following ramblers and tourists. Anyone headed to Glennamong – mostly locals, in my experience – will instead turn left at the top of the lake and drive round its north-western corner to the start of the glen. Here the tarmac gives way to a stony track built by the state forestry body. In motoring terms, you soon reach a dead-end in the forestry plantation, and anyone exploring this area will eventually have to set out on foot.

As you do so, you enter a disjointed, partly defunct network of remembrance and meaning, one that is typical of a landscape where the old, Gaelic vernacular has died out and where scholarship has only partly salvaged its main lines of reference. The 400-metre mountain guarding the eastern rim of Glennamong like a portal column is marked on my map, variously, as Tirclieu and Torc Shléibhe, the one sounding like a corrupt Anglicisation of the other. A large white cross is set close to the top of this mountain, marking the spot where mass was celebrated by the native Irish in the days when Catholic observance was outlawed. The cross also symbolises this area as an outback beyond the reach of law in a wider sense, for it was here, during the Troubles, that the IRA had one of their main training grounds. The valley is bounded on all sides by cliffs and ridges and was easily guarded by a look-out on top of Torc Shléibhe. Stories abound in local lore of men arriving at night at safe houses, of guns stored in cottages, and of IRA volunteers constantly outfoxing the law.

I went back to Glennamong recently to investigate a newly discovered placename on a ridge to the east of the glen: *Carraig an Iolra* (Eagle Rock). There are scattered references to eagles in placenames in Mayo, where golden eagles and sea eagles used to breed before their extermination in the early twentieth century, and I had set myself the task of checking those sites to see where the birds might have bred.

It was a morning in late February, during a spell of high pressure after a dismal winter of rain and storms. There was still frost on grass in the shadow of the hedges, and smoke drifted lazily from chimneys where early fires had been lit. Before I got to Lough Feeagh, I stopped to examine a mixed deciduous woodland, to see what winter colours might be revealed in the bright light, before spring growth took over. The tops of downy birch were fluffy smudges of wine beside the yellowish-grey of oak and the shiny, dark-green flares of holly. In a sign of what was to come, hazel catkins had already extended their bright yellow tassels to collect a tribute of sun for their loyalty to this setting after three months of rain and louring skies.

Around Lough Feeagh itself, there are only a few relict scraps of mixed oak/hazel/birch woodland, with some willow in the wetter hollows. Where birch predominated in one small stand, there was a particular elegance in the fine white lines of the trunks scored vertically under the wine-coloured canopy. The general impression elsewhere was of rocky barrenness, where sheep forage in the meagre growth of these moorland slopes. Here and there a tatty hawthorn tree broke the monotony, its browse line festooned with swabs of fleece.

Only when the road rises over the top of the last ridge, known locally as *brae*, do you see the bright sheet of Lough Feeagh, a silvery blade cutting through the yellow-brown of the hills. That morning, in the calm conditions, the lake was trying some upside-down impressionism on its surface, as the muted colours of the far shore took on reflected shape. At the top of the lake, the slope under the cross at Torc Shléibhe had a more varied, sharper palette: dark-brown heather at the top where the land was fenced off; a grey scattering of boulders farther down, with the ginger of dead bracken, and the yellows and greens of sedges and grasses where the ground was overgrazed.

As the road ran out, giving way to untarred track, I thought that I was leaving traffic and disturbance behind, but as I stopped to open a line of sheep fencing strung across the road, I realised that there was another car behind me. Two cars in such a remote spot felt like a complicity of sorts, so we both stopped and chatted, he a man in his fifties like me. As Glennamong was our common destination, it gave a special context to the conversation: I floated the common knowledge, that the IRA had trained here during the Troubles; that remark was the cue for the other to give his own history of Anglo-Irish relations. 'They were fighting a war,' he said. 'Two lads were shot by the British one day in Belfast. They had been here that morning.' Glennamong had taken away my liberal vocabulary, my need to correct this man's references to a war, as he glossed over what became the IRA's murderous sectarian campaign. It was soon a relief to move on.

After the sheep fence, the track curves to the right and overlooks the meandering stream that runs out of the glen into the lake. There are still the remains here of a few stone cottages, and the outlines of fields constructed from the bog using gravel and sand from the outwash of the river. As I drove in, I noticed one jeep and sheep-trailer parked beside the plantation; my follower had parked behind me, for some obscure purpose of his own.

Following the river upstream, the road soon comes to a new concrete bridge built by the foresters a few years ago to take lorries in here for the first felling of the crop. By my count of rings, the first plantings were in the 1970s, when the Northern situation was at its worst. The plantation covers the entire floor of the valley west of the river up to the 200-metre contour. It is composed of the usual staples of lodgepole pine and Sitka spruce, with a few stands of larch. Just across the river from the bridge, a ruined cottage with its outbuildings is now shaded among mature larch trees; at a casual glance you might think that the cottage had been built in a larch wood; in reality, this unusual scene marks the indifference of the planters to the visible heritage of the families who once farmed these lonely glens.

When I had parked near the bridge, I set out across the bog towards the slope of Torc Shléibhe. I was going east, away from the plantation, but I hoped that my climb of that small mountain would give me a new perspective on those conifers. I walked the spongy ground of sphagnum mosses and molinia sedge that had already dried out somewhat after the abundant rainfall of that winter. The countless little streams and trickles of water, added to the noise of the river, all amounted to a vast, diffuse sibilance echoing off the slope. The only break in that soundtrack was the rush of air in ravens' wings as birds flew past.

As the slope took me higher, the river's last few meanders into the lake were like a plate from a geography textbook, with one small ox-bow pond perfectly formed where an old loop of the river had been abandoned. Lough Feeagh appeared foreshortened, as if the lake surface were spread on a vertical, not horizontal, plane in front of me, a curious effect of hazy atmosphere that I have often observed. It was now shaped roughly like a map of England, with the bay at the mouth of Glennamong like the bulge of East Anglia.

In the calm, slightly hazy air of midday, the deep-pile carpet of conifers stretching below me was a yellowish-green. Several areas had been clear-felled in the last few years, leaving gaps and wide clearings among the dark stands. Close-up, these wrecked and sterile spaces have always appeared to me like a no-man's-land from some First World War scenario, but from a distance, the abandoned lines of brash from the cutting formed a pattern like the rough weave of a doormat; where these areas had been replanted, the new lines of saplings appeared as a dark pinstripe across a warm, brown tweed. It seemed an anomaly that these woodlands were understood by many people as part of a wilderness: walking in the coniferous State forest has been promoted for years as a healthful excursion, which I suppose it is; but I have always struggled with feelings of loneliness and desolation in those sites of havoc and those narrow corridors of dark green needles.

I had walked among those trees at ground level before, on my way to investigate another possible eagle site at the very head of the glen, where the map showed some steep slopes and cliffs. That visit was in late May, when the gnarled and worn hawthorn bushes along the way had been transformed by a blizzard of flowering. Having parked at the same spot near the bridge, I was greeted by a male stonechat calling from a clearing to announce his ownership of that territory. As I followed the forestry road on foot, I passed a large area that had been clear-felled very recently and showed the usual desolation. However, the grim economy of forestry does not entirely monopolise these areas: lodgepole pines had seeded naturally along the road and stood like miniature sentries, forming a guard of honour for the walker; each was neatly decorated with new flowers, like baubles on a Christmas tree. At another point, a row of four cedars grew in a regular line parallel to the track, in what appeared to be a purely decorative gesture. And there was a neat stone channel built with elaborate care, which took a stream down to a culvert running under the thoroughfare; the feature had a decorative charm, and I was reminded of it a few days later when I saw a Zen garden featured in a report on the Chelsea Flower Show.

These comforts and distractions fell away after a couple of kilometres when the gravelled track ended at another sheep fence. After that, my journey continued through a wide firebreak, where the ground was a peaty mess from rain and the trampling of sheep. I cursed the economy that had planted all those spiky, impassive trees in the upland valleys and gave subsidies to farmers to put hundreds of sheep on the hills, thus wrecking the vegetation and ecology. Although the worst of the EU subsidy madness was a thing of the past, there were still too many animals, and too many marks of their presence.

This plantation, I discovered, was also a site of scientific data gathering. The Irish state's Marine Institute was monitoring rainfall and run-off levels in the forest and had set instruments in many places: solar panels, rain gauges and troughs in the bed of drains to measure flows. These troughs, about ten feet by two, with an aluminium spout, were full of pale ale that day, topped with a beery froth: rain was intermittent, and my binoculars had fogged up with moisture. The weather was having an impact on my mood, because I thought that these studies, along with others on salmon and sea trout populations, and on the acidification of streams, were just hopeless, state-sponsored autopsies on a body whose life had passed away. I was angry at the inability of these agencies, despite all their confident statistics, to do anything about the decline in salmon and sea trout numbers in places such as Feeagh.

My angry reflections were interrupted when I glimpsed an accipiter hawk in the air above the firebreak: brownish, with a flash of bright undertail coverts. It moved away to the left to avoid me, a blue nuisance at the edge of its vision; but then it came back and reappeared for an instant to check that it got me right first time; after one more turn, and a brief air-dive like a wood pigeon, it returned to the fastness of the tree tops, and I saw no more of it.

In its final performance I got an impression of bulk saying 'goshawk' instead of 'sparrowhawk', but its appearance was so fleeting that I could not be sure. Instead of a confirmed goshawk, that day I recorded a *ghosthawk*, one of those rare raptors that our imagination yearns for, and which the wet day and the impossible perspectives of forestry trees overwhelm.

Since the spread of non-native conifers in the west and south of Ireland, there has been a small dividend of bird species taking advantage of the plantations. Crossbills are an occasional treat for the watcher, passing overhead through the grey stillness; coal tits, siskins and chaffinches are also at home here; and blackcaps and grasshopper warblers are regular in the deciduous thickets of birch and alder along forestry margins. Goshawks are as yet barely a rumour in the west of Ireland, but they have done well in similar landscapes in Wales, and there are a few pairs established in the north and south of the country. The chance of a seeing a goshawk in the Mayo forests is too remote to warrant a whole day's hunt, but the thought is nonetheless there at the edge of other concerns.

Eventually, following a stream, I reached the upper edge of the plantation, where spruce grew close to each other and created shade and shelter. The floor was deeply carpeted with fallen needles, making the ground spongy underfoot and relatively dry. I thought it would be a good pitch for a tent, under a dense canopy of low spruce branches. I had camped out as a young lad in a place like this, with trunks of conifers clustered round the light of my campfire. I had left home on a reckless impulse, to travel for a few days during schooltime, like the Irish author Pádraig Ó Conaire, who caught thrushes in a wood at night and roasted them on his fire. My own efforts to emulate him failed on that occasion: I raided a wood pigeon's nest for its eggs, but I didn't venture to eat them, thinking they might be developed.

These were some memories that added to the view of Glennamong as I looked down on that forest on that February day. Close to the top of Torc Shléibhe, there was a sheep fence running across the spine of the mountain that kept me away from the cairn at the summit: a neatly stacked affair with several quartz blocks on top, suggesting some ritual impulse. The lonely call of a golden plover haunted the sky for a while, an early bird tempted up to that summit in search of a territory. And I also came upon the precious find of a pile of fresh grouse droppings where a bird had roosted under a low peat bank. Just past the summit, a pile of old, tarred fenceposts left over from the work and abandoned gave me the struts to build an improvised stile and cross the fence. The cliff I wanted to examine was on the far side of the ridge, facing away north towards the plantings and peatlands east of the Nephin Beg mountains.

Twenty minutes of searching along the steep edge of the mountain brought me to a point overlooking a slope with deep heather and sheer rock faces. A few ravens had quartered the cliff and were turning in the emptiness below me. This was still sheep territory, but there were many corners and ledges where heather grew in profusion as a reminder of what these hills would look like if the pressure of grazing were removed. I scrambled down as far as I could, across woody stems of flattened heather, to get a view of Eagle Rock, an inaccessible bluff on the face, with a secure ledge deep in growth, a perfect spot for an eyrie. From here, the golden eagle eye had a commanding view of mountain and moor, and of the flow country to the north. Today, that view has changed because of afforestation: this part of Mayo was the site of an extensive planting programme by the Irish state following the Second World War. The optimism of those years still haunts the silence of the conifers, and could not halt the decline of communities in those remote places. A deep, dark-green pile has spread across the lowlands where eagles used to hunt hares and grouse in the open.

Much of the forest in that vista is now part of a new designation as the Wild Nephin Area, confirming conifers as a constituent of wilderness in Ireland. New planting in that area is due to cease, and road access restricted, so that the walker and camper will have an undisturbed wilderness experience. A ghosthawk in a glade, the call of a grouse near a campfire in the evening, a pine marten scurrying across the track. The wilderness will reveal itself in such moments. Beyond this, history rears its head with a different story of degradation, decline and loss – but who would want to spoil a day out with such thoughts?

Hidden Places

THE LINCOLNSHIRE WOLDS
Fiona Stafford

There was no wardrobe, and no fur coats. Only the sliding metal door of the big garage that had once been a stable block. On the chalky walls you could just make out faded frescos with *trompe l'oeil* frames: vanishing landscapes and faint portraits painted by the soldiers who had been billeted there during the Second World War. These blank faces unwittingly stood watch over the way into the woods. The door was heavy and instead of gliding, it stuck reluctantly in the overhead runner, but with a bit of determination and a good pull it would suddenly slide open enough to let the light in, and those inside, out.

Once through, it all depended on the season. The world beyond might be sky-blue bright with buds opening like the pincers of a crab, or thick with heavy August air and flecks of chaff from the harvested fields, or surging with the green of full leaves, rinsed by summer rain. Sometimes, the grey, dank air clung to the trees as if to drag their yellow rags down into the mud, at other times they stood resplendent still in the morning sun, as the first frost crisped the last fringes of gold. Rarely, but most memorably, the familiar shapes were so bloated with white that you could scarcely tell where one stopped and the next began, the air so quiet that even a cloud of breath threatened to wake these great, undefined forms from their deep winter sleep. Whatever the month, whatever the weather, the force field was overwhelming.

The paths through the woods were very different in character. One way led up the short, rubble track into the parallel line of yews where undergrowth never made any inroads. Here the ground was always covered in parched, rust-red needles, untouched by light or rain. Though perpetually shedding invisible showers of thin nail parings, the dense canopy never ran short – the thicker the bed beneath, the darker the covering overhead. This was the place to seek refuge from a summer cloud burst, where you could listen to the rain swishing through the surrounding tree tops, but remain dry and quiet by the flaking trunks of the yews.

If you headed instead into the silver birch wood, crossing over to where the taller, smoother beeches seemed to step back and let you pass by, you came to a stream, clog-edged with willowherb and couch grass, but pouring on down its narrowed channel nevertheless. A fallen ash formed a slippery bridge over to the far woods, but here ferocious brambles tangled with blackthorn and holly. It seemed impenetrable at first, but a little way further along the bank, a pair of oaks kept the undergrowth down, making it possible to slip through. There the ground dipped suddenly into thicker leaf mould, half concealing the fungal-covered stumps of older trees. The smell was heavier here, and on the other side of the hollow were great, yawning holes, fanged by dirty roots. If it looked like the entrance to the underworld, closer inspection suggested that it must be a badger sett, though the residents were too shy or shrewd to confirm their place of abode during daylight hours. After dark, it was impossible to find.

In early summer, unfamiliar birds of prey came together here, gliding silently from hidden places and then gone again, as if for ever. The dead leaves concealed deep hollows and rises, making this part of the wood rather hazardous on foot; like the great birds, the sudden dips were more visible in the neighbouring field, defying the plough and preserving the character of centuries past. This was known to be the site of a lost village, one of those utterly emptied during the Black Death and never revived. The long deserted forms were home to rabbits and thistles now.

There were other directions to follow. If you took a left turn from the garage door, the track led across a small yard towards a farm gate, which hung incongruously between a pair of grand, stone-capped columns, admittedly rather pitted and worn around the edges. The lower branches of the horse chestnuts hugged at the green-stained stone as if to greet the ivy, as it crept higher and higher up the damp brick plinths. The surrounding ground was ankle-deep in wet ivy, though still the trees shot up, jostling for light. A little way in, you could just make out a leaf-covered platform, which marked the top of an air-raid shelter that had never been refilled. On the far side of the gate was a cobbled drive, mossed, blotched, but more or less intact, with low walls along one side to keep the woods in check, and, a few hundred feet further on, the ruins of a house.

The roof was long gone and many of the rooms, too, but some tall walls remained, oddly patched with old wallpaper, ragwort and wild poppies. A few of the roof timbers still balanced across the void for squirrels taking short cuts, and on what must once have been the polished slabs of a kitchen floor, broken slates lay in untidy heaps among the nettles. Bushes of elder burst from the corners and the doorless space in the far wall framed an ebullient sycamore. The empty windows seemed to stare down in surprise at what had happened to their house.

You could see right through the old mansion, from the unshowy brick quarters at the back, through what might have been a dining room, grand hallway and wide drawing room beyond, and out across the spreading park with its great oaks, where a herd of Lincolnshire reds just got on with their grazing. It was all too precarious to venture inside, but walking round what was left of the building, almost every corner was clearly visible. As you followed the cobbles under the arch, its crest eroded by Siberian winds from the East coast, the grand facade was still plain to see. Handsome, even with half its countenance collapsed, the golden stone still defied some of the elements.

The woods concealed their secret well, for the house stood far from any road, come upon only by following the mossed cobbles at the rear, or the grander sweep that led to the stately portico. Far away down that grassy drive was another, larger archway, capped with petrified foxes, each supporting a chipped escutcheon in perfect symmetry.

And all around, the ruins of a carefully planned garden tumbled about, at once liberated and suffering from severe neglect. You might be pushing aside a low-growing elder in the middle of a half-concealed path, when a disconcerting drift of orange blossom would reveal a mass of overgrown syringa trees. The rhododendrons ran wild, dying patches of the woods cerise and ruby at times when everything else was spring green. The great landowners who had laid out the grounds with symmetrical beds and specimen trees would have been dismayed by the way their plans had turned out. It was as if, unchaperoned, their charges had loosened their stays, unbuttoned their boots and shaken their hair out into long, unruly tresses. What must once have been neat circles of cypress saplings had burst into huge, matted, inverted tassles, as each vast tree outgrew the original bounds. High above, a shrill, hardly audible call told that what seemed the movement of tiny, dead leaves in the breeze was really a pair of goldcrests. Things were always stirring quietly in the dense trees, unnoticed and just out of reach.

The woods stood in tiers around the house, creating an arena for the rams whose pasture was once the rose garden. The sound of their horns clashing in the spring echoed through the stillness of the trees. In early summer, when the night held back its blankets, the whole space filled with the liquid notes of nightingales. Later in the year, pale barn owls swept across from the field, to add their discordant screeches to the soft, brown voices of the tawny owls among the chestnuts.

At the heart of the garden was a beech tree, which towered above the ha-ha, marking the line between the park, the garden and the woods beyond. The distant oaks, the old stone steps, the rows of tumbling rhododendrons all spread from it like the points of a compass, forming a vast counterpart to the Victorian sundial that had somehow survived nearby. The trunk of the stately beech was wider than outstretched arms and under its benign boughs were two small headstones, bearing the names 'Lucy' and 'Chloe'. No one knew what the stones meant, though someone once said they might be the graves of the old family's pets and, from then on, dogs were known to be buried there. I never thought they were.

There had always been partings in the woods. What sometimes seemed to go on for ever would unexpectedly pause, where light filled a clearing or the trees gave way to a little dark, limpid pool. No route led there deliberately and they were easy to mistake. Deep in the ruined garden, far away from any obvious path, an iron gate stood as if holding back time. On the wrought-iron, lichen-patterned bench beneath, everything was suspended and the air felt thick with the breath of those who had never really left. The soft ground admitted no trace of old footsteps and the trees kept things to themselves, but still the haze of lost summers lingered and the echo of laughter caught on a dead branch.

One morning after a rough night in early March, the bright sunlight fell on the wrong patch of grass. The great beech tree had fallen apart and the garden had disappeared. Somewhere under the mountainous twisted tangle of twigs and limbs, the sundial, the stone steps and the small headstones lay buried. Many months passed before the vast trunk and massy branches were moved and then all that could be seen was starved grass and broken stone. The grass recovered soon enough, but the garden had somehow lost heart. Even the sheep tended to avoid the spot, preferring to strip the bark in the old orchard instead. Gradually, the broadleaves began to close in, growing closer together, as if to draw a decent veil over time's undesirable victory lap. The woods conceal their secrets well.

Arborotopia

NEW FOREST, HAMPSHIRE

Philip Hoare

Recently, I flew home from Scotland to Southampton. The plane slowed as it approached southern Hampshire and its coast, as if to acknowledge the approaching sea. In that moment, the motorways and towns of middle England gave way to acres of the trees and heathland of the New Forest. It was remarkable to see how 'empty' this space was, even as it was so close to what we might call the Home Counties, as if there were any other kind.

As the plane banked over the Forest and towards Southampton Water, that great inseminal inlet, the trees were as abruptly replaced by another kind of forest: the sprawling acres of Fawley Refinery, seeded with towers, spires and gantries, metal trees rising up out of the industrial site. In the winter, when I swim in that water in the dark before dawn – the hour between the wolf and the dog – I watch the ever-present flames burning off the refinery's excess, like some monument to an unknown warrior. Those artificial trees refine for consumption the products of their ancient, organic counterparts that abut the site. Meanwhile, their roots infiltrate the rest of the country, pumping, rather than drawing, their petrochemical products like some vast intravenous system, fed by docile super tankers which pull alongside the terminus to have their tarry udders sucked dry.

It was in the shadow of this ever-burning, ever-producing petropolis – whose inception, in 1950, when it was Europe's largest such facility, coincided with one of the dates given as the start of what we now call the Anthropocene – that I had my childhood experiences of the Forest. My grandmother lived in a bungalow, built in a vaguely Indian style (as if to reflect the memory of my grandfather, then long deceased, but who had served in Meerut during the First World War). It was a dark place, made darker by the veranda that ran around it, like a shady ledge. Inside, Nanny, fragile as a bird, sat with her lisle-stockinged legs across, while my uncle, her eldest and unmarried son, sat in his 'parlour' next to the kitchen.

As far as I could work out, the two never even spoke together; I used to imagine that they didn't even see one another from day to day, living out their demarcated lives in that shadowy house of ticking clocks and the football results intoned on the radio. Uncle Buffer, as we knew him, worked in the refinery. He had huge ruddy eyebrows which put me in mind of the nearby forest; he might have been a woodsman as much as an overseer of pipelines. (I think I made the link because of the plastic troll with shock-headed hair that hung, inappropriately naked, on his parlour wall. I still wonder how or why he came by it. Perhaps it was a lover's gift.)

My uncle was then younger than I am now, but he seemed old, and I wasn't surprised when, coming home from school one day, I was told by my mother that he had died of a heart attack, in the refinery. I pictured him felled to the factory floor, lying on its sticky ground. There in the void, face up to the sky. Those images of darkness and the past – the village itself was called Blackfield, an augury of what it had become, or might yet become if some disaster should overtake the nearby installation – became associated in my mind with the presence of the forest which lay next to the house itself: a beautiful but foreboding site, to which access was magical, and trepidatious.

In my grandmother's back garden, with its neat gravel paths and a stone bird bath and a blunt-nosed concrete bunny, all entirely enclosed by a tall privet hedge, was a gate at the far end which opened onto the forest. Walking through that gate was a transformative act – not least because we had been told not to stray. So of course we did. Through that gate, the suburban garden suddenly segued into wilderness. On the gravel path, we were in safety; one step into the forest, and we might as well be lost like the babes in the wood, their pathetic dead bodies covered with leaves by a blood-red robin. Later, driving back through the forest, I watched from the backseat of the car as a pure-white hart leapt out of the undergrowth, its eerie shape held heraldically in the bracken. I was, as you can tell, a child with an overactive imagination.

Yet it strikes me now, as I write in October, that we only think about the forest when it is dying, when its leaves turn into beacons of their own burning beauty. For a few short weeks we come to pay our respects, recalling our collective childhoods, remembering, perhaps uneasily, our vexed adult relationship with the natural world. As Richard Mabey notes in his *Cabaret of Plants*, we often only take notice of nature when it suits us, to feed our human needs; we seldom see it for its own sake. Trees, like other plants, have become commodities; an index of capital, rather than celebrated merely for being themselves.

The New Forest. The *New* Forest. Caught between Bournemouth's resort to the west and the industrial spires of the refinery to the east, backed by middle England and looking out to what was the ancient River Solent and the chalk-white Isle of Wight (where, recently, new petrified trees were found), 'the Forest' (just as the Island is 'the Island') straddles 144 square miles of heath and woodland. It is an hour and a half from London by car or train, and although one may still get lost in its depths, it is hard to see it as a primeval or even threatening place. Rather, it has become a playground where foragers gather supplies for distant deluxe restaurants, and where middle-aged men Lycra-ride five-abreast along lanes occasionally strewn with tacks by locals protesting at this appropriation of their land. 'Wilderness' would appear to be the wrong word; 'bewilderment' might be better applied to the long-running battle over its meaning and function. And how much better to be be-wildered?

In many ways, our modern concept of the forest itself has an apocalyptic genealogy. In his recent book, *What is Landscape?*, John R. Stilgoe, professor in the history of landscape at Harvard, describes how it was influenced by the ravages of medieval plague which removed one-half to two-thirds of the human biomass – already weakened by the Great Famine – from the British Isles and northern Europe and which resulted in cultivated land being overtaken by trees. This mass afforestation – in which trees seemed to supplant humans – created a new sublime locus for the imagination: an eerie, anti-Eden inhabited by brigands and murderers and witches. A folk memory of that fear could be felt even centuries later in the eldritch tales of the Brothers Grimm, which offered all manner of gruesome scenarios in the darkness of the woods. The forest was at the edge of that metaphorical darkness, the limits of civilisation and survival.

The forest has ever represented the other, in discrete cultures across the paleoarctic. It is a sensibility which translated to New England and emerged in the Gothic stories of Nathaniel Hawthorne and Washington Irving and all their witchiness. There are still parts of Massachusetts or Maine where ancient paths – created before the advent of Europeans and perhaps before the coming of humans – meander into thick woods which conjure up scenes of some past brutality continually being replayed, as if thrown through a flickering silent film. On the other side of the continent, the indigenous peoples of the north-west Pacific coast of North America preferred to travel by sea rather than venture inland. They had less to fear from orca and the open ocean than from impenetrable forests infested with bears and wolves – even as they invested these animals with anthropomorphic or even godlike qualities with which their shamans would be possessed.

The New Forest seems a long way from such visions, not least because it is now one of the most expensive places to live in England. But in his remarkable book, *After London*, published in 1885, the Victorian visionary Richard Jefferies imagined England after some unspecified conflagration, allowing nature to reclaim its own. 'By this time the brambles and briars had choked up and blocked the former roads, which were as impassable as the fields,' Jefferies wrote, invoking a kind of late Pre-Raphaelite science fiction.

'No fields, indeed, remained, for where the ground was dry, the thorns, briars, brambles, and saplings ... filled the space, and these thickets and the young trees had converted most part of the country into an immense forest ... By the thirtieth year there was not one single open place, the hills only excepted, where a man could walk, unless he followed the tracks of wild creatures or cut himself a path.'

In Jefferies' fantasy, the whole of England becomes a New Forest, a kind of inversion of the medieval plague and famine dystopia. Yet the reality of history – as opposed to Jefferies' imagined future – would prove the reverse to be true, as England was denuded yet further of its primeval forest in the modern era. Indeed, T.H. White, misanthropic author of *The Once and Future King* – which re-imagined its own medieval, Arthurian dream, somehow inflected by Julia Margaret Cameron's woodily sepia photographs and an applied Pre-Raphaelitism – and who was inspired by Jefferies, saw an entirely more dystopian, if not Orwellian, actuality. In the 1930s, by which time the octopus reach of London's suburbs had become irrevocable, White proposed that 'one day the New Forest will be the name of a tube station'.

This forest, which is not a forest (first-time visitors stand wonderingly at its blasted heaths and their lack of trees), has attracted many utopians and dreamers, ritual acts and mysterious narratives over its thousand years of history. But it was in the long nineteenth century – which began with most people living in the country, and ended with most people living in the towns – that the Forest became an antidote and an alternative to the gravitational pull of the city and the age of mechanical reproduction. Some resisted that pull, in sometimes extreme ways.

In 1871, an illiterate farm labourer's daughter from Suffolk, Mary Ann Girling, arrived in sleepy Hordle, a New Forest village, bringing with her 150 followers to whom she had promised eternal life if only they did as she instructed. They were to live together, like the apostles, giving up all their money and belongings to the sect – the Children of God, as they called themselves. Parents would live separate lives and abstain from sex. Children would be separated from parents and cared for communally. Women wore their hair in long, loose ringlets and wore bloomers, trouser-like garments that shocked their Victorian peers. Men too wore their hair long, under 'wide awake' hats. They lived by barter and the Word of God, and cut a bizarre vision when they walked the streets of the quiet forest town of Lymington. They resembled some seventeenth-century sect of civil war radicals, Ranters or Diggers reborn.

Most sensational of all were their whirling dancing rites, during which the women were said to undress themselves until they were dancing in the nude, spinning into a frenzy and falling in a comatose state on the floor, out of which they would awake – Mary Ann Girling promised – having died and been reborn to eternal life. Evicted from Hordle Grange on Vaggs Lane, the New Forest Shakers, as they had become known, ended up living in bare wooden huts on an encampment nearby, a strange cross between a village hamlet and a concentration camp; a processing plant for the ever-after. There, in those bare huts, many – mostly young women – succumbed to consumption even as Mrs Girling's mission became more urgent. She appeared to be quivering with the approach of the End Time. At one point, their 'Mother' emerged from her hut with eyes blindfolded and bleeding stigmata on her hands and feet, muttering in tongues. She might as well have been Kurtz in the jungle as a self-proclaimed female Christ.

There was a sense of sacrifice to this drama, a revival of all the gods of the forest; of pagan rites in the middle of the Industrial Revolution, and of auguries of apocalypse and ladders of bombs, of wood henges and forest ponds in which offerings were made and unwanted babies drowned; of sky-clad covens and New Age travellers rehearsing their own myths, breaking new ground in ancient turf – only for the Forest to become one extended stockbroker belt, pricing out the untidy past and its bohemians and heretics, in favour of gravel drives, security systems, and Shaker kitchens fresh from Chelsea showrooms.

All this future, seen and unseen, seemed to spin around Mary Anne's futile, whirling Shakers, trembling in advance of what John Ruskin diagnosed as the 'Storm-Cloud of the Nineteenth Century', and a violent century to come. When, inevitably, she died and joined her followers in the local churchyard, the remaining faithful gathered round her grave, instructing the sexton that he was wasting his time filling it in, as their leader would rise from the dead in three days.

And as these scenes played out, in muddy fields and the pages of the national press, a few fields away a giant concrete tower was rising over the Forest. It was constructed by a wealthy retired barrister, Andrew Peterson, who'd returned from his practice in Calcutta fired with the new science of spiritualism – declared by the prime minister, William Gladstone, to be the most important advance of the nineteenth century.

Peterson's 200-foot tower, composed of cement from Portland's convict-harvested quarries and shingle stolen from Milford's beach, was to be a temple to this futuristic religion, with each of its twelve chambers, set one on top of the other, to be dedicated to a different aspect of the new art: clairvoyance, clairaudience, spirit writing, spirit photography, and so on, to the stars.

Peterson even envisaged a series of these towers reaching up to the skies, marching across the countryside. At the top of his inaugural construction Peterson proposed to fix the first outdoor electric light, to shine out like a spiritualist beacon across the country, advertising this wonderful new message for the world. Sadly, he was forbidden from doing so by the Coastguard, on account that nearby shipping might mistake it for a lighthouse; and its creator would end up interred in his own creation, his ashes buried in a basement chamber. His posthumous fate echoed that of another Forest-dwelling spiritualist, Sir Arthur Conan Doyle, who was buried in Minstead churchyard, after being disinterred from his original place of rest in Sussex, where he had insisted on his body being put in the ground upright, as if to be more ready for his own resurrection.

Looking back on these stories, it seems that a sort of Victorian psychedelia had invaded the Forest. In the parish church at Lyndhurst – where Alice Liddell is buried – the interior is decorated with a lavish fresco by Lord Leighton, and carved wooden pillars and beams reach into the roof like fantastical versions of the trees outside. Forest and building merge, one into the other, just as other churches were sited on ancient holy places, marked by immemorial yews.

The sense of the Forest as a refuge and an escape extended into the twentieth century. At its beginning, Ernest Westlake, a self-declared neo-pagan, attempted to create a Neolithic game park stocked with Stone Age fauna, although the magnificence of his ambition was somewhat undermined by the name of the place he chose, Sandy Balls. Meanwhile, close by, the utopian radical Auberon Herbert – a patron of Mrs Girling, and, as the first man to ride a bicycle around the Forest, the forerunner of all those racers – built his own compound, Old House, deep in the Forest. Hidden by the trees, Herbert added to his hideaway incrementally, 'a bed-sitting room, and then, bit by bit, as the humour took him … a room here or a room there until the crazy pile was completed.' He liked to sleep in a different room each night, and even built his own, more modest, observatory tower, painted red, each of its three storeys containing a bed, enabling its tenant to take his rest wherever he liked.

He may have been the son of the earl of Carnarvon, but Herbert was a resister, a non-conformist. He had opposed a Victorian attempt to do away with the place altogether, when the 1871 Treasury bill for the Disafforestation of the New Forest proposed to remove its very meaning. It was as if the relentless onward march of progress and the Industrial Revolution, of empire and capital, could not allow these anachronistic acres so close (and yet so far) from the nation's capital to stand in its way. But Herbert and his fellow liberals won, and in 1877 the New Forest Act – 'the Commoners' Charter' – enshrined the wilderness for posterity. At least, that was the intention. But in the dawn of the new century, Herbert saw a warning in the army manoeuvres he witnessed being carried out in the Forest. He duly protested to *The Times*, in an article, 'How the British Army Captured the New Forest'. Watching the troops swarming about the trees, 'as in a splendid diorama', he feared strange new alliances to come, and 'a perilous way'.

In his own way, Herbert was reflecting the Arts and Crafts aesthetic, much as another son of Hampshire, Heywood Sumner, did in his writings, archaeological explorations, and distinctive pen-and-ink line drawings and lettering which reflect a particular late Victorian/ Edwardian forest utopia. Indeed, preserved in the Bournemouth Natural Sciences Society – a wonderful Victorian villa and extended cabinet of curiosities – are Sumner's Tolkienesque drawings and a map of Hampshire which might as well be The Shire. Meanwhile, in the Society's geological room stand a series of prehistoric tree roots, more than 7,000 years old, found after excavations at the end of Bournemouth pier, as if they had supported some ancient concourse out in what was then the river Solent.

After Herbert's death in 1906, his Old House faced an even stranger fate: as a proposed home to a new sect of spiritualists and New Age thinkers, the Theosophists. Newspaper reports anticipating this latest invasion described Herbert's mysterious abode still standing as if he'd only just walked out into the trees. Surrounded by caravans on rusty trestles, and odd outbuildings with crumbling walls, the house's interior had been left entirely untouched.

Every table and shelf was laden with 'ordinary, valueless pieces of flint, taken from the gravel pits to be found in the forest … arranged on the expensive porcelain among prodigious tomes and even under glass-cases just as if they were so many precious gems. Books and flints, flints and books. They have invaded every room in the house, including the music-room, the bed-rooms, and the observation tower.' From there the visitor could 'look over the multitudinous arms of the forest, or, with a turn, down to the sea where the Isle of Wight lies glittering like an emerald placed on a silver dish' – while Herbert's grave itself lay 'beneath the shadow of the crazy house, within a little clearing surrounded by tall elms and poplars', not unlike Mary Ann's resting place.

Part museum, part junk yard, this was to be the site for a new utopia, re-imported to England from California. But in the event, and doubtless to the relief of the neighbours, the Theosophists failed to make their transition. Instead, war came.

With the approach of Armageddon, the Forest was changed forever. Its timber was cut down to supply pit props for trenches on the Western Front, assimilating nature once more into the maw of industrial warfare. It was as a result of the attendant shortages of wood that the Forestry Commission was formed, to ensure that a future conflict should not catch Britain unawares. And so ranks of uniform conifers marched across the heathland, awaiting their own sacrifice, much as William Rufus had been slain and sacrificed a millennium before, it was rumoured, in order to propitiate pagan gods; an autumnal sacrifice echoed in the dying of the woods. Meanwhile, at Brockenhurst, Maori soldiers with *moko* facial tattoos would lie in the local churchyard, brought from the other side of the world to fight the war to end all wars.

During the Second World War, while New Forest covens gathered at the coast to repel the Nazi invasion, hundreds if not thousands of night-time refugees from the Southampton blitz fled the town each evening to take shelter under its trees, as if they might atavistically protect them from the Luftwaffe's bombs that fell 'in ladders from the sky'. They joined and merged with the Forest's other itinerant inhabitants, the gypsies and travellers whom the artist and mage Sven Berlin recorded during his own stay in the woods.

Many had been living there for years. In 1927, the newly-formed Forestry Commission addressed the problem of the hundreds of people who were living wild in the Forest. Its solution was to confine them to compounds, where, like Native Americans on reservations, they could be corralled within a forest they had once roamed at will. Forbidden from erecting any permanent structures, these social rejects were issued with six-monthly licences which could be revoked instantly, should their behaviour displease the Commission. Their compounds were, in effect, arboreal concentration camps. 'Although nobody so far has proposed to liquidate these nomads after the Hitler style, is it possible that, in his own country, John Bunyan's people have been sentenced to a lingering death?' Augustus John asked.

These lives lived in the undergrowth thread unacknowledged through the Forest's history, like other anarchistic lives, from Anabaptists to Shakers; as unrecorded as mounds of briar or fungi whose growth lies underground, and as lost to history.

By the 1930s, the population of the seven compounds had reached nearly a thousand, swollen by the effects of the Depression. In 1949, there were still about 500 people living this way when Arthur Lloyd wrote a report for *Picture Post*, illustrated by the photographer Bert

Hardy. The grainy pictures, taken in the aftermath of war, reflect the greyness of the era and yet evince a sense of forlorn romance about these lost people living under canvas rags – or 'slums under trees', as the *Post* saw them: 'In the New Forest, tucked away from the birdwatcher and the week-ending stockbroker, hundreds of poor folk live in compounds, under Stone Age conditions.'

'Some call them gypsies, some call them dirty, some call them thieves. Most of them are none of these things. Many are decent people, with a strong wish for a better life, and a struggle before them to overcome prejudice.' These were insular communities, 'in-bred' and withdrawn from the world. At one compound, Shave Green, near Minstead, Sven Berlin came to live with the forest-dwellers, painting them as they 'moved in their green underwater world of summer, moving like drowned men.' But soon these land-bound drowned would be re-housed in faceless council estates, assimilated into the rest of humanity, the memory of their free Forest days far behind them.

In their place came the modern Forest, a much changed place, for all that it looks the same. Just as the cells of a human body are entirely replaced every seven years, so this place is filled and emptied with its myths, reinvented in its own image, or in the image of the humans who have shaped it. The factory-forest created in reaction to the First World War has its counterpart in the refinery at Fawley. The New Forest, cleared of its peasantry for Norman nobles, has been cleared anew for a new nobility. Meanwhile, as Richard Mabey notes, trees, like other plants, have become 'a biological proletariat working for the benefit of our species'.

But in some future world, Richard Jefferies' vision may be made manifest. The gravel lanes and tarmac roads will disappear, just as the train tracks have done. The Co-op shops will collapse, the multifunction cables rot in the earth, and the ivy and wild boar run wild over dual carriageways. Pylons will falter and topple; the refinery will dry up; and slowly but surely, the Forest itself will resort to its rightful wilderness. Not that any of us would be around to see it.

Chanterelles

PANKHURST FOREST, ISLE OF WIGHT

Evie Wyld

In the video you can see that Willie is in love with your mother. You never see Willie, he's holding the camera, but you hear his voice. And you can see from the way the camera is always following her. The part you rewind to watch the second most: his wife, Barb, stands under a sweet chestnut in a clearing. Late summer light bleaches her hair and face, but you can see she's smiling broadly, embarrassed. She does a pose, like she's pointing for that old quiz programme, the one with the wheel.

You tried to talk to Aaron about television, but he just said he couldn't remember and got annoyed.

Barb does her pose and the second she does it, the camera pans away to your mother. She doesn't know the camera is on her and there's something about the way she's standing, looking at something out of the frame that makes your chest ache. You want her to turn around, but she never does. A late woodpecker sounds high up in the tree, and you like to think your father looks up at it, to save Barb's discomfort as she suddenly becomes aware of the gangliness of her wrists, of her bright orange fleece and sensible boots. He watches the green leaf tips as they tremble in the breeze. Perhaps, you think, he notes the odd honey bee cutting through the space, holding on to the last moments of summer, feels a flush of optimism.

The camera is your secret. You only watch the video at night, with your sleeping bag pulled up over your head, the screen of the camera pushed up against your eye, so the images blur and the light spills in.

The video cuts out and when it comes back the camera finds your mother crouched on the floor, all in black, like she is ready to hide in the dark. She doesn't appear to feel the camera on her, is sifting through the leaves on the floor with her fingers.

'What you looking for there, Chrissy?' Willie is the only one who ever called her this – she didn't like it. She is Christine, but back home they can't stretch to the full name. Your mother looks up at the camera, shielded by her dark glasses

'Morels,' she says, smiles widely, goes back to it, waits for the camera to look elsewhere.

'English More-els,' says Willie. 'What's that? A nut?'

Your mother laughs.

'A mushroom.'

'An English More-el Mushroom,' announces Willie and remains focused on your mother. She looks up to the sound of a passing propeller plane.

'There are none here.'

Airplanes are just one of the things you find you cannot explain to Aaron. You remember it is something about the shape of the wing but he asks you how big they were and when you tell him, you can tell he doesn't believe you. And more and more they are coming to seem like another thing you dreamt of.

A scene change – a gravel path alongside dense woodland. The sky late morning blue. Willie plays some camera tricks. He gets Barb to stand on the pathway, framed by dark Scots pines either side. You can hear his breath. Barb disappears. Then reappears. 'The amazing disappearing woman,' says Willie. Barb disappears again, but this time remains gone. Cut to black.

Inside the dark spined forest, the camera adjusts itself to the changing light levels. There is the heavy tramp of the four of them walking over needle mulch, sticks cracking dryly several layers down. It is hard going walking on the forest floor, there are small sharp stumps that burn into the arch of your foot, and twist your ankle.

Today was a difficult day. It rained and you both spent the entire day soaked. The long grass heavy with water, as you squatted, waiting and listening before running across the road. The furthest East you have ever been. The trees are close enough together where you stopped that you risked a fire. Aaron laughed as he ate his can of beans. 'It's warming up my stomach!'

The camera concentrates on the forest floor, up and down, up and down. Willie has a bad knee, and so perhaps this is exaggerating the swing. When the camera glances up, your father is ahead – you see him for just a moment, his swagger, like a Georgian Dandy, he has what he refers to as his foraging stick – a thin piece of varnished ash with a forked top. Your mother finds the stick embarrassing, occasionally picks one up from the floor and waves it at him to illustrate how all sticks can be used to fossick in dead leaves. Your father when she does this stands proudly with one hand on his hip, toe pointed out coquettishly, and his thumb resting in the Y of the stick. He lifts his head nobly and clears his throat.

In front of your father, the flash of orange that is Barb is talking to your mother. Your mother is invisible because she is wearing black, and it is dark inside the forest, even though the time and date at the bottom of the frame have it as 1.45 p.m., August 25 2017. You hear the words 'adventure park' and 'grandchildren', and 'No'.

You have thirty batteries left in your bag. The camera takes six. This is probably enough for another year, if you ration yourself. You might find more somewhere, but there hasn't been anything of that sort in the houses for a long time. You don't think about those long nights without the camera.

A pheasant craws close to the group and the camera jumps a little. Willie says 'What in tarnation?' The camera is still on the forest floor, but your father says, out of shot, 'A pheasant.' He can be heard to go on to say 'They breed them to shoot round here,' but Willie has turned the camera on himself so that you can see his long red whiskers from below, and he says 'An English peasant. Here in Parkhurst Forest. On the Isle of Wight, England.'

A glade in the pines at 2.37 p.m. Barb sits on a tree stump and looks at the floor, doesn't lift her head to the camera. Perhaps she is tired. Your father walks past the camera, doing up his fly, glances sideways, wondering, did Willie film him relieving himself behind a tree, dismissing it as inconsequential. For the first time the dog is in shot – beforehand she will have been trying hard to bag herself a red squirrel, but she does not like this glade in the forest and always keeps close by ears low and tail protectively between her legs. Willie follows her, zooms in loudly, and she senses it, slinks lower still to the forest floor and finds your mother. 'Dust the dog,' says Willie. She looks at the camera with unhidden violence. Your mother is also close to the ground, but this time, as the camera finds her, she lets out a shout. The zoom is too close in on her and Willie has to pull out quickly to focus – 'What is it Chrissy?' Willie is unable to keep the alarm out of his voice. Your mother turns to the camera, 'Careful where you step!' She looks crazed, pulls something carefully from the ground and holds it out to the camera cupped in both hands.

'Chanterelles,' says your mother.

You ate the wrong sort of mushrooms once, the both of you. You lay, burning and vomiting, calling out, you for your mother and father and Aaron for you. And that was when you realised Aaron didn't remember them.

The final shot on the film is of the ferry ride back to the mainland. It's a bright day, the other passengers are in shorts and T-shirts, your mother as she drifts in and then quickly out of shot holds a tray of bottled beer. Willie films the whole crossing. His crook knee is perhaps a little worse, or maybe it's the roll of the waves, but the camera is never steady. The ferry turns and at the front as the mainland gets gradually closer, you'll hear your father saying 'It looks like something's on fire.' And the camera pans to look across the sea, to where dark smoke hangs. And then the camera is switched off.

Your favourite part, the part you watch last is at 3.20 p.m. They are still in the glade. The camera zooms in on your father's large, red-spotted handkerchief which has been spread out on the ground, and is almost hidden by a pile of the orange fungi. The shot is long. And then 'The English Shantrel.'

'Chanterelle,' your father corrects Willie and the camera lifts. Your father has taken off his hat and is wiping the sweat from his forehead, 'thought of as one of the most important and best edible mushrooms. We can eat them fried in butter this evening.' He goes on to describe some wine that will compliment the meal; if you listen closely you can hear the words 'citrus' and 'woody', and 'rather delightful' but Willie's gaze drifts upwards, skipping over Barb's turned back some distance off, and up the columns of Scots pines to their black brush tips, until he reaches the sky, white now. He zooms up to it, and the whirring of the camera drowns out completely the sound of your father speaking.

'And there we have it,' Willie says close to the microphone. 'Somewhere the sun is still shining.'

Oak tree and ruined cob cottage
HALSDON, DOLTON, DEVON, 1980
by James Ravilious

Archie Parkhouse cutting trees
ADDISFORD, DOLTON, DEVON, 1974
by James Ravilious

In 1986, Common Ground started work on **Trees, Woods and the Green Man,**
*a project which invited different artists, sculptors, photographers, illustrators, poets,
cartoonists, playwrights and writers to explore the natural and cultural value of trees,
and worked to deepen popular concern and practical caring for trees by publishing
pamphlets, a newspaper called* PULP! *and several books, as well as commissioning
plays and initiating art exhibitions at Tate Britain, the Natural History Museum and
The South Bank Centre. During 1989 and 1990, Common Ground commissioned
James Ravilious to photograph the orchards and woods of the West Country, and to this
day his extraordinary photographs continue to be exhibited nationwide.*

Pines
WOODLEIGH, DEVON, *c.*1990
by James Ravilious

Frosty Twigs
HALSDON, DOLTON, DEVON, *c.* 1990
by James Ravilious

Green Man
ELY CATHEDRAL, *c.* 1335
from the Kathleen Basford archive

No. 749

ISTANBUL ARCHAEOLOGICAL MUSEUM, SIXTH CENTURY
from the Kathleen Basford archive

Kathleen Basford and the Green Man

Kathleen Basford (1916–1998) was a British botanist with a special interest in genetics, but was also known for her research into the cultural significance of the Green Man in the British Isles and around the world. In 1978 she published The Green Man, *a landmark exploration of how the foliate head has been used as an ornament in building since the fourth and fifth centuries, first borrowed from antiquity and modified to express particular ideas and meaning. Basford herself called it the 'spiritual dimension of nature' in architecture. The collection of photographs that Basford amassed during her research and writing of the book was left to Common Ground to become part of the charity's wider art collection.*

Mesopotamian Green Man
THIRD TO FIRST CENTURY BCE
from the Kathleen Basford archive

From Hatra, or al-Hadr, the ancient city in the al-Jazira region of
Iraq – it is not known whether the motif has survived the demolition of
Hatra begun on 7 March 2015 by so-called Islamic State of Iraq and the
Levant (ISIL).

Roof bosses in the Cloister
NORWICH CATHEDRAL, FOURTEENTH OR FIFTEENTH CENTURY
from the Kathleen Basford archive

Why Woods Matter

BADBY WOOD, WARWICKSHIRE

Fiona Reynolds

Running up the hill to our favourite glade in the woodland, my four sisters and I never failed to whip ourselves into a state of collective excitement. Shrieking and calling to each other, we whooped and skipped until we reached the see-saw tree – a huge trunk, lying prone, with smaller branches lying across it, not literally see-sawing but scarily mobile, a place for daring and adventurous games with endless variations and unpredictabilities. We crept and balanced, hid and slid, playing among its limbs until we were exhausted. We loved Badby Woods, a regular Sunday afternoon haunt for my family, not far from our home just outside Rugby, and often varied by a walk in one or more directions. Always the see-saw tree figured.

Thus, though I was a child in the 1960s, a time assailed by the Beatles, the mini-skirt and other stimuli beyond my comprehension, my memories are of soaring beeches, magisterial oaks and the joys of a woodland year. Every season brought different experiences: the crisp-cold of winter, bare trees gaunt against the sky; the unfolding of the spring, leaves almost yellow in their brightness soon followed by drifts of bluebell and wood anemone; the delicious warmth of a summer's day, our skin cooled in the shade as we lay flat on our backs, squinting through the canopy far above us; and magical piles of dry leaves in autumn, ripe for kicking, throwing and hiding in. Oh, and of course the numerous rainy days when clad in raincoats, wellies and plastic rain hats (no fancy outdoor gear then) we returned home filthy, wet, tired and happy.

Growing up near woodlands meant I was always disposed to love them, even the dark and sometimes mournful conifers we met on holiday in the Lake District and Snowdonia. I, however, always preferred the graceful birch woods, the stunted oaks bent by the prevailing wind, and the willowy rowan, its red berries gleaming, that we encountered on our increasingly adventurous mountain walks. I had no sense of the bigger picture: woodland was just there – robust and eternal as far as I was concerned.

But the next wood I got to know changed my mind. At university I was introduced to that most studied place, Hayley Wood, about 12 miles west of Cambridge. I was reading geography, and the department was still lingering under the influence of the recently retired great historical geographer, H.C. Darby. I fell for the discipline, steeping myself in W.G. Hoskins' *The Making of the English Landscape* and soon came across the work of Dr Oliver Rackham, a young botanist with a passion for woodland history. He had begun recording Hayley Wood's flora a few years earlier in the early 1970s, identifying what was rare and distinctive – especially the true oxlip, by then confined to a few sites in East Anglia – as indicative of ancient, undisturbed woodland. My mind was newly attuned by Hoskins to understand the vulnerability of the English landscape and I loved Hayley Wood and its oxlips, becoming at once captivated by this pale-yellow, large-petalled beauty and shocked by the realisation that this once-common flower had been almost wiped out by the destruction of ancient woodlands in recent decades.

That was my awakening to the vulnerability as well as the beauty of woodlands, and when I got my first job after leaving university, as Secretary to the Council for National Parks, the pace of my learning sped up. For I was catapulted immediately into a row about how farming and forestry were destroying the landscape and wildlife of Britain. In 1980, as I arrived, Marion Shoard's polemic *The Theft of the Countryside* highlighted how public subsidies were encouraging farmers and landowners to grub out ancient woodlands, ponds, wetlands and hedgerows and to plant conifers across the uplands;

while in Parliament. MPs and Peers were debating the Wildlife and Countryside Bill, whose modest measures demonstrably failed to grapple with the immensity of the conservation challenge. The irony, it soon became clear, was that when it came to woodlands they could be both good and bad: it all depended on whether the right trees were in the right place.

Ancient woodlands – those which have been in continuous existence since at least 1600 – like Hayley Wood were incontrovertibly good for wildlife and immensely important features in the landscape, but were disappearing under the plough in favour of the profits that could be generated by replacing them with cereal fields. In other places ancient woodlands were being under-planted with conifers, encouraged by grants from the Forestry Commission to make them 'productive', a process which also destroyed much of their historic interest and value for wildlife. And subsidies for planting and tax breaks for commercial forestry were driving the planting of conifers on heather moorland and other beautiful upland areas. Indeed, almost my first task as the new secretary of CNP was to corral the arguments against a peculiarly ill-judged, diamond-shaped new plantation on the slopes of the Brecon Beacons, stuck on the side of the sweeping hillsides of the National Park, bearing no resemblance to the native woodland of the valleys. We lost.

Immersing myself in CNP's files, I soon learned that there was a long history of fights against controversial afforestation in National Parks and that the battle was far from won. The arguments had begun in the early twentieth century, when the Forestry Commission (created in 1919 to replenish Britain's timber supplies) began its work. It looked for cheap land where the new breed of fast-growing conifers, particularly the American Sitka spruce, would bring a quick return. Its eyes turned to the hills. These had long been spoken of as 'wasteland', a derogatory term that ignored the writers, poets and artists whose admiration for their beauty had stimulated a love for the landscape and encouraged the early National Parks movement. It was not, therefore, long before there was a most fearful clash in that best-loved of all upland landscapes, the Lake District.

By the early 1930s the Commission had planted nearly 1.25 million larches and over 5 million spruce on 1,000 acres at Ennerdale and near Keswick. But it had not reckoned on the public's passion for protecting the Lake District, rooted in William Wordsworth's evocative defence ('is there no nook of England / secure from rash assault?') against the railway line to Windermere in the 1840s and John Ruskin's defence of beauty. A row over the drowning of Thirlmere in the 1870s to supply Manchester's citizens with much-needed clean water had led to the establishment of one of the country's first local pressure groups, the Thirlmere Defence Association, which, by the early twentieth century, had broadened its remit to the defence of the whole Lake District. The ugly conifer, in Wordsworth's words 'this spiky tree', blanketing the glorious fells, obscuring their natural lines and visual surprises and cutting off treasured public access, was already in its sights.

When the Forestry Commission provocatively acquired 7,000 acres of land in upper Eskdale, the Friends of the Lake District leapt into action. The author Hugh Walpole wrote to *The Times* describing the plans as bound to 'ruin it once and for ever', and in a House of Lords debate Lord Elton compared the proposals to 'planting a petrol station in front of an ancient cathedral'. After a petition was circulated attracting 13,000 names, many of them influential figures, the Commission was forced to think again. Finally in 1936, it took the unprecedented step of signing an agreement with the Campaign to Protect Rural England (Friends of the Lake District's 'parent' organisation) declaring that 300 square miles of the central Lakes would be exempt from conifer planting.

Nowhere else, though, received such exemption, and in the 1960s CNP's predecessor, the Standing Committee on National Parks, was still fighting the conifer. In March 1960, an article in *The Times* reported that a newly formed forestry syndicate planned to acquire 100,000 acres of 'bare land' in Devon, Cornwall and Somerset and to make a further 250,000 acres of existing woodland 'fully productive'. It was easy to work out that the moorlands of Dartmoor, Exmoor and Bodmin were in line for planting, and the precious ancient woodlands of the South West those that would be 'improved'. The

Standing Committee published a pamphlet urging that new planting be brought under planning control, but its pleas were ignored. Under pressure, the Forestry Commission agreed to pay more attention to landscape, wildlife and public access. It employed Dame Sylvia Crowe as its first landscape architect and had already begun to open its own plantations to walkers and cyclists, creating Forest Parks in its largest forests from the 1940s onwards.

The crisis that broke the stranglehold of bare-land conifer planting, fuelled by public subsidies, took place in Scotland in the 1980s. By now many sites in England and Wales (especially those designated as National Parks) were too controversial for major planting projects, but the Sutherland Flow Country, remote and inaccessible yet one of the UK's foremost conservation sites, seemed the perfect place. By 1987, a staggering 60,000 acres had been planted, around half by the Forestry Commission and half by private investors, encouraged by planting grants and generous tax breaks. Exceptionally, tax relief could be claimed by investors at two points in the forestry cycle: at the moment of planting, and when the trees were harvested, and these sums made what would otherwise have been an uneconomic pursuit extremely attractive. The RSPB called for planting to be stopped in 1987 and the Nature Conservancy Council (NCC) sought a moratorium while a conservation solution could be worked out. At CPRE (where I was by then working) we published a report setting out the perverse effects of forestry's generous tax subsidies, and in 1988, frustrated by the lack of progress, the NCC published a no-holds-barred report, 'Birds, bogs and forestry', highlighting the appalling damage being caused to the ecology and wildlife of the Flow Country by conifer planting.

The row that followed led to the break-up of the NCC and a bruising time for nature conservation in Britain, but it also stopped conifer planting. For on Budget Day in March 1988, the Chancellor, Nigel Lawson, unexpectedly but decisively pulled forestry out of its tax benefits. Overnight, the case for planting in the Flow Country and many other upland areas collapsed and the Chancellor called for a 'better balance' between broadleaved trees and conifers. The threat of large-scale afforestation in the uplands retreated and not returned.

The future of Britain's glorious ancient woodlands, though, was still on a knife-edge. And here the figures were even more shocking. In the first edition of his book, *Trees and Woodland in the British Landscape,* published in 1976, Oliver Rackham concluded that if the changes between 1950 and 1975 continued, there would be no ancient woodland left in the country outside nature reserves. In 1983 the NCC recorded that 46 per cent of ancient semi-natural woodland in twenty-three counties had been either cut down or replaced by conifers between 1933 and 1983. This resulted not just in visual and historic losses, but caused the catastrophic decline of woodland species of butterflies, birds, invertebrate species and flowering plants: a decline which was calculated in 2016 in the RSPB's 'State of Nature' report as being of the order of 53 per cent, with 33 per cent of species declining 'strongly' since 1970. Woodlands like my own childhood playground of Badby Woods, now thankfully a Site of Special Scientific Interest (SSSI), were disappearing or losing their character unless they were protected in statute or by conservation ownership.

Again the Forestry Commission was challenged, lobbied and eventually persuaded of the importance of protecting ancient woodlands, and its 1985 review of Broadleaved Woodlands Policy recognised for the first time the need for higher rates of grant to maintain and enhance pure broadleaved woodland, to protect ancient semi-natural woodland, introduce stricter controls over felling and provide better advice about the management of broadleaved woodland.

Slowly, the threats diminished and, by the 1990s, the benefits of well-managed woodlands, providing public access, wildlife protection and green lungs for all species, including people, were becoming widely recognised. New, sensitive woodland planting was also taking place. In the Midlands the National Forest was established in 1987 to create a new, 200-square-mile 'forest', combining planting with open glades and restoring the industrialised landscapes of the former coalfields; and new Community Forests around major cities brought woodlands for public recreation, green space and wildlife closer to people's homes. The Forestry Commission became the people's friend, opening its once forbidding conifer plantations in places like Kielder Forest in Northumberland, Coed-y-Brenin in Snowdonia and Grizedale in Cumbria, bringing recreational experiences and winning public support through generous access policies and good visitor facilities. Multi-purpose woodlands and forests, aiming to meet a number of public-spirited objectives, were in vogue and there was a genuine and growing consensus about the importance of woodland in people's lives and for the wellbeing of the country.

All the more surprising, then, that in late 2010 there was another shock when the new coalition government published a consultation paper proposing to sell the public forest estate in England. The public forest estate is that which is owned by the Forestry Commission. It is an estate of some 650,000 acres, around a fifth of the total woodland cover of England, and it comprises the major public-sector commercial forests, large areas of mixed and deciduous woodland, and the ancient former royal forests, whose ownership had been transferred to the Forestry Commission (not without controversy) in 1923. While there had been previous suggestions, repeatedly rebuffed by the public, that elements of the public forest estate might be privatised, never before had it been proposed that the whole estate might be sold off. The outcry was heartfelt, enormous and unanimous.

Though there was anger everywhere, it was most powerfully felt in the former royal forests: places like the New Forest, Forest of Dean, Cannock Chase and Rockingham Forest, with roots in medieval England, whose complex management structures and wooded landscapes reflected the intricate historic relationships that had evolved over centuries. It was strongly felt that these were not the Government's to dispose of but part of the public realm, deeply rooted in our collective cultural history. When the Government's plans became public, rallies and marches were held in these forests and many others, the banners declaring 'hands off our forest' and the protestors singing 'This Land is our Land'.

Given the Forestry Commission's unpopularity over many decades it was intriguing, though heartening, to see the case being rallied for its defence. But it was soon clear that the campaign was focused less on the Commission as an institution than on safeguarding the woodlands which were felt to belong to everyone, whether they were commercial, multi-purpose or historic, or all three. The Commission was their custodian but it was the woods that mattered.

The fight to protect them from privatisation was short, sharp and intense. And the Government was on the back foot throughout. It all came to a halt on 16 February 2011 when the then leader of the Opposition, Ed Miliband, asked the then Prime Minister David Cameron whether he was happy with the plans to sell off the forests. His response was pithy: 'The short answer to that is, no.' Within hours the consultation paper had been withdrawn and the newspaper headlines the next day spoke of 'forests sell-off abandoned' and 'Cameron U-turn'.

To answer the question 'what next', the Government set up an independent panel to advise on the future of forestry in England, chaired by the charismatic Bishop of Liverpool, the Rt Rev. James Jones. He was no bystander: he had spoken against the sell-off in the House of Lords, and was known as a passionate environmentalist. He saw it as the panel's job – I was one of its eleven members – to develop a vision for all the forests and woods in England, and for the next year he led an exhaustive inquiry into the state of trees, woods and forests in England, consulting widely on their future. And when our report was published, it won the rare accolade of being universally welcomed.

Our findings, and our vision, were clear and compelling. In the right places, managed for the right purposes, woods are good for people, good for the economy and good for the environment. So we can dismiss the tensions of the past and create woodlands which deliver multiple objectives, enhancing wildlife and people's lives while also earning revenue. At the same time, woods and trees will help us respond to and mitigate against climate change by stabilising soils, absorbing carbon dioxide and storing carbon. If we commit to using more wood for construction and in our daily lives – reconnecting with and reviving the woodland culture that had almost disappeared in this country – the benefits would get stronger.

My childhood experience of woodland was inspiring and motivating. It bred in me a love for woodlands that has never left me. But as quickly as I learned that the story was more complex, I learned that it was within our gift, if we work at it, to make sure that the right trees are in the right place, and fulfil their potential as inspiring contributors to every aspect of our lives. As we face a range of extraordinary challenges as a society this, at least, is one thing we can get right.

Forest of Eyes

BURNHAM BEECHES, BUCKINGHAMSHIRE

Paul Kingsnorth

When I was a small child, I thought that the biggest living thing on Earth was a blue whale. A little later, I discovered that I was wrong. The blue whale might be the largest animal, but the largest living thing, it turned out, was the giant redwood tree, which grew on the north-west coast of America. I ferreted out a picture of a redwood, and couldn't believe how huge, how wide and epic its trunk was compared to the puniness of the human being standing next to it. I spent fertile hours imagining whole forests of these things, how tall they would be, the view from the top of each tree of the untouched forests rolling away to the far horizon.

I seemed to spend a lot of my childhood fantasising about forests. I think that woods are deep in the imagination and soul of most people on Earth, at least people who grew up in a culture that came from forests. In northern Europe, we were a culture of forests until relatively recently, and the trees are in our bones. Our folk tales and fairy tales are set in the great rolling woods that once covered our lands, and in the tales the woods are sometimes threatening, sometimes welcoming, but they are always there, and they harbour creatures mythical and real. All of this entranced me. For a long time, as a child, I knew that when I grew up I would live in a pine forest, like a Viking or a wizard, or perhaps a Viking-wizard. To me, there was nothing quite like being in a wood. There still isn't.

When I was twenty-one years old, I spent two months working in the rainforests of Borneo. It was a life-changing experience. For the first time, I saw a forest as a forest was meant to be: as a living thing, as a network of life, as a life itself. The trunks of the great trees were as epic as anything I had seen in those pictures of the redwoods, and the gibbons hooting from the banks at dusk, the orangutans crashing through the canopy, the toucans and parrots and snakes and spiders, the danger and beauty; all of it made everything back home, including the English woodlands, seem as puny as that man standing by the redwood trunk in those childhood illustrations. Most of all, the great rainforests of Indonesia seemed more than the sum of their parts. In some intuitive way, some inexplicable but very real sense, these places were *alive.*

It was only very recently that I learned I had been wrong about the giant redwood. It is not, after all, the biggest living thing on Earth. I only realised this recently because it was only discovered recently. The biggest living thing on Earth is not a tree at all, it turns out, but a fungus; or to be more accurate, a fungal mycelium. The mycelium is the underground network of filaments that connect the fungal spore bodies which we see above the surface, the mushrooms and toadstools, the strange shapes growing on the tree trunks. These are just the tips of something very much greater; something buried.

Networks of fungal mycelium connect most of the world's plant species and form an integral part of them. They are to be found under the soil of every wood and forest, and scientists are only just beginning to realise how complex and wide-ranging they are. Ecologist Stephan Harding says that fungal mycelium are 'the most important nutrient transport system on the planet ... which control underground nutrient flows in ecological communities, and also determine which plant species can live in them.'

This is interesting enough, but pioneering mycologists – that is, people who study fungi for a living – are beginning to suspect that there is more to the mycelium even than this. Mycologist Paul Stamets, who has dedicated his life to studying them, believes that these networks of filaments, which connect the roots of every tree in every forest on the planet, are more than simply a food delivery system. In his book *Mycelium Running*, he describes them like this:

> The mycelium is an exposed sentient membrane, aware and responsive to changes in its environment. As hikers, deer or insects walk across the sensitive filamentous nets, they leave impressions, and mycelia sense and respond to these movements … The sensitive mycelium membranes act as a collective fungal consciousness … Like a matrix, a biomolecular superhighway, the mycelium is in constant dialogue with its environment, reacting to and governing the flow of essential nutrients cycling through the food chain.

A collective fungal consciousness: it is quite a claim. If Stamets is right, the notion that a forest is more than the sum of its parts may be borne out. It could be that a woodland is not simply a collection of trees, bushes and birds. It could be that a woodland is, after all, alive. In some sense, it is a being. And it is watching you.

It's interesting to compare this emerging scientific knowledge about the abilities of fungal mycelium with much older, indigenous stories of forests as living entities, in relationship with the humans who exist in and with them. Anthropologist Richard Nelson spent many years working with the Koyukon Indians of Alaska. This is now he describes their worldview:

> Traditional Koyukon people live in a world that watches, in a forest of eyes. A person moving through nature – however wild, remote, even desolate the place may be – is never truly alone. The surroundings are aware, sensate, personified. They feel. They can be offended. And they must, at every moment, be treated with the proper respect.

A forest of eyes. It is, surely, a fascinating prospect that cutting-edge ecology may be bearing out the intuitive understanding of very old worldviews such as this. *The surroundings are aware, sensate, personified.* Is this not another way of looking at the work of those underground networks of mycelium? Are these not two different methods of parsing the same reality?

I felt, when I was in Borneo, that I was in a forest of eyes. I have felt it in European woods too. I have felt it in Britain, even in tiny spinneys and copses. I have felt, in short, that a woodland represents more than can be explained in the kind of straight-backed rationalist language we are all supposed to use these days; and especially more than can be explained in the language of price, resources, or utility. If a woodland is alive, after all, if it is watching us, if in some sense it is aware, then our relationship with it changes – or should do.

Next time you go for a walk in the woods, reflect on this. Reflect on the possibility when you walk through a forest, the forest can feel you. That it knows what kind of creature you are. That it is sending out signals, that through the mycelium, the trees are communicating with each other. Some mycologists have suggested they can warn each other of threats and opportunities based on what they sense. *Here comes a human: be aware.* Think about that for a minute. Internalise it. Next time you find yourself in a wood, be aware of the reality that at some level you are not simply an observer of the wood, but are being observed by it. Just as in the old fairy tales, the woods have eyes.

If this is true, we might ask ourselves: what should our relationship with a woodland be? I don't think that this question, and the understanding that prompts it, should prevent us from utilising the woods where necessary: coppicing the trees, logging and replanting in a responsible manner, enjoying the place. Like the other species that live in a wood, it must be possible for humans to take advantage of its bounty, if they are able to do it responsibly. But are they? There is a big difference between seeing a wood simply as a collection of resources we can harvest to exhaustion, and seeing a wood as a living place we can have a mutual relationship with. In the latter case, we can still take, but we also have to give. That's how mutual relationships work, after all.

Perhaps this all sounds a bit airy-fairy. I don't think it is. I think it is necessary, and not a minute before time. If there is one thing that the current ecological crisis teaches us it is that we have got our relationships wrong, with woods as with nature more broadly. If we see a wood as a machine, we will behave very differently to the way we would behave if we saw it as an animal. Alive or dead, resource or living place: our attitude, our understanding, directs our behaviour.

Perhaps the old indigenous ways of seeing and the new revelations from scientific investigation might slowly help to change our attitudes, which in turn may help to change our behaviour. It might be a long shot, but it seems the best shot we have; maybe the only one. And I think it begins in the place where so many of the best and the oldest stories do: in the woods.

Speaking Wood

CAE'N-Y-COED, GWYNEDD

David Nash

Cae'n-y-Coed (field in the trees) is a two and a half hectare parcel of land sloping up from the valley floor on the south side of the Ffestiniog Valley in Gwynedd, North Wales. Owned by the Oakeley family (also proprietor of the largest slate quarry in Blaenau Ffestiniog at the head of the valley), the land was planted from the late-eighteenth century to supply timber for the estate, growing oak, ash and beech. In the early 1960s, the estate was broken up and sold in separate 'parcels' at auction.

In 1971, a local woodman suggested to the owner of Cae'n-y-Coed that some of the larger trees were ready to be felled, and it was agreed that he could buy and extract the mature trees. In the event, the woodman (who was a notorious rogue) cut down virtually everything leaving only the smallest trees and a single stand of birch. Only the trunks of the felled trees were hauled away; all the branches and brush were left and the effect was one of wanton destruction. The valley is part of the Snowdonia National Park and felling of this nature is illegal without permission.

Around this time, I had been to a retrospective exhibition of David Smith's sculpture at the Tate Gallery in London and had been struck by the ease with which he handled steel, cutting, heating, pounding and welding it as if it were clay in his hands. David Smith spoke steel. I realised I needed to try to be as fluent with my material, to learn to 'speak' wood and to allow the material to lead me. Hitherto I had been treating wood as a dumb, inert material, using it to invent forms without understanding or taking account of its origin.

The devastation at Cae'n-y-Coed presented me with a significant opportunity. I had just started working with unseasoned wood, and here were two and a half hectares of branches, some very large. So, it was agreed that in exchange for any wood I could use, I would clean up the mess and replant. For three years I spent time at Cae'n-y-Coed whenever I could. Without chainsaw or tractor, and with only hand tools and block and tackle, the clearing was a big task. I built a small hut where I could shelter from the rain and spent whole days simply sorting through the tangle of branches. As I cut them to manageable lengths and stacked them, I became conscious of shapes, diameter and length, bends and forks and the specific form, weight and texture of each tree species. The growth principles for all trees are the same. Each year their branches divide and lengthen so as to increase the number of leaves and the area of leaf surface, and their girth thickens with a new layer of wood – the annual ring. But each species has different characteristics that are consistent with that particular species throughout the world.

In axing, splitting and sawing by hand I had to engage with these qualities: some trees resist splitting – elm, sycamore, yew; some split willingly – willow, beech, chestnut; some resist handling – oak, hornbeam; while some seem to welcome being worked – lime, birch, beech. They also smell different; the smell of birch is clean, lime is dry, holly has a strange tang to it. Oak smells of vinegar, elm can be sour and vile. Beech with honey fungus has a smell of honey right through it which will fill the air at a work site.

I started by chopping and splitting fresh, unseasoned wood and deliberately kept my mind on the physical process rather than on the outcome. Soon I was looking for a way of working the linear shapes of branches into simple, self-supporting structures; searching for a method that followed from the nature of the material. I was using an axe and wedge, lever and rope, and later saws – methods of handling timber that go back thousands of years. Working continually on one piece of land allowed me to experience at close hand the progress of the seasons through the year and to watch how trees naturally regenerate – some growing from the stumps of felled trees, some from seed; meanwhile the bracken was spreading now that it had more light, and brambles too.

I was in my twenties, and giving up the colour constructions and theories of art I had learnt at art college: I was finding my art, and letting the land show me the way. The practical work showed me that there was 'thought' in physical movement and physical matter. The contact that my body and mind had with this raw material stimulated new and different ideas. My thinking/feeling senses were meeting the deeper 'thinking' of natural forces. Each branch that I pulled, sawed and stacked contained its journey from being part of a living, growing plant to becoming a separated object paused between life and decomposition. Each branch echoed the character of the species from which it came: a pile of ash branches is so different from a pile of beech, the feeling of ten oak twigs held in the hand is quite different from the feeling of holding ten birch twigs. Numbers also took on new meaning, became alive: one branch, two branches, three branches. One branch = alone, independent; two branches = balance, even, calm, complete; three = uneven, outward, alive; four = a balance again; even number = passive; odd number = active. Maths, geometry and algebra had excited me at school; they were the languages I could readily learn. Now at Cae'n-y-Coed these languages became truly alive. Shapes and weights began to demand to be put together, and I followed where they took me. Cae'n-y-Coed became for me an access point into vitality and dynamic thought, enormous in its simplicity.

Once I had started working with wood, it soon became clear that when wood is taken inside – inside a home, inside an art galley – we borrow it from its natural cycle, we remove it from the extremes of the environment that nurture it in growth and break it down in decomposition. So I asked myself a question: how can a viable wood sculpture exist outside?

I began with the assumption that a sculpture outside had to stay the same, to resist change. Clearly I could not change the nature of wood, but I could perhaps change assumptions about it. Engaging with and celebrating the potency of the elements rather than regarding these as a negative force was a liberation. I quickly saw a distinction between a tree growing or 'coming' and wood decomposing or 'going'. The *Ash Dome*, conceived in 1976 and planted in 1977, was my first 'coming' engagement and the *Wooden Boulder*, which began its journey in 1978, became my first 'going' engagement.

While I was working through the debris at Cae'n-y-Coed, natural regeneration had already started, mostly birch, willow and holly. I felt the need to add other broadleaved trees – oak, ash and beech, much in the spirit of information. Somewhere I had come across stories about Chinese potters laying down clay in pits for the use of their grandchildren. Another striking story I heard around this time concerned the British Navy during the Napoleonic Wars: finding that they were running out of oak to build ships they imported Indian teak, but this made ships that were too buoyant. And so, in an extraordinary act of long-term planning, oak was planted all over the south of England to build the fleet in the twenty-first century.

One of the jobs I had when labouring locally for a forestry company was planting Norwegian Sitka spruce in long, straight rows. I was paid six shillings per hundred. It was awful work, but even worse was the result over time of bland, alien plantations taking over the hills and moorlands. They were even replacing mixed deciduous woods, which were being felled because of the tax advantage of planting conifers. So when it came to planting trees at Cae'n-y-Coed I knew that I did not want spruce or straight lines.

Not planting in straight lines made me think about the eventual relationship between the trees once they were mature, which in turn led to visualising the space between them. Space is a fundamental ingredient of sculpture, and I soon realised the potential of growing a 'shape of space' over a long period of time. This idea answered a small problem I had with the itinerant nature of land art. An intervention in a usually remote area is documented and then abandoned. When I planted the ring of twenty-two ash trees in February 1977, with the intention of growing a domed space, it was conceptual artwork, and I presented it as such. However, I reckoned that it would take thirty years to grow the space, and this added a physical commitment to the conceptual action. Taking people there to see the ring of small saplings was asking them to visualise and conceive of an intended form. Over thirty years the concept has become a reality.

The idea was untested, but I assumed optimistically that both I and the trees would survive the thirty years, and that I would have cajoled them into wrapping themselves around and over a domed space. Another Chinese potter story I had heard was that the potter kept his mind on a form of space and coaxed the clay to enclose that 'form of nothing' – the 'something' and the 'nothing' giving virtue to each other.

A dome form seemed most appropriate as it was clearly a human intervention and it reflected forms already in the immediate landscape. There was only one space level enough at Cae'n-y-Coed for this project, and it was itself slightly domed. To the north were the curving foothills of the Moelwyns, and to the east, the dome forms of Manod Mawr and Manod Bach.

My main source for research into which species of tree to use was hedgerows. I noticed that ash was resilient and vigorous and recovered most readily from being pruned or fletched. And in the woods I observed that ash trees could lean a long way from their roots in search of light. (And there was my name Nash, apparently derived from someone living near ash trees Near Ash, N'ash, Nash.)

Twenty-two seemed to be a practical number with no mystical associations; this was sculpture not shamanism. I made a radius with a stake and string and measured twenty-two equal spaces around the circumference. I bought twenty-two ash saplings and planted them. Naively, I did not protect them and they were soon gone, eaten by sheep. So I started again with a fence and rabbit guards. It's tough to be a tree with so many predators. Mice, sheep, rabbits, cattle, deer, and squirrels (the last being the worst) will all nibble the bark off young trees. I also planted birch on the west side as protection from wind as well as inside the circle to stimulate the ash (the trees would compete for light). I took the birch out a few years later when their job was done.

The material and processes involved in the *Ash Dome* are the same as those deployed in making and sustaining a hedge. Interestingly, some people are discomfited by the *Ash Dome* and the controlling, interfering nature of my process. There is a sense that it is OK for hedges but not for art. The environmental movement was split in the 1970s between a belief that the human being is an alien parasite and that nature would be better off without us and a conviction that we are all an essential part of holistic nature, if we can work with it rather than attempting to dominate or conquer it. Forests are healthier for some extraction of trees but suffer grievously if there is over-extraction. 'Man gets along better by collaborating with Nature and not dominating it' is one of Lao Tzu's aphorisms.

Princess Forest

COILLE NA BANA-PHRIONNSA, NORTH UIST

Alec Finlay

How many ships sailed in the forest?
What anchor struck in the deep of the wood?

Where is the oak soaked and the ash awash?
Where are the pine needles encrusted with salt?

What is that sound: the shush of the wind in branches,
    or ebb of a riddled tide?
Where are there tillers, where once there were antlers?

Can you hear wolfhounds baying?
How are deer to be hunted in the sea?

Whose is that turf-roofed house?
How did the hearthstones get pockled with barnacles?

What am I doing showing you a forest here, on the west shore of a tidal island, attached by a causeway to the west coast of a larger island, looking out on the Western Ocean? Behind me Uist's dub moors are brocaded with sea lochs, some so intricate their coastlines exceed 100 miles in length. The bog is a book filled with pressed pollen; an archive recording the Hebridean outlier of a prehistoric savannah that we know as The Great Wood.

Place-names bear witness to The Wood's decline:

Tom Fhreumhaigh
Pine-roots Rise

Coire nam Freumh
Pine-roots Corrie

Tom a' Bhranndair
Root-tangle Knowe

The roots and names recall a millennial *pibroch*. The lament of the *ùrlar* ground: *Scots pine*; the grace of *birch*; bass of *juniper*; and the habitual inventions of *siubhal – birdsong*.

We own our forebears' destruction of the forest as a sin against nature, which science has translated into the measured guilt of biodiversity and species depredation. In expiation we are committed to the regeneration of the native woodland.

Why are there no trees: because there are no wolves, nor lynx; nothing to deter the browsing deer. *Deer and trees go together*, goes the old forester's saw, but togetherness can only occur after a cull. The Wood will not be regrown by carbon offsets, native wildwood reserves, and the promissory notes of SSSI.

The archaeologist's map shows a surprisingly bulbous Western Isles basking alongside Britain – though it will be centuries before the mainland is known as that. The separatist sea has recently released Kent from the continent.

Peat ash and one charred hazelnut shell are the cosy data marking the arrival of a band of hunters this far north and west: we don't know the name of their clan, and, if we could hear them speak, we wouldn't recognise the language. They followed elk and reindeer north, took to their coracles and crossed The Minch, perhaps calling in at the bloodstone quarries of Rum.

As soon as they arrived these wandering hunters began burning the woods – as early as 700 BC – gaining heather-moor and grass to encourage the deer they fed on, and worshipped.

Beyond the beach the trees!

There is, of course, a story that answers the riddle of the forest; otherwise why would I have dragged you here in the first place? There were once trees growing under these waves, forming a mythical wood said to extend all the way to St Kilda. It had a name, The Princess' Forest, Coille na Bana-phrionnsa. And some say that she – The Princess – is the first named person in Scotland, far older than Calgacus, *The Swordsman*.

Take a walk across Uist, through the confusion of inlets, or make your way by canoe, as two friends did, for a ploy; dip your fingers in its waters: you can never be sure when the taste will be briny. For thousands of years the sea has breached and reduced the Hebrides. In his study of North Uist, Erskine Beveridge reckoned the beach I have brought you to, Baile Sear, *The East Township*, must have had a partner West Village, now lost under the sea. This would help to explain why old field names have, perplexingly, become attached to skerries. Locals still tell how, at low tide, 'the stumps of ancient forests may be seen projecting above the sand.' There are sunken peat-mosses at Vallay and Kilpheder, and a friend found roots on the beach at Stoneybridge. Two centuries ago a horse and cart could cross the miles from the bright rock of Heiskir at low tide. Fishermen tell of 'moss, trees, and masonry' brought up by their anchors at 'fathoms'.

Geologists are willing to go some way with the folklore: a few millennia ago the westward coast-line was far out to sea – some even refer to a 'lost continent' stretching 40 or 50 miles, joining together the jigsaw pieces of Baile Sear, Heiskir, Hirta, and Harris.

As to the character of The Princess' Forest, the climate was more genial but, with squalls and salt spray, imagine nothing more substantial than scrub brakes and thickets – a forest, in the old sense of a tract of hunting ground.

The myth survived because Martin Martin recorded it on his voyage to St Kilda in 1697. The islanders showed him a drystane turf-roofed hut up on the Glen Mor shieling, Taigh na Banaghaisgeich, which he translated, 'The Amazon's House', though 'Female Warrior', or 'Huntress', is more accurate. Martin said:

> This Amazon is famous in their traditions: her house or dairy of
> stone is yet extant; some of the inhabitants dwell in it all summer,
> though it be some hundred years old; the whole is built of stone,
> without any wood, lime, earth, or mortar to cement it, and is built
> in form of a circle pyramid-wise towards the top, having a vent in
> it, the fire being always in the centre of the floor … the body of
> this house contains not above nine persons sitting; there are three
> beds or low vaults that go off the side of the wall, a pillar betwixt

each bed, which contains five men apiece; at the entry to one of these low vaults is a stone standing upon one end fix'd; upon this they say she ordinarily laid her helmet; there are two stones on the other side, upon which she is reported to have laid her sword: she is said to have been much addicted to hunting, and that in her time all the space betwixt this isle and that of Harris, was one continued tract of dry land.

Myth wears away. The most recent archaeological survey dates the hut as seventeenth century, but the islanders' practice was to add walls to existing buildings, so there may be an earlier dwelling, or dwellings, absorbed in the walls – whether Gaelic, Pictish, or pre-Pictish.

Martin reports the discovery of deer antlers buried on the east hill, Oisebhal, with a 'wooden dish full of deer's grease', a reference to bog butter – the traditional interment of vessels of fat, sometimes accompanied by a deerskin bladder. Some archaeologists explain this as a way to preserve food – rancid, at that – security against raiders; but, as deer were not native to St Kilda, the antlers suggest a ritual aspect. The artist Joseph Beuys certainly thought so when he embedded a lump of stork margarine in Rannoch Moor, as an offering to one of Scotland's totemic lost forests.

Everyone knows The Hebrides have been treeless for centuries. The islanders once explained that the woods were burnt 'by a witch' at the command of a Norse princess, 'betrayed in love'. Blame is a comfort, but it grows no woods.

Did the myth of The Princess' Forest arise out of the destruction of the woodland; a picture of better times, when an earlier people ran with the deer; or was the myth a way to explain the mysterious hut and ritual burial, as some suppose fairy knowes to be a memory of the patterned folk we call Picts, and their barrows? Is the simpler explanation that The Princess' Forest was woven together from the evidence of a real drowned forest that appeared at low tide?

Does it matter if the existence of the deer-mad huntress can't be proven? Her name leads between the known knowns of science and the unknown knowns of ancestral memory. Like those drowned churches off the Suffolk coast, whose bells are said to toll the tide's method, here, on the beach at Baile Share, the mind's-ear listens for siskin, and chiffchaff. The lattice of purposelessness of the wood hides in the humdrum pointlessness of the sea; lost songs pipe from the birds' narrow throats and rise in bubbles to the surface. In time it will turn out that myth is a trustworthy record: we may not know the origin of the tale, but we have only to wait a few years, a decade or two at most, to return to her forest. The world is drowning, just as the waves flooded over the machair in the cataclysms of the Mesolithic, creating a spume of charcoal, ash and branches.

Tom Fhreumhaigh TAUM REE-AVI
Mound or hillock of roots

Coire nam Freumh CORRA NAM FREAV
Corrie of the roots

Coille na Bana-phrionnsa COILE NA BANA-FROOSNER
The Princess' Forest

Tom a' Bhrannder TAUM A-VRANDER
Mound or hillock of gibbet

Ùrlar OOR-LAR
Floor or ground

Siubhal SHUAL
Travel (as in the musical term for variations)

Bale Sear *Baile Sear* BALLA SHERR
Eastern Township

Heisker HEY-SHKIRR
Bright rock

Taigh na Bana-ghaisgich TOY NA BANA-GASHKISHI
The House of the Heroine

Oisebhal (Norse) OSHIVAL
East Hill

Medieval Survivor

CHALKNEY WOOD, ESSEX

Simon Leatherdale

C halkney Wood clings to the valley side in deepest Essex, a rare survivor in a landscape ravaged by pre-Roman farmers, Churchillian military installations and post-war agriculture and forestry policies. Today, the wood is in two ownerships: one third is owned and managed by Essex County Council (since 1974), the remainder by the Forestry Commission (since 1956). The county council holding of 60 acres is ancient semi-natural woodland, a gem of an example of lime and hornbeam with a carpet of bluebells. The Forestry Commission area of 120 acres *was* similar, with the added interest of four, small valleys cut into the slope by spring-fed streams.

The war treated the two halves rather differently. The county council side contributed much needed underwood (coppice) to the war effort but the Forestry Commission side gave its timber trees in addition to underwood. There were only five timber trees left on this side by 1946, two oak, two ash and a sweet chestnut. So when acquired, their respective parts were very different in character and condition.

The county council, from the outset, adopted a policy of traditional 'coppice-with-standards' management which continues to this day and results in a wood of outstanding beauty and character.

The Forestry Commission side fared differently. What they acquired in 1956 was, at the time, termed 'scrub', so it was decided to replant. The standard practice of the day was to opt for fast-growing conifers.

This would usually mean planting a very limited range of species (often monoculture) thought to be suitable to the site conditions. Essex famously has a climate which is literally 'drier than Jerusalem', so the choice was probably pine (Corsican and Scots). What actually happened was somewhat different.

The Forestry Commission woods in this part of East Anglia were grouped together and managed as 'Honeywood Forest', later amalgamated with others in Suffolk to form 'Lavenham Forest'. This forest was very much a backwater, far removed from the mainstream Forestry Commission operations in places like Thetford Forest. As a consequence, when local foresters put in their requests for plants to Forestry Commission nurseries they were relegated to the bottom of the pile and were only fulfilled at the end of the planting season. When the plants arrived at the forest the numbers were usually correct but this was achieved by gathering all the species left in the nursery beds at the end of the season, so it was somewhat of a mixed bag (literally). The result was that these small woods got planted with a much wider range of species than was originally intended.

Chalkney ended up with Corsican pine, Scots pine, Douglas fir, hybrid larch, western hemlock, red cedar, Lawson cypress, Norway spruce, sweet chestnut, hybrid poplar and beech. Only five acres were left unplanted, the rest (116 acres) was planted between 1959 and 1961 with a mix of this array of non-natives (even the beech is not native to this area).

In order to achieve a good start, the native 'scrub' was comprehensively sprayed with a cocktail of chemicals to kill it off. A scattering of larger scrub trees were retained to provide dappled shade for the infant conifers (these would be poisoned later when the conifers were deemed to have established themselves, usually after ten to fifteen years).

Several chemicals were used on the scrub, notably '2-4-5-T' (a derivative of the notorious Agent Orange used in Vietnam) and Paraquat. The dappled shade trees were injected with 2-4-5-T via a 'Jim-Gem' tree injector (a large metal syringe-type device) or frill girdled with a billhook and ammonium sulphamate applied as crystals.

By the late 1970s, one could be forgiven for thinking that you were standing in a conifer plantation with few clues that it was in fact an ancient wood. The contrast with the county council part of Chalkney was dramatic and could not be more stark.

Oliver Rackham (an East Anglian born and bred) was familiar with Chalkney at this stage, and with his good friend Colin Ranson had studied the wood in depth, both on site and in historic archives. It was for them a great sadness to see this once fine wood brought to its knees from an ecological perspective and they both had all but written it off as an ancient wood. This is what Rackham termed the 'locust years'. By 1986 the Nature Conservation Council (NCC) had deemed it so damaged that the Forestry Commission part of the wood was de-notified as a Special Site of Scientific Interest (SSSI) – the ultimate disgrace. It was very clear from the rides and paths in this part of the wood that the public were voting with their feet: all the paths on the county council side were heavily used while those on the Forestry Commission side were rarely used at all.

Rackham published *Trees and Woodland in the British Landscape* in 1976; the frontispiece shows a map of Chalkney in 1598. The shape of today's wood is unchanged. This work gained a wide readership and established 'ancient woodland' as a valid concept in forestry circles. Indeed, in 1980 came his seminal work *Ancient Woodland* which again heavily featured Chalkney. From this point the value of ancient woodland, both ecologically and culturally, was being recognised and tentative experiments by local Forestry Commission staff showed that all was not lost, as these woods were capable of regenerating themselves if the introduced species were removed in time. In 1986, the Forestry Commission built a logging road into the wood enabling the planted crop to be harvested commercially – so began the first small removals of the conifer crop. With light let in, the ground erupted with shoots from buried seed, and shoots sprang from long-suppressed remnant coppice stools that had hung on through the locust years; Natural England (the successor to the NCC) re-notified the Forestry Commission part of the wood as an SSSI.

At this point Rackham began his Field Studies Council courses at Flatford Mill. Always over-subscribed, this course enthused, educated and inspired hundreds. For years his views were at serious odds with those of the Forestry Commission, but in a delightful turn about they asked him to run additional courses at Flatford for its own staff. These were five-day residential courses running late into the evenings, a fascinating and inspiringly intense week. The result of these latter courses was that an entire cohort of Forestry Commission managers were brought up to speed on ancient woodland issues and management techniques. Oliver used Chalkney for site visits on all his Flatford courses and hundreds of people from all walks of life went from Flatford with their eyes opened to the possibilities of restoring ancient woods that had been planted with alien species.

These people have since spread far and wide and suffused virtually the entire woodland management sector in the UK. Oliver's subsequent books have been read by many thousands, so his ideas and passion continue to spread to this day.

In late 2011, English Nature performed one of their regular SSSI condition assessments on the Forestry Commission part of Chalkney. The result was that it was now classed as in 'favourable condition' (the highest rating). From de-notification to favourable condition in twenty-five years – the first plantation on an ancient woodland site in England to achieve this.

So on a cold and windy day (8 December) in 2011, Oliver was once again in Chalkney, this time wielding an axe rather than a pen. He was there to fell the last conifer, a sizeable Corsican pine (33 centimetres in diameter and weighing nearly a tonne). With him were a group of people closely associated with the wood over the years, a small contingent from the media and a motley gathering of nervous Forestry Commission staff. The nervousness came from the thought of a seventy-one-year-old felling a big tree with an axe in a high wind in front of a crowd complete with the press and numerous cameras. The tree had been pre-cut by a skilled chainsawyer, leaving a small tab at the back of the tree to be severed with the axe. The risk assessment was complete, the felling area taped off, the steel toe-capped wellies and helmet donned and the axeman briefed – what could possibly go wrong? Well nothing did, it all went smoothly, though it took Oliver a few deft blows to get through. He stepped back. A cheer went up and the tree came down with a very satisfying thud. Photos were taken, speeches made and souvenir discs chainsawed from the butt for all those that wanted them.

To misquote Mr Churchill, this was not the end of the restoration process, nor even the beginning of the end, but it was the end of the beginning. The wood will never be how it was before it was planted with conifers. All woods change over time, and climate change is likely to exacerbate this. However, the wood is now in a much more natural and sustainable state and more able to adapt and cope with future change. Give a century, and it may look a little like it did in pre-war days.

If you visit the wood today you would need a very keen eye to spot any evidence that the conifers had been there. It looks for all the world like an unmolested ancient wood. There will be some losses with the demise of the conifers, some sensitive bryophytes won't tolerate their going, crossbills will find no cones to open and the delightful smell of hot pine resin on a summer's day will be sadly absent. The price, though, is well worth it. Go on a day in late April and marvel at the show of ferns, bluebells and pink campion and listen to woodpeckers and nightingales. The public have returned too – the paths are now well used and even dog walkers play a part by deterring deer that would otherwise browse the coppice regrowth. The plant communities here have direct lineage going back into the mists of time. Take a moment to stop and think of the continuity stretching back to before the Romans, even as far back as the last ice age.

Oliver Rackham influenced so many via his writing and teaching, including the managers of Chalkney. He was a woodland historian who became a significant part of woodland history.

Don't Look Back

PILES COPSE, DARTMOOR FOREST

Gabriel Hemery

Dictascript: Flek#101/December/2050/Devon
Interviewee: Dr Gabriel Hemery, Forest Scientist
Location: 50.444467,-3.909212 (Piles Copse, Dartmoor Forest, Devon)
Time (at start): 050-12-13-0.4.873
Recording length: 00:33:26:40

Interviewer: If it's OK with you, I'll start recording now *[panting and footsteps]*. I was surprised that you chose this place for your interview. You've been involved in so many projects during your career, I suppose I'd expected you to suggest we meet in Oxfordshire, at Paradise Wood, or the Jaguar plantation. Or it would have been easier to have met in one of the city-fringes of the Domesday Forest. But instead, here we are. A remote wooded valley on Dartmoor. Why here?

GH: Well, I'm eighty-two years old so getting here took more effort than it used to! Mind you, Dartmoor used to be pretty barren – it offers so much more shelter now. Some called it a wilderness but it was never that. Well, not since mankind first settled here 5,000 years ago and started clearing its trees.

   I suppose, to answer your question, Piles Copse has always held a special place in my heart, being a woodland that seemed to feature regularly in my life. You might say we grew up together! It used to be one of only three woodlands on the high moor; not exactly remnants but miniatures of the wildwood that once covered these hills from the end of the Preboreal chronozone. During the twentieth century these woodlands – Wistman's Wood, Black Tor Beare and Piles Copse –

were surrounded on all sides by livestock; sheep, cattle and ponies that grazed everything. Only the clitter protected the trees; no wonder the area was barren for most of the 954 square kilometres that made up the national park at the time.

I came here first in about 1974. I would have been six years old, and probably wearing flared cord trousers with a home-knitted (and itchy) polo neck jumper. [*Laughs*] My father, Eric Hemery, was an author writing about the history and topography of Dartmoor and I spent my formative years following him around every square mile of the moors as he completed over ten years of painstaking research. In part, I guess that's what gave me a love of the outdoors.

I remember exploring the tortured and dwarfed trees that characterised this small woodland; not these big oaks you see round us today. The huge granite boulders in the clitter seemed even bigger then as I scrambled over them with my little legs, searching among them for pixies and imagined Bronze Age treasures. I don't remember a great deal from that first visit except that it was bitterly cold; so cold in fact that my fingerless woollen gloves were hopelessly inadequate, and my toes froze in my thin rubber wellies. I remember the trees though – they were fantastical.

Interviewer: When did you next return?

GH: I lived about 15 miles away and I passed by here from time to time, often on walks (I started solo wild camping before I was twelve years old) and later, on my mountain bike in the late 1980s. In my late teens I volunteered with the Dartmoor Mountain Rescue Group, and we scoured this area, whose features were so often deceptively veiled in mists. It made search and navigation quite tricky, especially at night, which it invariably was. Of course those mists are infrequent now, with our warmer climate.

One of my most memorable visits here – for many reasons – was in August 1990 when I was just twenty-one. I came here as an undergraduate to study the ecology of the woodland for my final-year thesis. It was when the tree bug first bit me. I was with my girlfriend, Jane, having convinced her not only to help me with my fieldwork but to experience a long-stay camp for the first time. I got to know the woodland really well, and we got to know each other equally well, I can tell you. I remember one moment vividly: it was during our first full day – we were completing the first of many line transects up through the boulder-strewn slope, measuring and plotting the trees. I had placed my clipboard on one of the moss-carpeted boulders to measure a tree, and on picking it up was shocked to find it alive with hundreds of crawling tiny ticks. I had inadvertently found a swarm of the blood-sucking creatures. That was an omen. Later in the evening, by the light of a torch in our tent, Jane picked off 111 ticks from every conceivable warm crevice of my body. We got married two years later!

Interviewer: [laughs] How was the copse different in 1990 than it is today?

GH: Well, sixty years is a considerable period in ecological time. The landscape was almost unrecognisable from today. I would say that the environment was, simply, familiar, in the sense that it was bare and exposed like much of Britain's uplands. There was stark beauty to the high moor, which, owing largely to the absence of people, felt wild. It was only later, as I developed what you could describe as a deeper environmental awareness, that I gained true insight into the nature of Dartmoor's landscape.

I completed my undergraduate report, noting that the future for the woodland was positive, providing that grazing animals continued to be kept at bay by the clitter. I was well aware of the ecological significance of Piles Copse as an island of trees in a moorland wilderness. I think it was beyond my comprehension, however, that the copse was more akin to an oasis in a desert.

Actually, I brought a copy of my report with me; would you like to see it?

Interviewer: Oh really? Yes, that would be great. You mentioned clitter earlier – what is that?

GH: [Rustling is heard as Gabriel searches in rucksack – recording required digital enhancement]. Clitter is a local name for the boulder fields that can occur below the rocky outcrops or tors, that dominate many of Dartmoor's hilltops.

Interviewer: It looks like it has been produced on a typewriter...

GH: Yes it was, and you can see how the trees were stunted and deformed. They were not dwarfed to the same degree as those at Wistman's Wood, which is higher in altitude, but nonetheless the trees were less than half the height that you would expect for their age. The tallest were only 10.5 metres, even though well over a hundred years old. The main species was pedunculate oak, while a few rowan occurred along the woodland fringe, and alder on the river bank. It was just over ten hectares in area then. The next nearest woodland was three miles downstream in the Erme gorge.

So you see, Piles Copse really was very isolated. Did you notice while we walked here along the track that the trees amplified the roar of the River Erme? Well, imagine walking along the same track but being able to see for miles around. The sound of the river was usually swept away by the ever-present winds but you would have seen the river below, and the gentle sweep in the valley opening up in front of you to reveal the narrow corridor of trees that made up Piles Copse in the distance.

Interviewer: It looks incredibly different from these photos. In one way I suppose it's quite beautiful in that you can see the whole landscape.

GH: That's true I suppose. Today you would have to climb to the top of Stalldown Barrow to get a view across the whole landscape. From there the woodscape is a spectacular sight. It wasn't until subsidies were removed in the 2020s that things really changed on Dartmoor.

Interviewer: Tell me a little more about that.

GH: Ideas of rewilding had come to the fore early this century. It just made so much more sense to explore new options. Hill farming had become totally dependent on agricultural subsidies, while many people increasingly recognised the moorland for what it was: a manmade desert. Not everyone agreed of course – especially those who had farmed the land for generations and recreational users who were used to the wide-open landscape – but change inevitably came in many forms and at different paces. Removal of grazing because of economic realities meant that nature started to repair itself. In many places, incentives to enhance the environment through tree planting – often with water management in mind – helped considerably too.

Eventually, green fingers spread up Dartmoor's valleys; first came birch and alder (Italian), and later red oak, black locust and Japanese red cedar (which spread naturally from a nearby plantation). Milder and wetter winters favoured tree growth at higher elevations, and fecundity too. Sadly, the bearded lichens and mosses that once festooned the trees are gone from here now, owing to high summer temperatures, although they do still live on trees at higher elevations. We know from satellite imagery that by 2042 Piles Copse had become an ancient woodland among a mob of teenage trees that spread all the way from Ivybridge and the border country, right up to the edges of the blanket bog and craggy hilltops two miles further upstream. There are even a couple of common ash trees nearby, although their exact locations are not made public. It seems that the low footfall in this valley, together with prevailing westerly winds, has provided a little enclave both against ash dieback and the emerald ash borer, which have jointly decimated ash trees elsewhere in Britain.

Interviewer: I want to ask you about the last decade when . . .

GH: Sorry, before we move on, I wanted to mention another special moment in my relationship with Piles Copse.

Interviewer: No, that's fine. Please carry on.

GH: It was in late in the winter of 2015. I had been asked to write an essay focusing on a woodland that held a special meaning in my life. It was the year after my first book, *The New Sylva*, had been published, so I guess I was becoming better known as a commentator on sylvan issues. I chose to return to Piles Copse to write *in situ*. I remember it well, as I camped here again; this time accompanied by my two boys, who would have been teenagers then. You might like to see the sketch I made during that visit.

Interviewer: I find it almost inconceivable that this is the same place.

GH: Mmm. 2015 was a memorable year in many ways. When we visited here in December the ground-breaking climate talks would have just concluded in Paris. Politicians finally grasped the fundamental concepts of a low-carbon economy and climate-resilient society. For the first time it was widely recognised that we were already living with the future climate, and that those countries that invested in a green economy would emerge triumphant over the environmental laggards.

The same year I had led a survey of woodland owners, exploring awareness of environmental change, as well as actions and aspirations. It proved to be a turning point in its own small way in how we communicated with and supported woodland owners. After all, even then the vast majority of woodlands were owned privately (72 per cent), although that has changed now of course. Until then, policies and approaches were very top-down, and based on too many assumptions both in terms of the knowledge among woodland owners, and their motivations. Their voices were rarely heard. I remember one statistic – even now, thirty-five years later – that only 55 per cent of owners thought that climate change would affect the UK's forests in future. It was quite shocking even then. How times change. Perhaps I'm beginning to veer off course?

Interviewer: No, it's all interesting. I wanted to ask you to talk about the big picture. Since you mentioned 2015, how would you describe the journey we've been on since then, in terms of the evolution of society?

GH: We take for granted today that most everyday items are made from wood fibre in one form or another. Look at our e-comms for instance; all their components are wood-based, from the flexible screen inwards. After you picked me up from the seaport today we drove through Plymouth's suburbs, the residential blocks that towered thirty storeys above us being constructed entirely with engineered wood, while the superstructure of your car has been made entirely from bio-based materials. In 2015, we were only beginning to imagine these technologies. For instance, developments in the manufacturing of nano-crystalline cellulose were still in their infancy, but were beginning to show their potential as a replacement material to oil-based plastics.

Remember, 2015 was *only* thirty-five years ago, but we should recognise that cultural and industrial developments are ever-accelerating. If we imagine the lives of people back in 1915 – while Britain was at war, horses were a major form of transport and few people travelled abroad – and suggested then that in just thirty-five years life in 1950s Britain would be a post-war era (a Second World War no less), that most people would own a car, and the jet engine would soon make international passenger flight commonplace, it would have appeared totally fanciful. I suppose the term 'foresight' had yet to be coined by H.G. Wells!

Looking back to 2015 the same applies of course. We had little grasp then of carbon-negative construction, the notion of forest cities, wood-based, benign, carbon-capture technologies, and how to value natural capital. Wood was used in its most basic form, or even worse. For instance, you may not know that for a time the drive towards bioenergy meant that people were chipping and burning solid wood; can you believe that! Even worse, we were exporting our carbon and environmental footprints elsewhere by importing woody biomass (often, I would add, produced by plantations created in the place of precious tropical rainforest) to co-fire some of our coal-powered stations. So extraordinary, that if I'd not witnessed it myself I would count myself as a one of those eco-denialists!

I recognise that it is easy to criticise with the benefit of hindsight, but looking back we did seem to be slow off the mark. During the 1990s and 2000s, I worked as a tree breeder attempting to improve the genetic quality of some of our hardwood tree species. Scientists were advising decision-makers to account for the importance of the genetic component of our forests. However, entrenched views among powerful lobbying interests continued to peddle outmoded notions that 'nature will cope' with environmental change. Advocates of the emerging climate science were already warning that rates of change would be unprecedented, yet such projections were often unheeded.

I remember, too, being quite vociferous about the need to diversify species in our commercial timber plantations. Can you believe that the core argument was that sawmills would only accept a few principal species, mostly Sitka spruce of course? Rather than pursuing an intelligent discourse with sawmills, exploring the benefits of diversification and explaining the high risks inherent from assuming no change, we seemed caught in a feedback loop where the sawmills were reluctant to diversify, so the foresters planted and nurtured a narrow range of species. The commercial-forestry time bomb had been not only primed, but the fuse had been lit. It's no surprise that things came to pass as they did.

We were also planting what I termed 'green fuzz' everywhere. I got in trouble for that phrase at the time but I stuck by it as I believed the term captured perfectly the fact that trees were being planted with little intention that they would enhance society or support the green economy. New woodlands were often planted on good land, abandoned soon after planting with poor aftercare, with little if any mid-cycle silviculture. I believed, even then before our modern-day food rationing, that we would have been better off farming such land to produce food or biomaterials.

There was another dimension to our troubles, which proved to be the most problematic. This was the estrangement between much of society and the natural world, let alone our woodlands. I was a keen advocate of Forest Schools when they first emerged in Britain, while bringing environmental studies back into the secondary school curriculum was a long and hard battle. Fighting from the bottom-up for better environmental education was never going to succeed alone, not without changes to accepted paradigms. Eventually, when the penny dropped that the green economy was our future, then things started to change. Behavioural changes in wider society were nurtured through recognition of environmental citizenship, while investment in a future generation of green engineers started to bear dividends. I am proud that a disproportionately large number of environmental ambassadors from Britain now grace the world stage.

Interviewer: This is high-level stuff. How did these policies and global actions affect the environment at a local level, such as here at Piles Copse?

GH: You just have to look at the young woodland we've walked through to reach this ancient stand of trees. Already timber stacks from first thinnings line the road, consisting of many different species, both hardwood and softwood. Each stem has been selected for its intended market through precision 3D-scanning technology, linked to a real-time national wood inventory. Compared to the landscape that dominated before, methane-producing sheep have been replaced with nature's superlative solution to benign carbon management; namely the tree. The devastating floods that once tore through the lowlands have been reduced in frequency and impact, thanks to the trees now present in the water catchment area above us. Soil erosion, carbon-rich peat in fact, has been reduced too. Over 120 species of birds have been recorded in this valley alone, while rare woodland specialist flora and fauna are invading. It's inspiriting that this woodland provides a haven for wildlife and space for people to enjoy, while also being managed to produce the raw material essential for society in the mid-twenty-first century.

If I were a little younger, I would love to walk back to the Plymouth seaport. Did you know that you can cover the entire 23.3 km without leaving the shade of a tree?

Interviewer: Thanks Gabriel. I've enjoyed our wide-ranging discussion. I wish we had longer.

GH: My pleasure; I've enjoyed talking with you. Good luck with your book by the way. I'll send you a scan of this sketch if you like.

Thinning

KINGSETTLE WOOD, DORSET

Robin Walter

I still feel it's a weighty responsibility to authorise the felling of a tree, even after all these years and all my training. Sometimes I agonise, waver this way and that, then walk away unable to decide. Other times I mark trees for the chop with confidence.

Today, I am marking one of my favourite local woods, Kingsettle, for thinning. It will soon have bluebells and wild garlic in distinct swathes, but this early in the year there are small clumps of the delightful white wood anemone and a rare patch of town hall clock, not yet in flower, but with its clock-tower up and ready. Most of all, this wood has distinctive topography – steep banks, precipitous slopes, hollows gathering water and small streams running out into the fields below. Most likely, it is the wood's awkward landforms which have kept it wooded for centuries, while easier land around was cleared for agriculture.

Once part of a medieval hunting forest, this wood was probably used for low-grade timber and coppice until the 1960s. At that time the Forestry Commission was on a mission to convert 'scrub woodland' to productive use by planting fast-growing conifer species from Europe and North America. The land would have been cheap at that time, we needed the timber, we were investing in our nation's future, so it looked like a good idea.

They planted different crops according to ground conditions – Douglas fir, the quality king of conifers in Britain, on the greensand slopes; Norway spruce on the wetter flushes; Scots pine and beech on the drier tops.

Why do we so hate conifer plantations? Isn't tree planting supposed to be a good thing? Planting is the start of a tree's long static journey through time, rooted in this particular soil, weather, place. It also tells us something about ourselves, our aspirations and our values. Any kind of planting is an act of faith. But Jay Griffiths gives us a clue in her book *Wild* when she derives the word 'wild' as meaning 'willed' or 'self-willed'.

> Self-willed land does what it likes, untilled, untold, while tilled land is told what to do . . . Enclosed, land is no longer self-willed, and becomes listless, subject to the will of the owner, subdued in spirit.

The land has its own will, its own destiny and in these parts it is likely to evolve into woodland with oak, ash, hazel and willow. Few, if any, woods in Britain have been allowed to determine their own destiny; they have all been subject to the will of successive owners over the centuries.

But owners can exercise their will alongside that of the wood, respecting nature while tweaking some features and reaping a modest harvest. Felling an entire wood and planting something else is a completely different exercise of will, one with imperial attitude.

The resulting forests are unmistakably the work of a narrow and dominant intent imposed on the land – just one or two species of tree, all the same age, planted in rows, no variation, more like a military parade than a living landscape. This is industrial forestry, turning the landscape into a resource of raw materials for extraction and processing.

But these regimes can be difficult to sustain over the long decades. Perhaps there are pockets of resistance to the new order, now resurgent and overwhelming the colonists. These 'intruded broadleaves', as they are termed, used to be suppressed with 2-4-5-T herbicide with greater or lesser success. Some plantations bear no trace of the previous vegetation, so rigorous has been the suppression; other plantations bear little sign of the new owner's intended crops, so complete is their rejection by the natives.

Even a successful plantation crop will mellow with the decades as the will of nature reasserts itself. The mature conifers have acquired character and stature over their now long lives and these old giants are opening up to natural intrusions of young growth like tolerant old grandparents.

In the wood I am visiting, the planters have been very scrupulous. There are lines of beech planted on the bank and down over the edge on ridiculous slopes too steep to walk, let alone harvest timber. What were they thinking? By the time this is cut we will all be travelling by jet-pack? These beech have been left standing to attention long after the war is over. At ease! Stand easy!

A patch of land will generate a roughly constant growth of woody material. Left to its own devices, trees in a natural forest will fight it out amongst themselves over decades and generations. Strong growers suppress weaker growers; spindly trees may blow down; slow, steady trees, happy to grow up in shade, may emerge, tortoise-like, after the sprinters have had their day. We can reap a harvest from these natural forests and it will reflect the diversity of that forest in size, shape and species – a big oak log, some crooked birch and lots of ash poles perhaps.

So we foresters tinker with what nature offers and shape it to the needs of our times. All that woody growth can be concentrated on the trees we most value – so we keep the straight oak and fell the crooked birch, and the oak's annual rings grow fat in response to the extra light and root-space we give them, making a more valuable log for next time.

The needs of the day are filtered through the minds of foresters and into the fabric of the forest, favouring this tree over that when thinning – and when planting for that matter. Up till the twentieth century there was need of hazel for sheep hurdles and thatching spars, so acres of hazel were planted and grew like mustard and cress, with occasional oak standards. As the need for hazel lapsed, the oaks were allowed to grow up into high forest to provide logs; or perhaps the hazel and oak were swept away for conifer plantations like this wood.

So what do we make of these woods now, fifty years on? Do we still need this long-awaited crop? We are lucky here that the Norway spruce and Douglas fir have grown well and are sellable. But the beech and Scots pine are both poor quality and would only fetch a low price anyway. This first stand to mark for thinning is a mixture of beech and Scots pine, planted in close rows, three of beech then three of pine. The idea was the pine would grow fast and shelter the slower beech; the pine would be thinned in the early decades to provide a financial return while favouring the beech, which would grow on for a hundred years or more. It is one of the elegant systems of classical forestry, but it relies heavily on future generations to carry on the work and, most importantly, to value the enterprise and its products.

Here, changing owners have not kept to the rigour of the plan, partly because changing markets have not valued pine and beech as highly as was expected and partly because the current owners are not focused on timber. Lack of thinning left both beech and pine spindly and gasping for air. The beech has also proved to be of poor provenance, with repeated forks in the stem, so no grand columns of timber in this stand.

By chance another need has recently appeared – firewood for domestic stoves. Now these beech have soared in value as virtually any wood is good enough for the fiery furnace. But how long will that last?

I spray an orange paint spot on two sides of a crazily bent beech, swooping up into the sky amid its more sober neighbours. They might just be fit for sawlogs in a few decades time, if there is a market. Further on I mark a pine with a fork at ten feet – that tree will never get any better, but the one next to it might make good use of the extra space.

On the opposite side of the ride they planted just Norway spruce, now standing in straight bristly columns, the planting rows still clearly visible. It must have been quite a task to suppress the natives and establish this regime here, and not entirely successful. Alongside the spruce are growing numerous ash poles, their pale and slender stems weaving their way towards the light against the dark upright spruce. Where the spruce is dense and the shade unbroken, the ground is scorched of all vegetation. The dry earth bears only fallen needles and occasional moss.

Elsewhere in the wood where deciduous trees dominate, be they beech, ash or sycamore, there is still a mosaic of bluebells, garlic, wood sorrel, yellow archangel and pignut. They do their urgent reproductive work in spring before the leaves come out on the trees. In summer, they sit and ripen in the deep, leafy shade, protected now from invasive sun-loving bramble, grass and bracken.

But here in the spruce plantation the young trees grow up and out, forming a closed canopy of uninterrupted shade for years until the first thin. If the thin is early enough, some woodland plants may hang on long enough, even as seed, to re-emerge. Or perhaps an intruded ash has kept open a shaft of light for a patch of wood sorrel to survive; or a relic oak tree has gathered a congregation of plants under its sheltering limbs, witnesses to the old order.

When I was 'on the saws' I did some first thins in spruce. The forester marked the end of every seventh row and we cutters each had a row to do. The first tree was a bugger because it always fell out into the ride, its side branches heavy from gorging on sunlight. That meant lots of work snedding off the branches, only to reveal a knotty log for your trouble. And then you had to clear all the brash off the ride. The next tree would fall into the gap left by the first and so on along the row. It was a joy to see these shafts of light penetrate the still gloom. We worked away in our parallel rows, like miners following seams. I was never very fast, but some cutters handled their saws like plasterers' trowels, smoothing over the logs, removing branches and bumps to leave perfect cellulose cylinders.

What should we do with this stand now? We import 80 per cent of our timber, so perhaps we should take some responsibility for our insatiable demand and produce some more of our own. We could grow some fine spruce logs here.

But Kingsettle is on an ancient woodland site, meaning it has been wooded since 1600, or longer in this case. As such, it has retained its undisturbed forest soils, its characteristic woodland flora and who knows what other micro-organisms, something not found in more recent woods. Of the forests which once covered most of Britain, only a tiny percentage are left – these are our precious ancient woodlands. Where these were planted over, as has happened here, we have a Plantation on Ancient Woodland Site, or PAWS. These woods can retain many of the plants that thrive only in their long-stable soils, and sometimes harbour ancient trees, 'distressed' by centuries of events recorded in their grain.

So converting these woods to a more benign deciduous forest cover is a priority for conservation; restoring that seasonal rhythm of light and shade will let the vernal plant specialists in but keep the summer generalists out.

I am drawn to the spruce with my spray can. If we just felled them all now it would be simple and cost effective, but we would lose our protective canopy and leave our precious woodland flora at the mercy of invasive bramble, bracken and grass. So we must choose which to take and which to leave as our continuous tree cover.

This stand has had to sort out its own pecking order – some 'wolf' trees have grown big and sprawling, dominating and stunting those around. Others have lost the struggle for light and with it the will to live. Most are reaching up shoulder to shoulder with neighbours, their canopies interlocking. The question is, which trees have most to contribute to the stand from now on? The weedy ones will not recover their vigour and are best harvested now. Those wolf trees should have been culled years ago and should be removed now – except perhaps that one with a buzzard's nest in its storm-damaged crown.

Felling this rough tree and its stunted neighbours will leave a bit of a gap. Carving out this niche will provide an opportunity for a new generation of trees to grow up. Judging by the other gaps, it will most likely fill up with ash seedlings, some birch and willow and even a few spruce. Further on, another fine spruce has outstripped the others and reached its optimum size for felling. Any bigger and the sawmills will not be able to process them, so they begin to lose value.

A spongy bed of golden saxifrage covers a wet flush where several spruce have blown over. It is always surprising to see these root plates tipped up vertically. Not at all the mirror image of the aerial parts, the roots spread out wide and shallow like little model trees in a train set. Their roots cannot live in waterlogged soil and there is only sludge to grip onto. Leave them where they lie for the bugs.

This wet flush may grow up with willow and alder; trees whose roots can live in water. Back in the gung-ho days they might have drained areas like this, making the site fit their requirements. That wilfulness is less common now and you are more likely to find a forester suiting the trees to the land.

Further on into the stand is a little gap which must have been created during the last thin some twenty years ago. It has a bristle of little ash trees carpeting the ground. Their pale-green stems, the size of lollipop sticks, are ankle-high and already multi-stemmed, like crazy candelabras tipped with tight black buds. Deer have repeatedly nibbled the growing tips over the years, causing them to branch out from the side again and again. Held in check, they are shaggy with gathered moss. With less deer browsing they would send up slender shoots of new growth and resume their journey up into the light.

This profuse regeneration of ash offers a vibrant new component to the stand – columns of broadleaf trees rising up in these pools of light. But we now have to ask what future these ash will have – will Ash Disease blow in and blight them? And what of the relic ash and the intruded ash already here? If we thin the spruce to favour them now, will we be left with gaping holes when they too succumb to the fungus? Perhaps we should thin out the ash now and put our faith in the spruce? Or we could plant in the gaps, if there is enough light, with oak and impose our own little islands of intent. In fact, the notion of our controlling nature is often illusory. The landscape is littered with woods where our intentions have been gradually overwhelmed by nature's gentle might; human interventions now long forgotten.

Ash is the obvious choice for so many people wanting to grow woodfuel – a native tree, fast-growing, good to coppice, unpalatable to squirrels, its clean stem yielding easily worked poles, its low moisture content making it the best hardwood for burning. But when *Chalara fraxinea* was discovered in planting stock in Britain, it was a sobering moment for anyone working in forestry. It reminded me of the skeletal hedgerows left by Dutch Elm Disease and the trees felled at my parents' house – in particular the extreme difficulty of splitting the logs. Although, I was too young to remember a landscape populated with mature elms. Could this be repeated now, where chancing upon a mature ash in a remote wood will be a source of surprise and wonder?

Half-way up the slope is a mixture of Douglas fir and Norway spruce. Maybe they were hedging their bets here when they planted. Douglas is more valuable, especially in large dimensions for structural timber, but spruce might do better in the wet soil. Both cast dense shade. In this stand they have both grown well and there are sawlogs to be harvested from both – that will improve the income from this thin.

Ten or fifteen years ago you would have lost money on a job like this – it would have cost more to harvest than you could sell it for. Lots of thinning was delayed or abandoned at this time and the effects of that neglect are showing now. Sales prices were low because imports from densely wooded emerging nations such as Latvia were so cheap you could buy timber ready planked off the dock for less than we could harvest it here. Then they joined the EU, living standards rose, wages rose and prices went up. Also China has become a huge importer of timber, especially from Russia, so we have less flooding our markets. We used to have to pay to take our low-grade chipwood away; now the price is positive and rising as woodchip boilers hoover up available material. So a building boom in Beijing draws timber across Asia, triggers new patterns of supply in the Baltic and may affect whether this wood gets thinned this year and in years to come. It is still marginal on these steep slopes with poor access for road haulage and with a motley range of log sizes, but it is now possible to cover these high harvesting costs.

So I spend the day choosing between this tree and that, this spruce and that ash, this beech and that beech; my will, reflecting our current concerns, written in orange spots across the forest.

What governs this succession of choices? How do I know when to stop? Must every crooked tree go now? Classical forestry employs tables to measure increment and yield and thus arrive at the correct thinning intensity. But forests rarely conform to this ideal, so the forester's interpretation is crucial. This is particularly important where, as here, the original trajectory of the plantation is being diverted to new ends.

For me, thinning is creating a living structure in four dimensions. Keeping or removing a tree will affect the stand's overall structure and composition right now in 3D. Add to that the axis of time and you can imagine the whole forest evolving through the decades – the favoured trees swell to fill the canopy gaps you give them; the bigger gaps on the forest floor fill up with natural regeneration and new cohorts of trees surge upwards; the shading canopy is now permeable to light and the wood sorrel and bluebells can enjoy their brief months in the sun; the woody increment is accruing to the stems of greatest value; we are beginning to let go of our domination and let nature have a say in what happens next.

It is difficult to imagine and sustain complex structures over decades and centuries. It is more a case of setting the parameters and letting natural processes take over. For example, you may decide to have no more than one third of the natural regeneration as conifer, or none at all; or to introduce a new species like oak, which has few parent trees to reproduce from in Kingsettle Wood; or to harvest at a certain size; or to let nature take over completely and walk away.

But time is not what it used to be. When the forestry books were written they assumed the world would be the same in fifty or one hundred years time; markets might come and go and fashions might change, but the world itself would stay the same over time.

Not so any longer. Trees pushing up through the ground now will find the world is significantly different when they mature. In these parts they will probably have to endure hot, dry summers with occasional severe drought and wetter winters with more storms.

Our new climate will favour some species over others. Beech and Norway spruce may find it too dry on shallow soils, but Douglas fir and others may benefit from the extra warmth. To meet these changes, we should consider planting at least some trees suited to the expected future climate – perhaps common oak or even downy oak from southern France – as an insurance. How would that fit with conserving native woodland?

International trade has brought many pests and diseases to our shores which would otherwise have remained confined to other continents. Now a changing climate may also be creating favourable conditions for them to spread. Imagining and designing the forests of the future has always been a forester's job, but now it is particularly complicated; which species will thrive, or even live? Will they be resilient to future climate? What will they produce, if anything? What are they even for?

Could we not just walk away now and leave nature to sort it out? Might that work just as well as our tinkering? In some woods and for some objectives that would work fine, where the wood already has suitable species and there is no particular expectation of timber.

But here we have established dense shady stands over what would otherwise be a rich woodland flora and it would take several more decades to collapse of its own accord. We started it, so we should see it through.

If we want to make more use of natural materials in preference to concrete, steel and oil, it is important to retain some working woods and I am wary of just shutting the gate. I would be out of a job for a start! The story of human civilisation is largely the story of how we have enslaved the natural world for our benefit. As we reach the outer limits, there are movements to reverse this by 'rewilding' extensive tracts of land. But can we find a middle way between exploitation and abandonment, working with nature, reaping a modest harvest while leaving the wood's integrity intact? Living off the interest rather than gorging ourselves on the natural capital?

Now I am done with my spray can. Next the cutters will come to realise my imagined forest, wondering why I marked this instead of that, grumbling at how awkward I made it for them. The immediate aftermath can be sobering – too much cut or too little. Either way, the wood is one step forward in its evolution.

I am following a line of foresters, bringing my vision to the wood. I too will be followed by others, possibly wondering what on earth I was thinking, or hopefully seeing how they can work with what I have left them and guiding it onwards to meet the needs of that future day.

The Ramsbury Elm

RAMSBURY VILLAGE, WILTSHIRE

Peter Marren

Threaded village of Ramsbury, where I live, is best known for a natural landmark: a tree. It stands, or rather it stood, where four roads meet, in the exact centre of the village. On one side is the pub, The Bell, and on the other the High Street, curving gently away past the village stores, the post office and houses of locally-made brick and flint. At one time the tree was also flanked by Ramsbury Building Society, the trusted protector of village cash, which took the tree as its icon. Until recently the glass doors of its successor, the Portman Building Society, retained images of the tree in its prime: a billow of green spreading its branches to every corner of the square.

Ramsbury's tree was a huge Wych Elm said to be at least 300 years old. Indeed, you hear it said that the tree is actually older than the village which grew up around it, though that is nonsense for Ramsbury is a very old village; at the time of the Domesday Book it boasted ten mills when little Newbury had only two and no one had ever heard of Swindon. Most likely the tree was planted for its beauty and shade. Its crenelated, hour-glass-shaped trunk, broad at the base and at the top, indicates that it was a street tree, and, like the limes and planes of suburban London, occasionally cropped to keep its canopy tight and avoid overhanging the lane. Later on, to judge from old postcards, it was left alone to grow outwards and shade much of the square.

A century ago the Ramsbury elm was still a healthy tree, 12 metres tall and nearly 20 metres across its span. Villagers would sit beneath the comforting security of its boughs, gossip and watch the world go by. Children used to clamber up inside the hollow trunk, emerging at the top, far above the street. They knew the tree from the inside, every crevice and hold, the mattress of dry leaves at its base (useful if you slipped) and the smell of mould and sawdust. The hollow was also said to be the 'scene of countless romantic trysts and even conceptions within its hollow trunk'. And around the spread boughs, the life of a busy rural village went on, the cycle shop and the basket-maker, the cart taking a load of bark to the old tannery, past butchers and bakers and saddlers, and children bowling hoops along the cobbles.

The tree first began to show its age after the First World War, years that coincided with road surfacing and an increase in motorised traffic over its ageing roots. Elms shed their lower branches suddenly and without warning. Once one went, others might have been lopped for reasons of safety. At any rate, by the Second World War the tree no longer resembled its former grandeur. Only a few vertical branches now projected from the trunk, like brooms, and in summer the canopy was roughly the shape of a figure 8. But the tree retained its aura of venerability, a mighty tree from a distant age, another time. Around it the scene was changing but the tree was the one constant in village life. It seemed that it had always been there and always would, and this was in some indefinable way a comfort.

And then, in 1983, the old tree died. Some say that Dutch Elm Disease caught up with it in the end, but more likely its demise was accelerated by the overwhelming crush of buses and lorries on its decayed roots. Everyone knew the legend which told that when the great tree died, bad things would happen. For the Ramsbury elm was a Witch Tree. It had a curse attached to it. Perhaps the story originated in a confusion between 'wych', as in wych elm, and 'witch', although the former has nothing to do with black magic. 'Wych' is an old word meaning supple or pliant, and celebrates the quality of elm wood. But even so, the story was that, long ago, a wicked witch called Maud Toogood had lived inside its hollow and that her bones were buried within its roots. Like the ravens at the Tower of London, the fate of the village was bound up with that of the tree (as it happens,

Ramsbury means 'burg of the raven'). Of course we are not supposed to believe in witches or witchcraft any more, and so it was no doubt coincidence that the demise of the tree was soon followed by a rash of financial scandals, including the arrest and jailing of Ramsbury Building Society's investment manager for fraud. Even so, that stunning news marked the end of the trust and fellowship that had long characterised the village economy. So, to that extent at least, the curse came true.

The question now was what to do with the dead stump. Some wanted it to be preserved in perpetuity, perhaps by filling the hollow core with concrete. In the eyes of many, it was still the Tree, unique and irreplaceable. A referendum was held on its future but the result was indecisive. Nearly half the village (339) wanted it kept and the other half (356) wanted it removed and replaced. In the process the Tree became a story. TV networks sent their cameras to Ramsbury to report on this Clochemerle-like confrontation and reported on it as far away as New York, Sydney and Cape Town. It made, I suppose, a deeply English story. Where else would they make so much fuss about an old, rotten, and now dead tree? Why didn't they just plant a new one?

In the end they did. It was health and safety that decided it. The hulk of the tree was brittle and tinder-dry, and so was deemed a hazard to pedestrians and traffic. When the gang came to demolish it, the trunk departed the ground with ease, almost as if in relief, exposing the poor, crippled remnants of its roots. Unhappy villagers gathered to watch it come down. A few had sworn to prevent the desecration, but, as one witness recalled, in the end 'they allowed themselves to be led away as a loved one might depart from a condemned prisoner for the last time, knowing the situation was hopeless.' The pile of broken timbers was picked apart for mementoes. The most valued pieces were the circles of swollen wood around knotholes in the trunk that could be turned into picture frames – for pictures of the tree perhaps. I was given one of these by a friend – a ring of rustic timber as light as balsa wood – and I in turn passed it on to The Bell, whose customers had gazed out at the tree since the reign of Charles I. That, I felt, was the right place for it.

The promised replacement was not another elm – that would have been too vulnerable to disease – but an oak. Not a sapling but a young maiden tree carefully excavated from the earth of Epping Forest with its root-ball intact. To welcome the new tree, a day of celebration was planned, with bunting and a brass band and culminating with a folk group playing from the back of a wagon in the pub yard within sight of the new replacement. Much of the village turned out on a blustery late autumn day under a leaden sky, girls dressed as witches, boys as scarecrows. As the band began to play, children linked arms and danced around the new tree in the pattering rain. I wish I had been there to see it: it must have made a scene worthy of Goya, a splashy pageant of witchery and half-buried folk memories. It was as if the curse was being exorcised. And, indeed, after everyone had gone home, it was a wild night. The rain fell in torrents and a whirling wind ripped roofs from houses round about – but not, curiously enough, houses in Ramsbury.

The new tree thrives. It has not yet acquired the same mythic status of the great elm and perhaps it never will. It is simply a small tree, just over roof height, in the middle of a traffic island in front of the pub. At Christmas it is covered in twinkling lights and during street fairs and fetes it helps support the bunting. But only those who know their village history understand its true significance.

I have told the story of our tree in some detail because it seems to me to say something broader about relationships, between people and trees – or rather, a particular tree. We have never in this country adopted the continental practice of preserving ancient trees as monuments, but Ramsbury's elm was as socially significant as any memorial or carved stone. It was the village equivalent of the British lion, an emblem, an enduring symbol that defined Ramsbury's sense of what it was and where it was. It linked the past with the present and, like Tennyson's brook, seemed to say that 'men may come and men may go, but I go on forever.' To assert that the tree was valued is to understate the case: it lay at the very core of village identity. The tree, in that sense, was us.

I think this is one reason, possibly even the main reason, why great trees survive in such remarkable profusion in this country. Their custodians (I prefer that word to 'owners'), whether communities or families, admired such trees for their beauty and great age and took pride in them. They knew that their tree would outlive them and welcome generations yet unborn and become an ornament to the estate. On one level they took the credit for a tree of great character and beauty. On another, they saw that tree as a symbol of heredity, the core of ancient pith that runs through the generations. The tree was like the house: solid and permanent, or seeming so. It was family.

Another example of the deep feeling that trees draw from us lies just over the hill from Ramsbury. Savernake Forest, situated on a plateau of clay and gravel overlooking the town of Marlborough, is unusual in that it has never been bought or sold. It has remained in the same family (inter-linked by marriages) for nearly 1,000 years. From the early Middle Ages the lords of Savernake were also hereditary Wardens of the Forest. And among the woods, commons and enclosures of the ancient Forest were great oaks of unfathomable age. The greatest of all was the King Oak, monarch of Savernake, which stood almost at the Forest's dead centre, in its own glade, accompanied by a retinue of lesser oaks that would themselves be classed as giants anywhere else.

But although its position is still marked on Ordnance Survey maps, you will search for the King Oak in vain. We know what it looked like from old drawings and prints, and it was, by any measure, a mighty tree. According to Jacob Strutt, who included it among forty-eight of the nation's grandest trees in his *Sylva Britannica* of 1822, it stood about 90 feet high and spread its leafy boughs over a circle 60 yards wide. The tree was reputed to be more than 1,000 years old. Strutt imagined 'our Saxon ancestors' holding sinister rituals in the 'shadowy recesses' under its boughs. His engraving shows a great barrel of a trunk with a cave-like recess at its foot, supporting four or five enormous branches.

Back in 1822, the tree still bore a healthy canopy of leaves but there were already evident signs of strain. The then warden, Thomas Bruce Brudenell, Earl of Ailesbury, was a keen tree planter who also valued ancient trees for their picturesque qualities. Some years earlier he had been concerned that two of the leading branches of the King Oak had begun to split the ageing trunk. A fissure had appeared in the crutch of the trunk which the estate tried to patch up with a sheet of lead secured by nails – while relieving the weight on the trunk with a pair of great iron crutches. But the Earl feared that even this might not be enough to save the tree from splitting apart (and besides, someone was clambering up and stealing the valuable lead). His man, a Mr T. Young, thereby proposed to girdle the tree with an iron band, treatment that has since been accorded to another Savernake giant, the Big Belly Oak. It seems that the work was undertaken but that the band had been attached carelessly, and so slipped from its moorings. Mr Young was of the opinion that the tree nursing had not 'been of much service', or as we might say, it had all been a complete waste of time.

Despite concern for its future, the King Oak still appeared to be thriving in 1845 when the Rev. William Lukis, founder and first Secretary of the Wiltshire Archaeological and Natural History Society, sketched it in pencil. But over the next half century the great tree fell apart, whether gradually or suddenly we do not know. There came a point when the hollow trunk could no longer support the weight of its branches and down they all came. The last of its great limbs crashed to the ground in October 1872, the wettest month in a notably wet and windy year. By the turn of the century the fallen limbs had long been cleared away and all that remained was the shattered, leafless stump.

We can get an idea of what might have happened from another of the great oaks of the forest, the famous King of Limbs. That too was a huge spreading oak whose outstretched branches – its great 'limbs' – eventually proved too much for the rotting trunk. A photograph taken in around 1950 shows the tree still intact. Today, though, two of its five main branches lie broken on either side, leaving only the three more upright ones; though fortunately those seem healthy. One of the fallen branches has ripped away a large chunk of the hollow trunk exposing a veritable wooden cave of the kind that once distinguished the King Oak.

Like the Ramsbury elm, the King Oak was revered long after the last acorn and leaf had fallen. What remained was a still impressively gnarled and embossed hulk with a pinnacle of wood pointing skywards above the hollow at its heart as if to reproach the clouds and wind for its fate. The estate circled the stump with a paling fence and left it to stand in its decayed glory, a place of pilgrimage. Each successive series of Ordnance Survey maps marked its position (along with the smaller Queen Oak nearby). The stump appears on old sepia postcards and published photographs. They said that the bracken, which infests the other open spaces of the Forest, never touched this hallowed space.

When the Forestry Commission took over the management of the Forest in 1939, there was some discussion about what to do with the great trees. At the estate's insistence, the 'named oaks and other ancient oaks' were preserved. And, in a spirit of 'the King is dead, long live the King!', a 'new King Oak' was planted close to the original, taken from another historic oak in the Forest with small, bunched leaves known as the Cluster Oak. Alas, the new king has proved a sickly specimen and seems unlikely to survive its first century. Meanwhile, one final moment of posthumous glory awaited the old king. During the latter part of the Second World War, the Forest was used as an ammunition dump guarded by American servicemen (obscured by dense woodland, the dump was invisible to German aerial photographs). To these men the stump was a familiar landmark and perhaps something more. For when, in 1945, the time finally came for the removal of the hulk, many of the American soldiers took pieces of the trunk and brought them home, perhaps as souvenirs of the days they spent working in an English forest. It would be nice to think that bits of the King Oak still survive far away in the New World, perhaps in farmhouses in the American Midwest, or timber-framed homes in New England, or oceanside condos in California, or as objects in the local museum labelled as 'pieces of timber from an English oak, said to be 1,000 years old'. The great tree had become a symbol of these men's wartime experience and identity, so much so that they were willing to find precious space for a piece in their holdalls on the troopship home.

There is one more oak in Savernake whose very name invokes the sense of pride shared by past wardens and their foresters in their great trees: the Duke's Vaunt ('vaunt' is an old word meaning 'boast'). There is only one duke among the wardens of the Forest: Edward Seymour, Duke of Somerset and Lord Protector of England during the minority of King Edward VI. The tree is almost certainly old enough to have been the pride of a Tudor duke. Although now swallowed up among the lesser trees and hard to find, the Duke's Vaunt was once a prominent landmark set by the old road from Marlborough to Bedwyn. At one point a door was set into its trunk enclosing a space large enough for twenty choirboys to squeeze inside, and for a small band, including a violin, a hautboy and a bassoon, to offer tunes from within the compassing bark. Even by the early 1700s the Duke's Vaunt was in a 'decayed state', a testament to the prolonged old age of great oaks. Today, only the broken, hollow shell, some 30 feet in circumference, remains, yet it still supports a slender living bough, like a green flag flying over an ancient ruin. Half a century ago, foresters had tried in vain to save the tree from splitting by circling the crutch with the heavy chains that still hang from the stump. Shrouded in a post-war plantation, today's damp, moss-grown wreck excites pity more than pride. Yet the place still has an atmosphere. The last time I was there it was loud with crossbills feeding on the cones at the top of the spruces and larches that now far overtop the old Duke's pride. When no one is about, they say, the birds come down to the forest floor to drink from a natural trough left by a fissure in the Duke's last fallen bough.

All these trees meant far more to those who loved them than the physical volume of their timber or their harvest of acorns and elm-seed. Although two of them are only memories, and the third is near the end of its long life, their fame lives on; the relationship continues. The timber of oaks and elms is, of course, useful and even valuable. But the Ramsbury elm had no financial value, and no particular use either unless it was to provide shelter or shade. If the King Oak or the Duke's Vaunt ever supplied wood to the estate – for both appear to have been pollarded in the distant past – they had ceased to do so for the last few hundred years of their lives. In forestry terms they took up valuable space in which dozens of young trees might be planted. They were obviously valued for reasons beyond economy or profit.

In sickness they were tended as though they were loved ones, and in death their communities were reluctant to say goodbye. But what is it, exactly, that creates such bonds of love and fellowship with what is, after all is said and done, simply a big plant?

Personally I discount the Druids. The ancient Britons may have performed rites of worship in sacred groves of oak, but whatever they might have felt and believed about old trees has long been wiped out by centuries of Christianity. Nor do trees play any significant role in heraldry, unlike the English rose. As far as I know, the first person to make a fuss of England's great oaks and elms was John Evelyn in his groundbreaking work, *Sylva*, in 1664 (all right, there were Tudor texts on the propagation of trees but they seem concerned mainly with the practicalities). Our feelings for trees blossomed with the invention of landscape architecture and our discovery of the picturesque. It was only then, during the past 300 years, that we seem to have given names to favourite trees and brought them into our world and its networks of stories and beliefs.

So, granted they are valued despite being near worthless, what do great trees do for us? I think the key lies in what we see as shared qualities. We stare up at the lofty boughs and down to the stout, fissured trunk of a great oak and see – what? – Endurance? Strength? Power? As something so much larger and older than ourselves we can even see them as protectors (the embrace of those comforting boughs), as in the adoption of the great Tree by the Ramsbury Building Society, where the Tree meant, in essence: your money is safe with us. Today, oak has become a latterday emblem for countries and states across the world, whether it is the Golden Oak of Cyprus or the White Oak of Connecticut or simply a generic oak, not even a species but the quintessence of a strong and mighty tree.

Perhaps the most telling modern borrowing is the Conservative Party's symbol of a 'scribbled oak'. In 2006, under David Cameron, the former 'torch of freedom' was replaced by a stout British oak. The intention of the rebranding was to provide the party with a softer, friendlier, and above all, greener image ('We will be the greenest government ever,' promised Cameron). Open-grown oaks have a distinctively broad, squarish outline that is evident even in the £40,000 scribble created for the Conservatives by the Perfect Day design agency. The Tory oak stood for qualities that it hoped the British people still saw in themselves: 'strength, endurance, renewal and growth' – and perhaps they hoped some of this might rub off into Conservative economic policy. Soon the scribbled oak turned a more party political blue, and then, just in time for the 2015 general election, it turned into an oak-shaped Union Jack. Today, green promises forgotten ('green crap', said Cameron), the oak now stands for patriotism and the Union: flag and tree combined. Perhaps it also makes a few nostalgic minds think of Nelson and the days when Britannia ruled the waves in ships made of heart of oak. Trees do make versatile symbols.

Many old trees stand in semi-protected places called Sites of Special Scientific Interest, and valued as mini-ecosystems rich in lichens, mosses and rare beetles. But for most people science has little or nothing to do with why they are special. Our historic relationship with old trees has nothing to do with beetles. It is about us, about our sense of the past, and about pride in ourselves and our surroundings. Ancient trees fill us with awe, and perhaps, in an increasingly godless age, they occupy some of the vacant space in minds once filled with religion. They also help define our sense of place in the world. Ramsbury might be just another village in the Kennet valley, but Ramsbury had its Tree. Savernake might be just another big wood, but not every big wood has a King Oak or a Duke's Vaunt. For anyone and everyone who feels a sense of kinship with them, such great trees are 'ours'. And, one cannot help wondering, in the unimaginable ways in which a tree interconnects with its environment, are we not also theirs?

Two Storms

TEDWORTH SQUARE, LONDON

William Boyd

I was living in Fulham in south-west London on the night the infamous October 1987 storm hit southern England, and I have to admit I slept through most of it. I was aware of more wind-noise than usual but, possibly because our small terraced house was fairly well sheltered by adjacent buildings, the night didn't really register as anything out of the ordinary. The next morning, however, the news bulletins informed me of the scale of the devastation and Susan – my wife – and I jumped into our car to see if there had been any damage to the house we had recently bought a couple of miles to the east in Chelsea.

It was on the way there that we saw bits and pieces of the wholesale destruction that the news had alluded to. Cars flattened by trees. Streets filled with a thick fritter of leaves and branches and – most impressively to my mind – fallen trees impaled on the spiked railings of gardens and parks. Sometimes the sharp finials of the railings had been driven entirely through the trunk of the fallen tree. One got a real sense of the destructive force of the storm.

Our new house was fine, apart from a TV aerial teeteringly askew, and, in a way, that was the 1987 storm as far as I was concerned. Blocked streets were quickly cleared; flattened cars were towed away; the torn leaves and kindling were swept up.

There was one consequence, however, that was more of a slow-burn. I remember developing a curiosity about the wider effects of the storm.

I became more aware of the cost of the storm: the fifteen million trees that had fallen; the destruction to historic woodland; the landscaped parks wholly obliterated and so forth. Then I read a letter in *The Times* from one Oliver Rackham saying that this storm was no epic disaster but merely a blip in the lifecycle of trees, woods and forests. Many fallen trees wouldn't die, he wrote, but would live on horizontally. There was no need to tidy them away. He also pointed out that trees were unimaginably resilient – that, left unchecked and un-husbanded, the land would be entirely forested within a couple of generations. I cut out the letter and stuck it into my notebook. I date my concentrated interest in trees from that moment. Something in me had been piqued by that confident, controversial assessment of the notorious storm. I looked up this Oliver Rackham and saw he'd written a number of books about trees and forests. I bought and read them all.

With hindsight, I now realise that I'd always had this curiosity about trees – probably because I'd been born and brought up in West Africa. Unreflectingly, I had come to know the names of the trees in our large garden – the casuarinas pines, the frangipanis, avocado, guava, the flamboyants with their huge seed pods. Our garden was hedged by eight-foot-high banks of hibiscus and poinsettia. Step beyond that cultured boundary and you were in a version of tropical rainforest – hugely buttressed figs, teak, lianas, palms – and all manner of noxious wildlife.

By contrast, our family home in the borders of Scotland was arrived at via a tall landscaped avenue of mature beeches. The small tributary that flowed through the fields surrounding the house, and that fed the Tweed downstream, was lined with willow and black alder, ash and hazel. I was aware of these trees and wanted to know their names – in an idly curious way – but it wasn't until I left the city and moved (part-time) to the country that my relationship with trees and woodland changed – forever. It was a process that was accelerated by the second severe storm that I lived through.

This countryside was in south-west France, in the very south of the Dordogne, about an hour or so east of Bordeaux. In 1991, we bought a semi-ruined farmhouse that was set on a small hill and nearly surrounded by mature oak woods – huge trees, 80 feet high. The view west, the one quadrant where there were no woods, looked over undulating, farmed valleys – vineyards, sunflowers, maize. I've always thought of this part of France as the frontier between northern and southern Europe. The landscape is northern, lush and verdant – as the oak woods testify – but the buildings, like the local agriculture, are essentially southern in character – small clustered villages around an ancient church and scattered farmsteads of thick-walled, small-windowed houses with low-pitched, canal-tiled terracotta roofs. Summer days can be crushingly hot; winters bring iron frosts (rarely snow) than can last for weeks. The idea of being on a border between climates, landscapes and states of mind can be very pronounced.

At the very end of the millennium, on the night of 27 and 28 December 1999, France was hit by a storm of genuine hurricane force – Cyclone Martin, as it was officially known. We were warned by the Méteo and duly hunkered down. Storms are a feature of south-west France – they roll in off the Atlantic, winter and summer. Ferocious displays of lightning and hill-cracking cannonades of thunder often mean a loss of electric power for a few hours and a sumptuous soaking of rain. But this one was different. It arrived after dark and you could tell from the volume of wind-noise that it was in an entirely new category. The winds, we later learned, reached 180 kmh. We lost our electricity very quickly and lit candles – we already had a big fire roaring in the cheminée. The noise of the rushing wind was so deafeningly general that you couldn't make out anything of significance going on outside in the darkness. At one stage I peered out with a torch and flashed the beam around. The air was full of flying debris – leaves and branches. In fact it's very dangerous to step out of doors during the height of such storms. You can be clattered by big chunks of wood and whirling roof tiles. But I was shocked by what I saw.

Our house on its small hill was always identifiable from miles away by the towering cedar tree that grew beside it. My torch beam picked out the cedar, now uprooted and flattened, its tip a few feet from the front door. It had been raining all over Christmas and the ground was sodden. As an evergreen, the cedar's leafmass had proved a perfect wind-catcher and the sopping ground had loosened the earth around its rootball. It had come down with no noise, any thud of its falling obliterated by the cyclonic winds. I closed the door and we anxiously waited out the rest of the night until the storm subsided. I was worried about our trees.

We had planted a lot of trees around the farmhouse – cypresses, oaks (holm and deciduous), figs, maple, two acers, umbrella pines, a chestnut. Moreover, these weren't saplings – they were mature trees, ten to fifteen years old, bought from a nursery near Bordeaux, owned by a man called Bernard Roque. Monsieur Roque became my tree-guru. He advised me what and how to plant them around the house. In those days – the early 1990s – such nurseries were quite rare. Bernard Roque had discovered a method of uprooting, potting (in large plastic containers) and preserving mature trees. He was particularly proud of his oaks, trees that he dug up from a forest in Italy and shipped to his nursery. They weren't particularly expensive and it was a tempting bonus to plant them – you had an instant tree, no waiting – and, thus tempted, I had bought about two dozen of these mature trees from Bernard Roque and they had all taken well – were rooted-in and flourishing. By the time of the storm they had been growing around our house for some six years.

At dawn I went out to inspect. They were all standing, except for two cypress trees that were horizontal but unbroken. However, a huge mature oak had come down, along with the cedar and all the roof tiles of our open wooden barn (that the French call a *hangar*) were scattered in the meadow, some over 100 yards distant. These tiles must weigh two kilos – there was no more telling symbol of the storm's potency and the brute strength of the wind that had sent these tiles sailing across the field like autumn leaves.

Cyclone Martin wreaked havoc in France. We were without electricity for five days and, a week later on a journey to Biarritz, we passed through the pine forests of Les Landes where square miles of trees had been flattened and smashed up, as if some vast giant had tramped through the forests crushing everything in his path. Later calculations put the timber loss in France at 140,000,000 cubic metres.

On reflection, we had been lucky, just the cedar and an oak gone (we winched the cypresses upright and they seemed none the worse). When the cedar was cut up for firewood I counted the rings on the bole that was left and they came to a hundred. It was obviously a tree that had been planted to commemorate the arrival of the centennial change in 1900 – it had lasted an exact century before the storm brought it down.

In its place I bought more trees from Bernard Roque – three oaks, three lime trees, a mulberry, and planted them in a rough grove where the cedar had stood. Sixteen years later they've all flourished and have easily doubled in size. Bernard Roque's oaks seem to love our soil and situation. The 1993 oaks are now monsters, well over 40 feet tall now, densely foliated, that look like they've been there forever. Bernard Roque has retired now and sold his nursery, but when he's passing he stops by to check up on his trees and even he is impressed by their prodigious growth.

Thanks to Bernard Roque I've come to know, almost as individuals, all the thirty or so trees we've planted around our house in the last two decades. I see how they've fared, note how they've grown, inspect them for maladies, fret about them at times of drought, marvel at their new growth as spring moves into summer. And this familiarity has simulated an interest in trees in general, in London and wherever I travel, and in the many acres of oak woods around our house where I can see and study natural woodland flourishing and changing through the seasons (aided and abetted by the wisdom of Oliver Rackham) and always with the encouraging words of Bernard Roque echoing in my head: 'Planter un arbre – c'est un beau geste'.

Sand Forest

TENTSMUIR FOREST, FIFE

Jim Crumley

Tentsmuir Forest lies in the very north-east corner of Fife, where the open North Sea defines its eastern edge and the final outpourings of the Tay estuary its northern edge. In the north-west it rubs shoulders with a magnetic little wetland fragment called Morton Lochs. Its western and southern approaches betray none of that, for they plough through the dull and dead-flat margins of agricultural Fife, and confer on the Forest something of the aspect of a dark-green cliff.

I have known Tentsmuir all my life, for I was born and brought up in Dundee on the Tay estuary's far shore, and although my writing has mostly preoccupied itself with the landscape and wildlife of Highland and Island Scotland and occasionally with a handful of other cold, wet, northern countries, I am an east-coast mainlander by instinct and inclination. Tentsmuir is a restless landscape in a constant state of change, and I have lived long enough and walked here often enough to have witnessed a few of them at first hand. But the twenty-first century has bestowed two gifts on Tentsmuir, gifts that are in the throes of changing everything – sea eagles, and at least one beaver.

The Forest has no great age. It was planted by the Forestry Commission on sand dunes and moorland in the 1920s. Mostly, it is Scots pine and Corsican pine, and being Forestry Commission pines they are dead straight, having been taught in their crowded youth to reach for the sunlight. If the Scots pines you dream of are wide-boughed and flat-crowned and sustain a birch or a rowan sapling from the pool of discarded needles trapped in its deep fork, and have cast an ever-broadening, ever-lengthening shadow on the land for 200 years, you're in the wrong forest, and I urge you north to Rothiemurchus or Abernethy or Glen Affric. But as Commission woods go, Tentsmuir has many charms, and is something of a mould-breaker. The Commission has had to up its game here because its sea and river margins and Morton Lochs constitute the Tentsmuir National Nature Reserve, and many of the Forest's visitors are also nature reserve visitors, and wildlife and its habitat are high on their list of priorities.

One of the consequences is that some of the longest-lived, well-thinned trees now embrace some of the most spectacularly dense, naturally regenerating Scots pines anywhere in the land. Another is the tangible sensation of a landscape on the move. There are places where it looks as if the trees are wading out among the captivating mix of sand dunes and heath, hell-bent on the three-mile-long beach, the surf, and the sandbanks, where both grey and common seals haul out, and – occasionally – fight to the death. Elsewhere, it looks as if the dunes are invading the Forest, like landing craft up from the beach, an illusion lent particular credibility by the ungainly survival of long rows of 'dragon's teeth'; free-standing concrete cubes deployed as anti-invasion defences during the Second World War. The idea of Fife being invaded by Germany is moderately laughable now, and the guffaws of two unseen green woodpeckers from the edge of the trees lend body and soul to that illusion, while behind your back, skylarks embellish the defences with tall columns of song.

A final dividing line, a kind of no-man's-land between the pines and the dunes, is occupied by a long string of wizened alders, a frail buffer, it's true, and nature's doing rather than the Commission's, and symptomatic of the fact that the water table on this edge of the forest is very near your feet.

I have walked in most of Scotland's best-known woodlands, and many of the unknown ones, and I can think of nowhere else where worlds change both utterly and immediately by the simple act of stepping into or out of the trees. Outside, the sky (like most east-coast skies) is huge and blue, and the sea is stunned by sunlight. Within the trees, the sky is riven into narrow strips and shards and parallelograms, and the presence of the mostly unseen sun is diagnosed by a forest of shadows. Then the sound of the sea is snuffed out and the scent of ozone has metamorphosed somewhere behind you into the scent of pines, and you did not notice it happening. You start to hear the sound of your own footfall. All this creates a rare species of natural tension around the seaward edge of the wood.

Getting lost in the Forest is almost impossible because all the paths are tracks, discreetly signposted and colour-coded, and because the site of Tentsmuir is flat and there was never any need for the Forestry Commission to confront gradients with curves; all the tracks are more or less dead straight. A map of the Forest looks like a street map of Manhattan. But there are many different densities of trees, creating different atmospheres, different shadows, different light, different habitats. There are also different ages of trees (mercifully, the Commission's penchant for clear-felling is not a management option here), and although none is truly old, there are many of middle-age, of youth, and of infancy. There are interlopers, too, and these tend to make camp in colonies – the most prevalent are beeches that form up in 'avenues' along some of the trackside straights, hollies thrive in the coolest shadows, and birches crop up almost anywhere (in Scotland, a birch wood is nature's default position), mixing it with rowan, willow, and alder. The deeper into the woods you go and the quieter you move, the more intently you watch and listen to the landscape of the forest heartland, the Forest is likely to confide its secrets; Tentsmuir is a red-squirrel enclave, and – like many of the other wildlife tribes that shy away from the well-trodden tracks around the forest edges – redsquirrels like the long straights of the heartland tracks to move around. And if you tire of these long straights yourself, you can always go off-piste, cut corners, explore the deepest depths, and sooner rather than later you will hit another straight track parallel to the one you abandoned.

So here is a long straight forest track. It bisects the wood from south to north. Tentsmuir Point, where river meets sea and seals and eiders cavort, is three straight forest miles away. And there is the first red squirrel on the track, moving towards me. Freeze. Be a tree. Hint: wear tree colours. You can get away with this I-am-a-tree strategy surprisingly often (a badger once peed on my wellies while I was wearing them: I felt anointed), but you cannot fool all the woodland creatures all of the time. The squirrel stops dead, an inch-long, four-footed skid, like a Tom and Jerry squirrel. It gives me a two-eyed, black-eyed stare from 30 yards away. I remember thinking that a bear once did that to me too, a grizzly bear on Kodiak Island, Alaska, only it was a few yards closer. But the purpose was the same – she wanted more information, a better scent, a clearer sight.

'What's she doing?' I had asked my guide.

'Oh, just taking a look.'

'At us?'

'No. At you. She knows what I look like.'

Back in Tentsmuir Forest, the red squirrel (again, like the bear), chooses discretion, vacates the track, climbs the first eight feet of the nearest beech trunk at squirrel speed then stops dead again, four feet splayed wide, head pointing up the trunk, tail down it. Suddenly the position is reversed – head pointing down, tail up and flat against the trunk, feet still splayed wide. How do they do that? The manoeuvre is executed in a second, too fast for human comprehension. I want to slow it down frame by frame to see how it works. From its new position, it contrives to raise its head almost ninety degrees, taking a look. At me. And now, its eyes are pretty much as high off the ground as the eyes of the standing bear on Kodiak.

It is, I have noticed, a peculiarity of walking these long, quiet forest straights that my mind tends to go off-piste a little more to compensate, which is another reason why I like them. The squirrel reverses its position, contours round to the blind side of the trunk, reappears high in the topmost branches, from where it transfers in one short aerial swoop to the next tree, then vanishes.

A mile drifts by, scrolled with wren song, brightened by the voices (you could hardly call it song) of four kinds of tits and by the tinily berserk roller-coastering of a pair of tree creepers. Far off, at the edge of my hearing, a mistle thrush sings. I stop to silence my footfall and improve the listening. It's the jazziest of singers, which endears it to me. Bluesy triplets, repeated twice, then discarded in favour of a tricky double-stopped flourish that reminds me of Stan Getz, which is one of the highest compliments I know. The clarity of the song is astounding for all its distance, which makes me wonder if these long, narrow airspaces above the tracks funnel sound in some airy acoustic fluke that I don't pretend to understand.

The track kinks slightly at a junction with an east–west track. Here the trees are suddenly taller, the beeches and birches and the rest have vanished and big pines gather round. From one of these a buzzard casts off and unfurls a down-curving woodwind plaint, answered at once from a hundred feet above where her mate circles, a sunlit copper insignia on a flag of sky blue. Soon there are three buzzard voices and there is a two-second glimpse of a tumbling frieze of birds, patterned underwings aglow and all the shades of sunlit brown that nature ever invented, before they too disappear. Only the ubiquity of buzzards counts against them, somehow seems to demean them in human eyes and diminishes our valuation of their undeniable grace and beauty. They thrive despite us.

But now they have tilted the cast of my mind somewhere beyond the reach of the trees because they have planted the image of eagles there. Preposterous as the idea would have seemed for all of my life until ten years ago, the Tay estuary is now a landscape of eagles and one of the best places to see them is just beyond the last of the trees, on the beach at Tentsmuir Point. The white-tailed eagle – the sea eagle – was successfully reintroduced on Scotland's western seaboard between 1975 and 1998, then, as part of a programme to try and reinstate it throughout its former range, the north-east of Fife was chosen as the base for an east-coast reintroduction programme between 2007 and 2012. The first eaglets in 200 years have flown from east-coast nests.

Suddenly, there are tall, thin, ragged windows of blue among the trees in the north, and now the track has narrowed and grown green and sinuous, and now the northern edge of the forest is in sight. One last rank of pines, then you burst onto a short bank of rocks and down onto a mile-wide, puddled plain of low-tide sand. And now you have changed worlds again. The Tay estuary is two miles wide here, and there, on its far shore, is Dundee, where I come from. The long, introverting walk through the trees had erased even its possibility from my mind, so that the last thing I am thinking about when I overwhelm the no-man's-land of the Forest edge is the proximity of a city. But there it lies on its accustomed shore, swathed in sunlight, its twin hills towered over by piles and piles of bright-white cumulus. Once again, for what could easily be the thousandth time in my life, I renew my acknowledgment of what a fair situation it occupies, and once again, for perhaps only the tenth time, I think, 'Eagles, here!' and shake my head at the wonder of it. As if to underscore the sentiment a curlew gives heart-rending, anthemic voice and a squabble of oystercatchers twenty or thirty-strong drowns it out as it takes to the air. Without a backward glance at the wood, I go looking for eagles.

Out on the ever-widening expanse of sand (heading east now to where the estuary's beach performs a dramatic right-angle turn and becomes the North Sea beach with Denmark across the water instead of Dundee), the sense of liberation is a jolt between the shoulder blades, and the Forest has become a dark, brooding deadweight all along the beach's western fringe. It is time to check out the fence-less fenceposts standing out on the sand. It is hard to know now why someone thought fences were necessary out here considering how often they must have been submerged, not to mention wrecked, by high tides and high winds. But if you have never seen a sea eagle standing alone and erect and at a distance on a beach (and most people have not and will not), it resembles nothing so much as one of those old fenceposts, broken off at about waist height. Yes, human waist height. This is a BIG bird with an eight-feet wingspan and a curved yellow beak that suggests nature has fashioned a lethal weapon out of a banana. Unlike the golden eagle, which is a shunner of humankind and all its works, the sea eagle is unafraid to come in among us, and to compel us forcibly to reappraise the possibilities of what an eagle looks like and what it does. And now, for example, we know that it nests in a tree not very far from here, opening up a new frontier of nature where the edge of the Forest and the edge of the sea meet in a crumple zone of dunes, and binding the two elements together by its everyday journeys in a way that no other creature does. It makes for astounding birdwatching for beach and forest walkers. It makes serious trouble for the Tay's internationally significant population of eider ducks – once (not here but at Talisker Bay on Skye) I saw a sea eagle lift an eider drake from the surface of the ocean with the ease and grace of a barn owl carrying off a vole. You do not lightly forget such things.

Which leaves me with the beaver. Scotland has been dipping its toe in the water of beaver reintroduction with a scrupulously observed five-year official trial in Argyll. Meanwhile, on Tayside, a rogue population has grown from wildlife park escapees complemented by the generosity of what we might term the provisional wing of the conservation movement. The result has been spectacular, and from a stronghold in east Perthshire and Angus on the north side of the Tay, they have spread far and wide, and at least one foray has reached Morton Lochs, Tentsmuir Forest's wetland love child. It is a perfect site for beavers, and enlightened conservation policy in the national nature reserve would have been to allow this exploratory presence to establish, to watch and learn, and to marvel at the beaver's capacity to transform and expand wetland, which is after all our most fragile native habitat. Alas for enlightenment, official policy removed the beaver (or beavers). The Scottish Parliament has yet to give its final blessing on the project, and as I write, it is legal to shoot beavers from the Tayside population, and farmers are doing just that, and post-mortems have shown that they have been none too careful or selective in the shooting, as pregnant animals have been counted among the dead.

Likewise, the sea eagles have not been unanimously welcomed, and young wandering birds have met ignoble ends and at least one nest has been destroyed. But nature is better at these things than we are, more persistent, more opportunistic, and more liberal, and where the heartlands prove troublesome it finds ways of insinuating itself into the edges – the edges of the Lowlands, the edges of the Highlands, and that no-man's-land where the edge of the woods meets the edge of the sea, and where eagles prosper and beavers will be back.

Wood Woes

UP THE FOREST!

Sue Clifford

S tanding on the halfway line at the City Ground on a Saturday afternoon, the tension heightened just before three o'clock as the sound system belted out the theme from *The Adventures of Robin Hood* (a favourite TV series in the late 1950s). Teenage girls, much outnumbered by men of all ages, standing watching Nottingham Forest run out on to the pitch shared a mingling pride of local lore with men in shorts who, at that time, had the kudos of holding the FA Cup (1959). Heady days. The rare hearing of that same theme still brings a tingle to the spine.

What I never realised was that The Forest, where we played school rounders on the other side of town, had been saved from development by the 1845 Nottingham Inclosure Act: 80 acres of flattish ground with a steep wooded slope became a recreation ground evolving through race course, cricket green and the first pitch for the fledgling Nottingham Forest, who were named after it in 1865.

Some way out of town, I grew up around Eastwood, where, beyond our imagining, Carboniferous forests had grown, died away and been squeezed to 28-inch coal seams. I even remember catching buses full of men with the blackened faces of work deep underground. We all breathed the burning residue of these older-than-ancient trees and ferns while the living trees tried hard to keep up with carbon overload. Mining and heavy industry was interwoven with houses, fields and woodland. We didn't know it then, but change was soon to overwhelm us. After 1945, the race for economic development meant that the little pointed hills planted with conifers, revealing in the fingernails the detritus of coal mining, would soon be overshadowed by massive coal tips from increasing exploitation underground.

Not far away, the earliest opencast mine in England was opened, followed by a rash of activity as out-of-scale machines dug into field and wood. Protected amongst the graveyard dead, big trees held on, as did those huddled in gardens or serried as town avenues, and wriggles of streamside trees kept diminishing flocks of long-tailed tits in food and home.

As the massive holes were backfilled, new hedges of solely hawthorn – regimented planted sticks between fence and ditch – created new field boundaries, not long before rich with oak, rowan, hazel, holly, willow, elder and more. There are still no tall trees, old names of fields and woods have been lost, old shapes rationalised, soil compacted and bereft of richness, few worms, much clay, all the old subterranean communication lines gone.

Not only surface mining stripped the remnant woodland from the scene for, as the engineers pushed through the M1, many copses were felled and displaced foxes were driven to raiding the hen-runs miles away. Or so the tales went.

Meanwhile, up the road a new forest was emerging. Landowners seized subsidies to plant conifers as government policy sought to replenish the lost tree cover of centuries. Here on the Magnesian Limestone, neighbour to the Coal Measures, hundreds of acres of conifers were being planted. Now, driving up the M1, passing the Misk Hills, I look west and indeed the forest is tight filled, dark and forbidding. I also see the ghosts of deciduous woodland and copses, through which I think I hear the baying of foxes of generations past and worry that deer might start across the motorway.

Further east, I can take you to Sherwood proper. Its minster in Southwell shows off the High Medieval feeling for the spirit of woodland. Its arches echo its old habitat, recognisable curls of foliage, oak, maple, hawthorn, are carved reverently in stone and the chapter house is full of Green Men; Nikolaus Pevsner, in *The Leaves of Southwell* (1945), argues that these 'assume a new significance as one of the purest symbols surviving in Britain of Western thought, our thought, in its loftiest mood.'

And this is the heartland, the greenwood, of Robin Hood whose stories tell of older times but are first mentioned by Langland in the 1370s referencing the (anonymous) ballad of 'Robin Hood and the Monk' which begins:

> In somer, when the shawes be sheyne,
> And leves be large and long,
> Hit is full mery in feyre foreste
> To here the foulys song:
> To se the dere draw to the dale,
> And leve the hilles hee,
> And shadow hem in the leves grene,
> Vnder the grene-wode tre.

The many tales of Robin Hood place him and his merrie men (and women) in a sanctuary of their own finding, here in summer when the woods are shining, the leaves big, and birds singing. He is an outlaw from the middle of England, but he is loved across the world as a just and honourable man, his goodness aligns with that of the Forest. Beguiling tales of hiding, disguise and outwitting, taking from the rich and giving to the poor, fantastic marksmanship, humour and humiliation, love and friendship all associated with Sherwood and the greenwood.

Men in green populate our religious houses and our stories. Woodland is their habitat and they render it benign, mostly. Shakespeare plumps for forest as haven in *As You Like It*: 'Are not these woods / More free from peril than the envious court?'

What do we see in Sherwood or Arden, Wirral or Peak, Epping or Bowland? Do we see the forest as a haven or the place of terror and danger so often depicted in fairy tales of northern Europe? The word 'forest' may imply dense woods to us now in England, but in medieval times it was understood as a place reserved for royal hunting. Harsh Forest Law extended over places of scattered woodland in open heath or moorland, a place of sometime sanctuary for deer, when the king and his henchmen were not out with the chase.

Apart from Robin Hood, outlaws were rarely benign champions of justice and care. Medieval travellers, facing the northward trek out of London, must have shivered as they approached Hampstead Heath. Footpads lurked, highwaymen took advantage from the shadows. Hampstead Heath is still widely wooded (plant records date back to 1629), and its protected 750-odd acres is a place of play and joy as it fills with summer music, autumn goodbyes to the swallows, winter ice, spring kite flying. It is home to creatures of many kinds, it helps the city breathe, offers an expansive lookout over the territory of millions of people.

Down in the streets, trees are scattered, a different take on savannah. They offer foil to the hard surfaces of pavings and buildings. They give welcome summer cool, tangled shadows of winter branches, yellows under the peeling bark of the London plane purifying the air of pollutants, boughs animated by the circling of squirrels or by blackbird song under a midnight light and still the occasional lime hawk moth. The squares, such as Gordon, Russell and Bloomsbury, open at their feet, but with more aerial greenery than the coverts of the Cotswolds, are small woods that give many of us brief sanctuary from the day.

I walked into WC1 and through these squares on the morning of 16 October 1987. The serious storm that raged through the night had caused much damage, many boughs and some trees were down; amazingly, most of the huge old London planes stood. In Russell Square a small group of young children clambered gleefully through the boughs of one plane now lying across the grass as individual grown-ups sat, some quietly crying. I watched as a stunned blackbird, sitting at the roots of a standing tree, reminded one that their night must have been terrifying.

That storm added to my understanding of woodlands and change, appreciating through a new kaleidoscope of fragments as I saw the fallen in Camden, on Hampstead Heath and the scattered matchsticks beyond London across the south of England. Common

Ground set up a cry to echo across the south-east: 'Don't chop them down. Don't chop them up.' We printed and dispersed 56,000 postcards to try to stop people tidying them away. We knew nature would repair in its own way and that we all had a lot to learn. Of course, trees across roads, small gardens and buildings had to be removed, but in woodland, non-commercial orchards, some parks, we felt it wiser to wait and watch. Virtually, our only vocal ally was Oliver Rackham, who later reported that much more damage was done in the aftermath, in cutting perfectly viable trees and by heavy machinery traversing the sodden soil. As research revealed, the emergence of the heavy logging horses and the simple leaving alone proved sounder practice for the land and the dependent creatures.

Then in 2008, *New Phytologist* carried an article by Rackham, *Ancient woodlands: modern threats*, in which he was positing that

> An increase in storms is likely to be wholly beneficial, through counteracting too much shade and through fallen branches adding to the habitat for deadwood animals and fungi. However, it challenges the assumption that the normal state of a tree is upright. Future woods, like those of south and east England after the storm of 1987, may be full of uprooted, horizontal, living trees.

Change snags on our emotions when it happens so suddenly. In the 1970s and 80s, the tendency to tidy after disease may have deprived us of persistent low-living elms. We must be aware that gentle watching and sharing of knowledge will serve us well if Ash Disease and Sudden Oak Death really spread.

Hundreds of years of persistence and change can be read on our maps as placenames. They whisper past (and future?) tree cover: Alderwasley in Derbyshire, Ollers in Yorkshire, Orleton in Cheshire, Alrewas by the Trent in Staffordshire – all remember wet woodland full of alders.

We can draw on a wide vocabulary to particularise smaller woods: shaw, copse, covert, hanging, grove, avenue, orchard, tanglewood, underwood, spinney, dene, coppice, holt, plantation, thicket, inclosure, carr, lea. In the New Forest, another old royal hunting forest, patches of wood are separated by expansive areas of heath. In some parts the woodland has grassy grazed clearings here known as 'the launds' – hear the echo in our word 'lawn'.

Not all words are ancient. Oliver Rackham spent his life researching and imagining 'the wildwood' – a term of his coining. Scientists add so much to our appreciation. It is not long since we have begun to recognise deep-hidden connectivities in woodland. Finding toadstools in the woods reveal but fragments of their social activities. Below ground, fungus roots (mycorrhiza) may link trees across many acres, exchanging food, information and protection for mutual benefit.

Artists nourish our imaginations too. Sculptors including David Nash, Giuseppe Penoni, Ai Weiwei have taken us inside trees and woods – reassembling what we thought we knew. David Hockney has given us colourful trees from California to the Yorkshire Wolds, in paintings and stage sets. Long before, Constable impressed upon us the woody ways of Suffolk. Andy Goldsworthy has made us look at leaves and boughs as never before.

Paintings by Paul Nash of Wittenham Clumps remind one of the importance of landmarks and groups of trees that welcome home or offer orientation. The Caterpillar (looks as it sounds, especially in winter with the sun rising behind it on the ridge) watches from the downs to the east of the Blackmore Vale in Dorset. Far from home in 1917, Ivor Gurney yearned for 'May Hill that Gloster dwellers / 'Gainst every sunset see'. May Hill with its sprouting Corsican pines (replacing earlier Scots pines in 1887 for one of Victoria's many jubilees) still draws the eye from the M5. It not only marks the border of Gloucestershire and Herefordshire, but its visual reach serves as the perimeter of those tall pear trees known to produce proper perry.

There is more than one May Hill – the name is a reminder that festive occasions and assertion of long-held rights draw us to woods. By Great Wishford in Wiltshire, celebrations on Oak Apple Day begin around dawn with the cry 'Grovely, Grovely, and all Grovely' up in the eponymous forest. In the village, oak boughs hanging on every door, celebration and reassertion of the rights to collect wood go on all day.

Not far away, near Stonehenge, by the A303 north of Amesbury, beech trees are configured in clumps, not to mark horizons but to commemorate and trace Nelson's ships victorious in the Battle of the Nile in 1798.

Littoral woodland is amongst the most beautiful. Picture the massed trees that kiss the water along the edges of the drowned valleys of the south Devon coast graced now by egrets, the woods paddling along the beaches of Scottish lochs and high tarns in the Lake District.

Much like mangroves (though without the heraldic crabs rampant and insects *accorné* of Queensland tropical forest) alder carr stands buttressed by tangled roots that will endure long periods of inundation; indeed, they have a role to play in slowing down the rush of floodwaters along overtopped watercourses. All woodland intercepts precipitation: falling rain is slowed down by the boughs in winter and more so by the canopy of leaves in summer, and water is sucked up through the binding roots and out via the leaves as water vapour. In tropical climes the felling of forest brings flood, then drought and desert; in our circumstance woods help against landslides, loss of soil and floods.

The woodland edge is amongst the richest of nature's places: the ecotone – where the plants, insects and animals of the wood meet those of open land or water. And the edge is often where we feel safest: as Jay Appleton asserted in *The Experience of Landscape* (1975) it presents *prospect* out over open country or water – we can see what is coming; and *refuge* offered by the trees, into which we can melt away unnoticed, into the safety of the known greenwood.

There is no natural, undisturbed woodland on this hard-worked island. People point to Wistman's Wood on Dartmoor and its tortured, stunted oaks, some perhaps 500 years old, and a few other remote enclaves but even they have been sheep nibbled and increasingly walked through. The formal definition of ancient woodland claims persistence since *c.*1600 – plant indicator species include bluebell, dog's mercury, wood anemone. But historical and archaeological research in Norfolk is casting further doubt on the continuity of tree cover in some of these places. Nevertheless, the whole point being made is not that these woods are not worth their title, but that our partial knowledge is leaving out little-understood woodlands that need our care. As Gerry Barnes and Tom Williamson point out in *Rethinking Ancient Woodland* (2015), we need more safeguards over a wider variety of dynamic woods.

We certainly need to believe in natural regeneration – free trees growing where they want to grow as well as trees continuing life while reclining. The wholesale import of young trees for planting has shipped in disease and a thinning of immunities, plants have been drenched in chemicals that persist in the soil and we have so often planted species that bring little long-term benefit to places.

Reading the richness of Local Distinctiveness would help guide us, even if we know little of the mycorrhizal undertow: Derbyshire's limestone ashwoods and those of the Mendips; beech on the Chiltern chalk; upland oakwood with birch amongst the high hills of Cumberland and Westmoreland, Argyll, Gwynedd; boreal forest scraps of Scots pine. Wood pasture – parkland with ancient trees such as the massive oaks of Moccas Park in Herefordshire which host beetles unique to themselves, and Richmond Park which supports 1,000 different beetle species – is, like all the rest, an artefact, a working memory of us and nature. We have let our knowledge wither: in so many places we no longer know how the locals went about coppicing, pollarding, charcoal-burning, fence-making, house-building, boat-making, bodging – working with woodland and sharing it.

We need to make anew the relations between story, history and natural history. And working woods are edging back into fashion, not least because a different carbon balance needs to be struck. Planning and extending woodland, planting and coppicing deciduous trees offers old ways to achieve new goals. With more carbon fixing comes richer habitats for bees, butterflies, birds, badgers and the gradual ecological and sensual enhancement of places written off as ruined by industry (including agriculture) only decades ago. Our relations with nature need new cultural impetus. Yet the more climate change deranges weather systems, brings bigger winds, intense rains or none, the more we seem entrenched in economic models that warmed our toes and smelted our steel on the Earth's geological rendition of great forests.

Back around Eastwood, coal mining lives on through memories, traces in the land and in literature. D.H. Lawrence tied *Sons and Lovers* and *Women in Love* so strongly to the place that many of us can recognise the descriptions as well as the sentiments. Brinsley Colliery hosts long defunct mining headgear (sadly from another place) and a footpath along a now bosky railway line. Beside the traces of Moorgreen Pit a new habitat is developing. People of the vicinity have planted and are nurturing 'Colliers Wood'. Taking their cues from the local, they are endeavouring to help nature build back a richness not seen here in perhaps 150 years. The name offers tribute to those who hacked at 300 million-year-old forests underground and who, convalescing from the working day on return to the light, knew more about the woods of the Anthropocene than most of us.

Mayor Oak
HIGH PARK, BLENHEIM, 1987
by David Nash

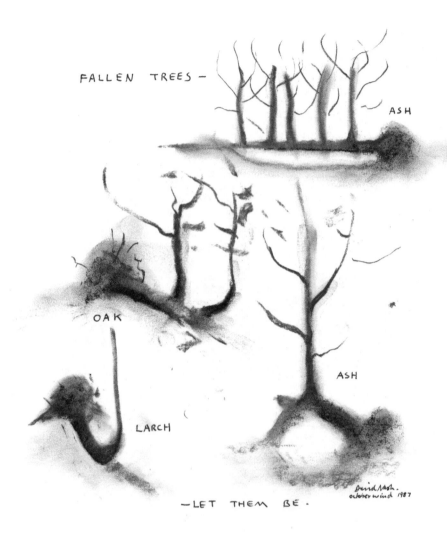

FALLEN TREES –

ASH

OAK

ASH

LARCH

– LET THEM BE .

David Nash.
october wind 1987

In a Nutshell by David Nash, 1987–1989

*The Great Storm of 15–16 October 1987 transformed the landscape
and lives of many, unleashing a great swell of public affection
for trees and woods but also a sense that an entirely natural
disaster was only reparable by human intervention, by tidying, by
chainsawing, clearing away the tilted or fallen trees, even if they
were still alive and growing. On the morning after the storm,
Common Ground turned to the artist David Nash and asked him to
work on several charcoal drawings that could be printed as postcards
– 56,000 of them were eventually distributed within a month of the
storm, all with a simple message: a fallen tree is not a dead tree. This
collaboration with Nash continued when he created the artwork for*
In a Nutshell, *Common Ground's 1989 'manifesto for trees'.*

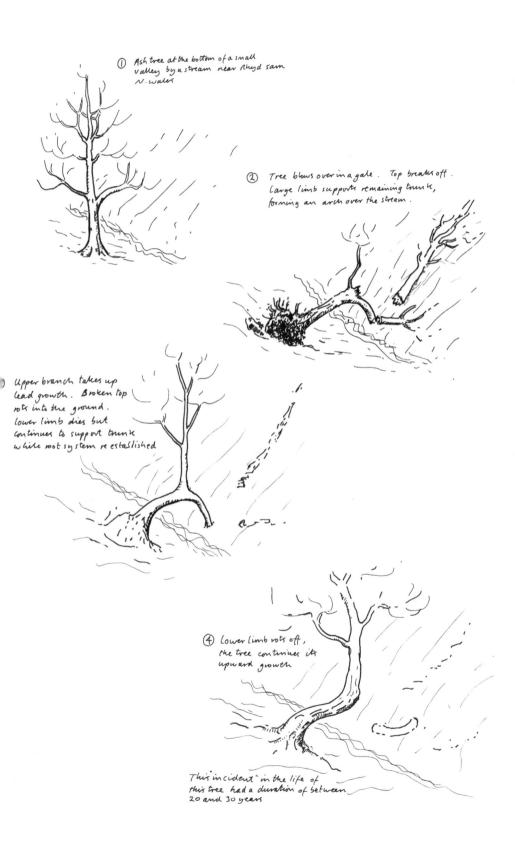

① Ash tree at the bottom of a small valley by a stream near Rhyd sam N. wales

② Tree blows over in a gale. Top breaks off. Large limb supports remaining trunk, forming an arch over the stream.

Upper branch takes up lead growth. Broken top rots into the ground. Lower limb dies but continues to support trunk while root system re established

④ Lower limb rots off, the tree continues its upward growth

This "incident" in the life of this tree had a duration of between 20 and 30 years

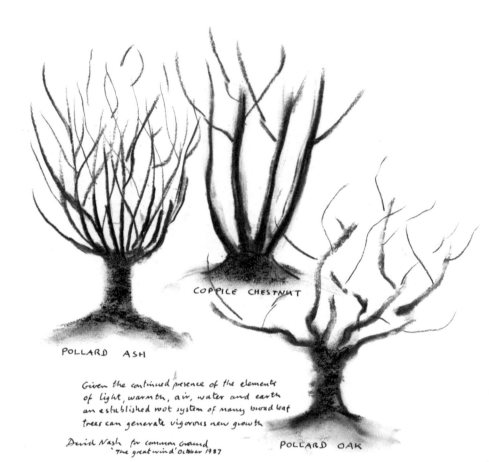

COPPICE CHESTNUT

POLLARD ASH

POLLARD OAK

Given the continued presence of the elements
of light, warmth, air, water and earth
an established root system of many broad leaf
trees can generate vigorous new growth

David Nash   for common Ground
        'The great wind' October 1987

Ash

FARNLEY ESTATE, HUDDERSFIELD

Simon Armitage

Reader, allow
the poet to elegise
the ash:

that bank of saplings
on Farnley Estate,
rankled with blight

after two seasons;
this felled centenarian
culled with an axe –

on a muted tv
some Danish backwoodsman
opens the bark,

reaches in
through the flaked timber
and breaded grain,

scoops out
with his pink hand
its pulped heart.

Nine Oaks

CURRIDGE, BERKSHIRE

Adam Thorpe

Every tree is an interlude between applauses
of air, an upside-down splash or that lone cloud's image.
The limbs go everywhere there is a taste of light.

My late father's liriodendron, for instance,
that took up too much space on our small lawn:
not banked on at all when he tied the sprig

those years before. I would like to be of a species
that lives much longer than we do, sentinel
of the centuries' passing, doing good turns

without moving ground. Harrumphing in wind,
or when a buzzard or the like takes off
from my kindly lap, my avuncular slopes.

Squirrel ladder. Cat trapeze. Lizarded
and lazy-leoparded, monkeyed around with
in squeals, like a hen party in a pub

of many rooms. You couldn't move for trees,
until recently. They'd crash, lightning-struck,
and everything would ken the clearing like release,

blinking in sun's floods, milk-parsley
jostling for position in no time
among the infant ginkgos. The forest

was its own dominion, a continuous
lisping of insects, no stony silences
bar the aftershock of a weighty clash, probably.

It tolerated everything: even fire, even
glacial pulverisations were only
temporary. The iconoclasm of the axe,

of the lustily screaming saw, makes it shudder
more deeply than anything before.
Hug the trees like a recovered child:

the sap bleeds the perfume of trauma.
The fenestration of the nine oaks, for instance,
in the field above us: long ago, but I kept

the slivers and shards in a bowl (the buds still
intact as fossils are), for whatever reason.
Each great oak in nuce, now, an anatomy

of arrested twigs I touch for inspiration
because, quite simply, I would sit far
below them then, in my leaf-vihara,

rooting myself to their trunk's itinerary.

Trunk

SPINNEY WOOD, CAMBRIDGESHIRE
Jackie Kay

The tree trunk is the colour
Of an African elephant's legs:
It has the feel of a cheese grater

Years later
I remembered them –
The lost children of the woods –
And their names came back to me:
Avia, Cheng Cheng, Aisha, Pavel, Bill P

By then I was an old woman,
My legs like those trunks, swollen
And all of my secrets locked away
In the old wooden trunk
From India in my living room,
Downstairs, where I hardly go anymore.

And my old heart is a wooden chest.
And my old feet are rooted to this place.

Andy Goldsworthy. Wind fallen branches. Forms for Hooke Park
HOOK PARK, DORSET, APRIL 1986

Andy Goldsworthy. Silver Birch. Forms for Hooke Park
HOOKE PARK, DORSET, APRIL 1986

Andy Goldsworthy in Hooke Park, 1986

*In the winter of 1985, Common Ground invited a young Andy Goldsworthy to London
from his home in Cumbria to work with his hands in the ice and snow on Hampstead
Heath. For six weeks, using only found materials – twigs, leaves, feathers, stones, ice and
snow – he created a series of ephemeral sculptures while visitors to the Heath watched.
This collaboration with Goldsworthy continued into Hooke Park, a 150-hectare woodland
and furniture school in Dorset (now managed as a woodland campus by the Architectural
Association). Here, in April 1986, he began making 'Forms for Hooke Park', a series
of small-scale experiments to attune himself to the landscape. This residency became
part of Common Ground's* **New Milestones** *project which, between 1986 and 1989,
encouraged several Dorset communities to commission different artists – Christine Angus
at Godmanstone, John Maine on Portland, Peter Randall-Page near Lulworth Cove
and Simon Thomas in East Lulworth – to make sculpture that expressed something
about their relationship with the local landscape. At Hooke Park, they settled on the idea
of making a gateway from roundwood, naturally curved trunks that would otherwise
be discarded or chopped-up for firewood. And in July 1986, over a period of four weeks,
Andy Goldsworthy created both a physical threshold and an invitation which encouraged
local residents to step inside and explore the woods.*

Andy Goldsworthy. Wind fallen branches. Forms for Hooke Park
HOOKE PARK, DORSET, APRIL 1986

Andy Goldsworthy. Constructing the entrance
HOOKE PARK, DORSET, JULY 1986

City, Trees, Water

AVON GORGE, BRISTOL

Helen Dunmore

I remember when the first row of plane trees was planted along the cobbled Narrow Quay in the 1970s. The Arnolfini Gallery had not long moved from the other side of the water into Bush House at the end of the quay. The saplings were among the earliest signs that Bristol's historic Docks were not going to fall into utter dereliction and disuse now that commercial shipping had left for Avonmouth. Few saw any beauty in the raw desolation of Bristol's port, but the seeds of its regeneration were already being sown. The planners who had wanted to send a splendid dual carriageway over the water were in retreat, even though buddleia still sprouted from disused warehouses, the demolition ball was swinging, Canon's Marsh was a huge and gloomy car park and the water of the Docks was a byword for filth. If you fell in, the story went, you would get Weill's disease from the rats which thrived while everything else decayed.

One night back then I walked from The Grove past the Arnolfini and along the quay. One of the freshly-planted saplings had been seized, bent over from its stake and broken. A torn-off branch lay on the ground, its leaves trampled. I willed the other trees to grow quickly, to put themselves beyond reach of vandalism. There is something in us that does not love a tree and makes it a target, and perhaps this is because we know the tree will grow so much taller than ourselves, and will outlive us. Then, it will take a chainsaw, knowledge and organisation to take it down. Now, any fool can destroy it.

That line of trees is more than forty years old now. There is no gap in it: another sapling must have been planted to repair the damage, or perhaps the tree, by some miracle, regenerated itself. The planes have come into their magnificence, while around the water more and more trees have been planted, and are still being planted. Leaf shadows ripple, people sit with coffee and beer in the shade or stroll in and out of the dappled light. Warehouse after warehouse has been converted into housing, restaurants, shops, cafés, museums, galleries, cinemas, and each time, more trees have been planted. The water quality is assessed regularly and the results posted up, because so many rowers, canoeists, sailors and paddle-boarders are at play on the water. Swans glide from houseboat to houseboat, knowing where they will be fed.

The raw glory of the Docks' working past has gone, along with its dirt, smoke, labour, venture, endurance, profit. Even its name has changed. To the satisfaction of the tourist industry and the developers of luxury waterside apartments, Bristol Docks are now Bristol Harbourside. But there is still the same intricate, brilliant engineering of locks and sluices to keep the water in the Floating Harbour at a level despite a tidal range of more than 12 metres. There is still the same voyage out through the lock that secures the 200-year-old Floating Harbour, down the River Avon and towards the sea.

It was a mild sunny October morning when I first made this voyage, more than four decades after I first came to live in Bristol. The ferry swung out from its mooring by the SS *Great Britain*. I was going to spend the next few hours travelling down the Avon Gorge to the mouth of the river, with commentary from the naturalist and broadcaster Ed Drewitt.

I live overlooking the harbour and its swans, cormorants and ducks are my garden birds. The Avon Gorge is familiar to me in every season: the electric green flicker of new leaves over black twigs in spring; the summer branches bearing their loads of darker leaves; the fire of autumn and the rich compost and mushroom smells of winter. But this was the first time I'd gone all the way to the mouth of the Avon by boat, following the river's twists along the deep limestone gash made by glaciers or perhaps by the giants Goram and Vincent in their battle for the beautiful Avona.

Few cities possess such wild places so close to their hearts. The centre of Bristol is not really its centre at all, because while the city has grown to the north, east and south, its western edge has remained much as it was, bounded by the river and the plunge of the Gorge, rimmed by National Trust land, by nature reserves and Forestry Commission woodland, by the Downs gifted in perpetuity by Act of Parliament to the people of Bristol, and by the publicly-owned estate of Ashton Court. There is a wealth of ancient green spaces and forest within walking distance of the city centre, and these spaces are knitted into Bristol life. They have their own rhythm of balloon and kite festivals, long muddy weekend walks, charity runs and mountain bikes rides, endless picnics and parties, sunbathing, fireworks and Dark Sky stargazing. When Concorde made its last flight home to the city where it was born, it swooped over the trees, the Gorge and the Clifton Suspension Bridge like one of the peregrine falcons that nest on the cliff face. Crowds of thousands lined the Gorge from the Observatory to the Sea Walls.

Like everyone who lives in Bristol, I have walked over the Suspension Bridge many times and stopped to gaze down 300 feet at the glisten of mud or the swell of a rising tide. I think of the ships coming in after long and dangerous voyages, centuries ago, and how the sailors would have snuffed up the smell of trees, sap, soil and blossom after months out on the ocean. I can't help thinking of the Bridge's sorrows too: the lives it cost to build it, the lives that are lost every year as people come to it in desperation to end their sufferings. From here the forest looks very dark. For once it's possible to see the trees as birds see them, their crowns visible, their trunks dwindling into the earth far below.

As our ferry left the harbour we turned to watch the final struggle of an eel in the gullet of a cormorant. Every so often the fish would show as a flash of silver in the bird's mouth while the cormorant gulped, head thrown back, in the throes of its swallow. Then it was the lock and the dank, mineral-smelling silence of the lock, the water level dropping and dropping as if it would swallow us too into this grave of water.

We came out onto the light of the river, and there were the trees on either bank, rising steeply above the rich mud. Oak, ash, birch, hazel, holly, guelder rose, yew, hawthorn, coppice hazel, small-leaved lime, dogwood and whitebeam of all kinds. According to the plant taxonomist Dr Tim Rich, there are more than twenty differentiated species of whitebeam growing in the Avon Gorge. There are two which are unique to this place: the Bristol Gorge whitebeam and Willmott's whitebeam. They flourish in the thin limestone soil, among the crags.

When I was young I would climb over the fence beneath the Observatory, 300 feet above the water. There were secret places in the scrub, where sun fell on exposed stone and there was no sound but the cries of birds. Even the traffic below on the Portway was stilled for months while a canopy was built over the road to protect it from rockfall. Opposite, there was the dark mass of Leigh Woods and far below, the glisten of mud at low tide. I would wedge myself in among low, knotted branches, eat an apple, read, close my eyes and feel wind and sun on my skin.

There is something entrancing about such wildness which is not only close to a city's centre but is also part of the city's breath and being, part of its understanding of itself. In spring, the encampments of hawthorn, blackberry and wild cherry on the Downs break into foam. It looks as if the blossom will spill in a tide over the roads. In November, the dense ivy which grows over these thickets is alive with the buzzing of innumerable honey bees, taking nectar for their winter stores. The light is low but in these sheltered places the sun is warm enough for the bees to cluster and suckle. In winter-time the naked trees reveal their beauty of line and structure. All along the roads across the Downs the avenues of horse chestnuts are bare. Generations of Bristol children have come to pick up conkers, or hurl sticks into the branches to bring them down. In spring, there are cowslips all over the Downs close to the Sea Walls, and in summer the meadows are mown for hay. There are harebells, scabious, ox-eye daisies, pimpernel and orchids, and rippling, exquisite grasses, bronze, thistle-blue and silver in summer twilight. In the background, always, the trees: the frame and protection of this landscape. And always, the eye is drawn back towards the 300-foot-deep gash in the landscape.

We sail under the Suspension Bridge. There are buzzards circling high above it, and from this angle the Bridge might as well be flying too. So much is visible, and so much is hidden. On either side of the Gorge there are Iron Age hill forts, built in defensive positions which gave a clear view as far away as Wales. Stokeleigh Camp, Clifton Camp and Burwalls Camp rose out of the trees and then returned to them. Their fires charred stones which are still buried somewhere under centuries of leaf-mould. The people who lived there cut down the trees to enclose their camp, and burned the wood to keep themselves warm. Stokeleigh Camp alone covered seven acres of land. The forest must have rung with voices, the clang of tools and weapons, cries of children. The people who lived in those camps have left behind pottery, a coin or two, a brooch. Like the buzzards they circle in a blue immensity of time, part of the world in which we live and yet flying in their own element. The trees grew back again, hiding deep ditches and raised ramparts. Roots dug deep into the wreckage of huts and walls.

Later there were foresters, quarries for limestone and celestine, charcoal burners working in their clearings. Generations of work, and the trees grow back over it. The 400 or so acres of woodland contain ancient woodland, veteran trees, wood pasture, coppice and post-war plantation.

We were on deck, watching as the trees slid past. Every so often Ed Drewett would swing up his binoculars and call out the birds that he saw long before we did. These woods are rich in prey and the crags are rich in birds of prey. We saw buzzards, kestrels and a peregrine falcon at roost in its limestone eyrie, invisible until we were shown where to look. I have only once seen a peregrine in flight over the Gorge, adrift it seemed on an updraught, its wings drawing energy from the wind with the most perfect economy. The peregrines hunt pigeon, starlings, doves, waders, swifts, thrushes, bats – and they are well fed here. The woods are full of birds. Nightingales, ravens, green woodpeckers, song thrushes, bullfinches, sparrowhawks, nuthatches. They reveal themselves only in glimpses, then go back to their secret, intricate lives. The woods hide and sustain them.

The river widens. There's salt in the air now, and seaweed clinging to the banks. We see redshanks and common sandpiper, shelduck and lapwing. Herons stand at strict, heron-regulated intervals, fishing their territory. The trees have thinned out. Everything is broad, tidal and suffused with light. We sail under the motorway bridge at Avonmouth and for a moment it seems possible that this little blue and yellow ferry might go on and on, trudging through wilder and wider water as river becomes estuary becomes sea.

But of course we go back. The tide has turned and is pushing us in with it. The trees run down almost to the water again. A golden fox slips out of the grass at the Gunpowder House. The Gorge is steep now on either side and cars drum along the Portway, echoing. This is where we see the peregrine, folded against grey rock, 200 feet above us. Another buzzard steers above the tree canopy, balancing, waiting. Here is the Suspension Bridge again, and soon we will turn into the lock. Now everything is in sight at once: city, trees, water, the dazzle of windscreens, a brutal flyover, a buzzard's looping flight.

Return to Ruskin Land

WYRE FOREST, WORCESTERSHIRE

Neil Sinden

We arrived at St George's Farm to start a new life at the heart of Ruskin Land in July 2015. We had left our busy lives in the East End of London, drawn by the lure of this magical place at the heart of the Wyre Forest and the hope of playing some useful role in its future. My wife, Lynne, had just finished almost thirty years teaching in the London Borough of Tower Hamlets, home to some of the most impoverished communities in the inner city and now one of the most successful education authorities. I was due to step down from a job I had held for almost fifteen years, campaigning to influence increasingly controversial reforms to the planning system pursued by successive governments.

Our move to Ruskin Land might be seen as a case of middle-class flight from city to country, but we had a real desire to be in this particular place at this particular time. For both of us the attraction was both historical and contemporary. What we knew about the Victorian visionary John Ruskin, his interest in art and nature, and his influence on the early environmental movement, was one inspirational thread. The more recent activities at Ruskin Land, particularly the work of the Wyre Community Land Trust, were another. A friend had been telling us of his role working with the Trust to develop a more integrated approach to the management of the Wyre Forest. Comprising mainly former oak coppice, the Forest is one of the largest areas of ancient woodland in England, yet remains relatively unknown outside the

West Midlands. We had only a superficial sense of the place before coming here. And what we didn't appreciate at the time was how we were retracing the footsteps of some fascinating pioneers who had made a similar journey more than a century before.

The area which has been known as Ruskin Land for over a hundred years, and identified as such by the Ordnance Survey, is now at the centre of our new lives. It is a name that signals a rich and complex history, and one that hints at its origins as a late Victorian utopian initiative. This was part of the irresistible lure of the place that attracted us here. And it is an experiment which has continued, with some diversions and distractions, to the present day. Its story is as remarkable as it is so little known. Having moved here, I needed to understand why the place held so much resonance for me, yet appeared to feature hardly at all in wider public consciousness.

One reason for the relative obscurity of Ruskin Land may be the controversy that surrounded its early years, as John Ruskin entered the final phase of his influential life. He had published what many, including Ruskin himself, consider to be his most important book, *Unto this Last*, in 1860. A critique of the approach to the 'political economy' at the time, it was ridiculed in the mainstream press but later became a major influence on the pioneers of the labour movement. It heralded a shift in his focus from art criticism towards a greater practical engagement with the social and political issues of the time. It is a book, despite its sometimes challenging language and construction, that has much to teach us today, particularly concerning the creation and distribution of real wealth, and the dehumanising effect of capitalism. Growing increasingly disturbed by the environmental destruction caused by the rapid industrial growth of Victorian Britain, and frustrated at the general indifference, even hostility, to his political writings, Ruskin decided he must take action and put his ideas into practice. As he said in 1869 in his influential lecture 'The Future of England', he resolved to address the question of 'what ought to happen' to correct the damage caused by industrialisation, rather than to dwell on 'what ought not to happen'.

In the years that followed, Ruskin's writing became increasingly focused on the need for social reform and his practical schemes. In the first issues of *Fors Clavigera*, his monthly letters to the workmen and labourers of England he began to write in 1871, he set out the idea of a 'National Store', of food, clothing, books and works of art, in contrast to the economic notion of a 'national debt', as a way to promote beneficial change. Later this became the 'National Company', providing the basis for what was to become the Guild of St George. After a lengthy struggle with officialdom, the Guild was eventually constituted legally in 1878, with Ruskin as its first Master. Its primary objective, set out in the Memorandum of Association was, 'To determine, and institute in practice, the wholesome laws of laborious (especially agricultural) life and economy, and to instruct first the agricultural and, as opportunity may serve, other labourers and craftsmen, in such science, art, and literature as are conducive to good husbandry and craftsmanship.' While the phrasing may be dated, the words remain relevant today as we develop plans for the future of Ruskin Land.

Although the cultivation of land was at its heart, according to Edith Hope Scott, the author and early supporter of Ruskin, the Guild had 'the appearance of a revelation – a sudden inspiration' and 'was certainly no logical and intellectually worked-out Utopia.' The sense of direction, though, was clear. Ruskin wrote that its purpose was 'the buying and securing of land in England, which shall not be built upon, but cultivated by Englishmen, with their own hands, and such help of force as they can find in wind and wave.' In this way, he stated, 'We will try to take some small piece of English ground, beautiful, peaceful and fruitful.' In a pamphlet on the *Nature and Purpose of St George's Guild*, published in 1882, Ruskin explained its role as showing 'how much food-producing land might be recovered by well-applied labour from the barren or neglected districts of nominally cultivated districts.'

A few years before producing that pamphlet, in 1876, Ruskin bought a 13-acre plot of land at Totley, near Sheffield, to rent out to a small group of industrial workers keen to establish an agrarian commune. They had formed a group a few years earlier to buy or lease some land to cultivate and use as a base for making tools, clothes and furniture. The property, which became known as St George's Farm, was owned by the Guild until 1929 when it was sold to George Pearson. Along with fellow socialist John Furniss, Pearson had taken over the enterprise at the suggestion of Edward Carpenter in 1884, after internal conflict had caused the original tenants to depart.

In its early years, the Guild attracted significant and loyal support from a limited number of individuals. Many of them were formally admitted as 'Companions', as Guild members are still known. It was one of the early Companions, George Baker, a Quaker and Mayor of Birmingham from 1876 to 1878, who offered Ruskin some land in the Wyre Forest to make a practical reality of his ideas. Baker had acquired 381 acres of woodland from a sale of Crown property in 1870. He originally offered seven acres to Ruskin the following year, increasing his offer to 20 acres in 1877, the year that Ruskin paid his one and only visit to the area. Ruskin stayed at Bellefield, Baker's home in Birmingham, and visited Beaucastle, Baker's country seat, an imposing Gothic mansion just outside Bewdley on the edge of the Forest about a mile from Ruskin Land. In Letter 80 of *Fors Clavigera*, written during this visit, Ruskin described his bequest with characteristic eloquence as set 'in midst of a sweet space of English hill and dale and orchard, yet unhurt by hand of man.'

It seems that Ruskin was initially ambivalent about what to do with the land he had been given in the Wyre Forest. It would no doubt have formed part of the oak coppice which was predominant there at the time but it is not clear whether it was being actively managed as such when Baker had acquired it. It didn't help that Ruskin himself was not considered to be particularly skilled in practical matters. Octavia Hill, one of the founders of the National Trust and an admirer of Ruskin, said as much and fell out with him as a result. Ignoring the likelihood that the land had previously been managed as coppice, Hope Scott writes that 'at first he decided to leave it in its ancient wildness to be a joy for ever in the Guild's hands safe from the menace to natural beauty, which was creeping over the English countryside.' But a few years later, in 1877, the year of Ruskin's visit, a local contractor was paid to clear five acres of the land of trees, which it appears took roughly five months, under the direction of George Baker. Despite this slow start, Ruskin subsequently devised plans for building on part of the site. Following his earlier initiative to establish an educational art museum in Walkley, a suburb of Sheffield, 'to provide training for the eye and the mind', he devised similar plans for the Guild's land in the Wyre Forest. According to Hope Scott his vision was for the museum building to be 'set there like a temple in the grove of oaks whose roots and stools were older than English history', drawing the workers 'to a double delight of natural beauty and of its spiritual and mental appreciation'. He duly asked George Baker to fell some oak and 'put it to season for years to come when he could hope to begin to build.' Despite appeals for financial support, his plan to build a museum was not actually realised, but Ruskin went as far as commissioning Joseph Southall, Baker's nephew and an aspiring artist (who later pioneered a revival of painting with egg tempera) to draw up plans for it. Those plans are now part of the Guild's collection.

Some insights into John Ruskin's approach to land management can be gleaned from his activities at his home in the Lake District. A few years before his involvement in the Wyre Forest, Ruskin had moved into Brantwood, a house on the shores of Coniston Water. Along with the then modest building, he had purchased 16 acres of land in 1871, 'half copse, half moor and rock' as he described it, on a steep hillside with views over the water to the Old Man of Coniston. The woodland there, as in the Wyre, had been coppiced for centuries. David Ingram, who has written on the gardens of Brantwood, suggests that coppicing was abandoned by Ruskin 'for aesthetic reasons', only to be reintroduced after his death. As well as creating a variety of distinctive gardens, however, Ruskin did much to alter the aspect of the woodland at Brantwood, including creating stepped paths, opening up vistas and re-routing streams. In Ingram's opinion, 'Ruskin always combined some practical social or intellectual experimentation with the desire to create an aesthetically pleasing effect.'

These experiments with his land at home illustrate Ruskin's belief in the possibility of a harmonious relationship between people and the natural world. He was not one to delight in wilderness untouched by human intervention. In *The Seven Lamps of Architecture* (1849) he wrote of the beauty of woodland 'dyed by the deep colours of human endurance, valour and virtue'. In the early years of Ruskin Land there was clearly a tension between leaving the Forest in its 'natural state', or 'ancient wildness' as described by Hope Scott, and intervening in some way. After a few years of prevarication, however, action was taken to carve out a clearing for a smallholding to enable some of his followers to start to make a living from the land.

While he recognised the use of the Forest for charcoal-burning and associated coppicing, Ruskin was unlikely to be aware of the way in which the Wyre Forest had evolved as an industrial landscape over the preceding centuries. By the seventeenth century, almost all of the Forest was being coppiced for iron smelting. Research by the Bewdley Historical Research Group shows that in the mid-nineteenth century, as well as providing a livelihood for wood-colliers (charcoal-burners), the Forest provided employment for sawyers, woodcutters, hauliers, hurdle-makers, bark-peelers, lath-cleavers, gatherers and sellers of firewood, basket and besom-makers, wheelwrights, coopers and carpenters. Towards the end of the century, however, as Ruskin's attention was drawn to the Wyre, the economic significance of the woodland was beginning to decline.

Shortly after Ruskin Land was cleared in 1877, William Buchan Graham, who was to become a key figure in its story, arrived to set about the task of establishing a smallholding. Graham, from a working class background in Glasgow, spent eight years toiling here and his experience, uncovered by some fascinating research by Mark Frost, is an illuminating one. Displaying the skills from his former trade as a lithographic draughtsman, in 1880 he made a detailed plan for an orchard to be established at the 'St George's Guild Bewdley Estate'. Shortly after, one assumes, he began planting the 180 or so fruit trees he specified, comprising mainly varieties of plum and damson, reflecting Victorian tastes, along with some apples, pears and cherries.

Sadly, Graham's time at Ruskin Land was not a happy one. He laboured here until 1886 without, it seems, much support. In a draft article written in 1887 but never published, he laments:

For eight years I worked on the Guild's land here, at Bewdley, situated in the heart of Wyre Forest – oak mainly, the property 20 acres in extent, 5 of which had been cleared in a slovenly fashion when I came; work redone by me and planting the patch with fruit trees. Thereafter I cleared 2½ acres more; made a road to the land; built some rough sheds and cots for pigs and appurtenances; grew crops of black oats and potatoes; tried growing beans and strawberries, by and by finding effort in any direction beset with insuperable difficulty.

The problems Graham encountered were bound up with the difficult relationship he had with Ruskin, initially a great inspiration for him, alongside a positively fractious relationship with George Baker. Conflicts with the latter involved complaints over his lack of regular remuneration, inadequate equipment and the use of part of Ruskin Land as a 'game reserve', contradicting the Guild's founding principles. There was a gulf between the classes in the nineteenth century, as Ruskin himself described, so it is difficult to draw firm conclusions about these personal relationships. Ruskin is known not to have been an efficient manager of practical detail and Baker must have been preoccupied much of the time with his civic role in Birmingham. Graham's story does suggest, however, a lack of understanding and respect for the physical and emotional commitment he made to Ruskin Land in its first decade. This was no doubt amplified by Graham's apparent unwillingness simply to follow his 'Master's' wishes, and to live uncritically with the hierarchical approach which then underpinned the structure of the Guild.

Crucially, there appears to have been some dispute over providing accommodation at Ruskin Land which, it seems, Graham had hoped for. In a letter to Baker in 1878 Ruskin writes: 'Since my illness I have given up all hope of instituting any modes of habitation on St George's ground: as long as the present Master lives, or is not deposed, or does not resign, the Company must be content with merely Vegetarian successes – for all the land at my command I shall keep under leaves.' Intriguingly he goes on: 'you may relieve your neighbour's dread of the threatened colonisation' and concludes; 'I am most thankful to hear of Graham's progress and good conduct'. These passages give an insight into the nature of relationships and local disagreements surrounding the early development of Ruskin Land.

Graham tried hard to resolve matters. He even visited Ruskin at Brantwood in 1881 to seek guidance on both how he should manage the land in the Wyre and handle his difficulties with Baker. During that visit he apparently pleaded with Ruskin to allow fellow Companion, John Guy (who had a similarly gruelling experience at Cloughton Moor where Ruskin had purchased land for him to work on), to join him in completing the task he had begun of establishing the smallholding at Ruskin Land. Getting nowhere, Graham eventually abandoned the project, the Guild and Ruskin. In the end he deeply resented his time trying to uphold what he understood the Guild's values to be through his work in the Wyre.

It wasn't until the late 1880s that the fortunes of Ruskin Land began to look brighter. In 1889, the first people from an expanding group of Ruskin followers, Margaret and Thomas Harley, came to visit the Wyre Forest from Liverpool. They settled just half a mile away in St John's Cottage built on land bought from George Baker. There they carved out a smallholding and inspired other visitors from Liverpool. Edith Hope Scott was to become their neighbour in 1908 after she had a house built, which she called Atholgarth, on land her father had bought for her, again from George Baker.

The Liverpool Ruskin Society had formed in 1883, meeting regularly at Mulberry Cottage in Wavertree between 1884 and 1901. The Cottage became a kind of communal sanctuary and host to both group discussions of the issues of the day and shared experiments in gardening. Members of the Society forged a strong bond that was to be critical in the later establishment of Ruskin Land. The Liverpool contingent were central to the survival of the Guild in the troubled times after the First World War, when its leaders openly speculated on whether the Guild was 'outworn' and had 'run its course'. Together they began to form the nucleus of a small community, at its peak comprising six households, in the forest immediately to the south of Ruskin Land.

Little is known of the activities at Ruskin Land itself during the final years of the nineteenth century. The orchard established by Graham was no doubt tended by the Companions living nearby and became more productive. But more significant developments were to come. In a letter written sometime in 1901 to Sydney Morse, following Ruskin's death the year before, Hope Scott expressed sympathy for the Companions in the Wyre Forest who, she said, 'I know are anxious for the Guild to do something with regard to the land to carry out the purpose for which Mr Ruskin founded St George's Guild.' And in a passage, which reflects the feelings of many of those involved with the current plans for the area, she went on:

> Bewdley has been tending to become a new Guild centre, and therefore seems the most suitable place for at least beginning any new Guild work. The Master (George Baker) lives there. The 20 acres of Ruskin Land are there. And two Guild Companions already own small plots of land there.

Hope Scott's thoughts, no doubt shared by others connected with it, appear to have galvanised the Guild. Shortly after that letter was written, in 1903, the Guild resolved to investigate building cottages for farm labourers on Ruskin Land. In 1908, St George's Farm – our new home – was completed and let to a local tenant whose identity is unknown. A few years later, in 1911, Frederick and Ada Watson, who had kept a successful ironmonger's shop in Liverpool, moved into St George's Farm together with their daughter Eva and two sons Harry and Willy. They had been drawn here by their friends, the Harleys, and Hope Scott. They must have experienced similar feelings, as we did more than a century later, on moving from a dense urban environment to an isolated rural dwelling, as it remains today.

Insight into the emotions of the early settlers at Ruskin Land is provided by a little-known and long out-of-print novel, *The Beloved*, written by Edith Hope Scott and published in 1921. It consists of illuminating, fictional letters from an early settler describing her response to the area, and the stories of other early inhabitants, including a Mr and Mrs Brown, whose characters are based on the Watsons. In it, Hope Scott describes the antiquity of the oak forest and its use as a coppice:

> The Forest is older than history, but only immense oak roots tell that, for the trees are seldom more than thirty or forty years old, and are surrounded with short dense oak scrub which grows on the oak stools and are periodically cleared, so that any year you may find a part of your dense and mysterious forest become a thinly wooded stretch of ground, bare of undergrowth except for the useless delights of honeysuckle and wild rose and all the other sweet wildnesses that are not to be bought or sold.

She also refers to the clearing of Ruskin Land, the establishment of the orchard and construction of 'the little red house' – St George's Farm – describing the smallholding and its fruit trees in blossom 'as a coral islet rising out of a sea of trees'. She dramatically captures the feelings of two visitors, in a passage which could have been written yesterday, on arriving at the farm:

> Then we turn off the high road, which after passing a few cottages, became more and more enclosed with trees; and it seemed to Molly and me that we were getting into a dark and dreadful forest such as we knew existed in fairy tales … It was nearly dark when we turned into a long steep lane, which seemed to go straight up a hill, and was bordered with tall, dark pine trees – We did not know what they were, but they looked like great giants standing in rows, and our hearts beat quickly – at least I'm sure mine did.

The Watsons stayed at St George's Farm raising their children and working the land, using a horse and trap to get to market, selling pigs, chickens, eggs, honey and fruit, for almost thirty years. There are a few surviving photographs of the whole family which give glimpses of what their life was like. Despite the passage of time, it is still possible to identify with the feelings she describes about living and working here. In fact, it wouldn't be too difficult to reconstruct some of the photos today, if we could successfully source the Edwardian clothing.

During the Watsons' time at St George's the Guild considered purchasing some forest adjoining Ruskin Land. This was inspired by concern over conifer planting by the Forestry Commission, which had been set up in 1919, that the Guild believed was a threat to 'preserving the traditions and crafts of the forest'. In June 1928, the Guild agreed that its work lay in the Forest and that a definite policy be developed for its landholdings there. Subsequently, in 1930, the Guild took the opportunity to purchase almost 100 acres of woodland, part of which is known as Shelf Held Coppice, along with Uncllys Farm, a neighbouring smallholding. This land connected the Liverpool settlers in St John's Lane with the original area of Ruskin Land, and stretched further north, down to the Dowles Brook which marks the border between Worcestershire and Shropshire.

In 1938, the Watsons returned to Liverpool, after Frederick had suffered a stroke, and the farm was passed to their nephew, the aptly named Ruskin Williams. Not much is known about what happened here during the Second World War but following the departure of Williams, who had apparently built up rent arrears, Jack Bishop took over the lease of St George's Farm. With his wife Nancy, he took over the smallholding in 1956, almost sixty years before our arrival.

Jack was employed by Brintons the carpet-makers as a 'loom tuner', a much respected expert in mending and servicing looms used in their factories in nearby Kidderminster and abroad. It seems he took on the smallholding as a part-time activity. With the help of grants from the Ministry of Agriculture, which were widely available at the time, he grubbed out the orchard which had been so carefully planned and planted by William Graham, and used the land for grazing cattle and making hay. In a personal reflection, Jack's daughter has expressed her ambivalence about our recent efforts to re-establish an orchard here given the hard work her father undertook to replace the original one with productive pasture land. In his later years, Jack also kept turkeys in one of the two main outbuildings near the farm, and leased a patch of land next to other outbuildings, a short distance from the main farmyard, for the storage of building materials. While Nancy died before him, Jack lived at St George's Farm until he moved into a hospice shortly before passing away in 2014. Jack was a respected character, who is still fondly remembered by the older walkers in the Forest and the scouts and guide groups that he allowed to camp at Ruskin Land. There is little evidence, though, that he had much interest in John Ruskin or the Guild of St George. While it provided mains water to the house and installed a bathroom in 1962, the Guild played a largely passive role during the Bishops' tenancy. Their main concern, it seems, was simply to ensure that the land was kept in good agricultural condition.

Alongside its apparent hands-off approach to the farming activities, the Guild was uncertain about how best to care for the woodland it had previously acquired. A report by the Master of the Guild in the early 1970s talks of problems with managing the oak coppice owing to 'the increasing difficulty of finding labour, and the need to protect its flora and fauna'. Help was at hand, though. A partnership with the Worcestershire Countryside Preservation Trust, involving the county council, the Guild and neighbouring landowners, led to the designation of part of the Wyre Forest, including Ruskin Land, as a Site of Special Scientific Interest. In 1978, after the Nature Conservancy Council had begun to purchase land in the Forest, 214 hectares of it was designated as a National Nature Reserve, making it one of our most important wildlife sites. Since then considerable effort has gone into encouraging the coordinated management of the Forest to enhance its value for wildlife and people, with the Guild and the Wyre Community Land Trust, set up by John and Linda Iles who live at Uncllys Farm, playing an important role.

We now have the opportunity to tell the story of Ruskin's legacy here and explore the potential for bringing his ideas to life in the twenty-first century. There are certainly lessons to learn from the past which has not been without its troubles and tensions, but there is great optimism among the people who work and volunteer here. It will be a big challenge to safeguard and nurture the distinctive character of this place while sharing it more widely. Protecting its tranquillity will be particularly important. We feel a strong sense of personal responsibility to the people that have lived and laboured here before us, as well as to John Ruskin's inspiring ideas about society, art and the natural world.

There are solid foundations on which to build. Over the past ten years or so, the Wyre Community Land Trust has started to restore the landscape. Working with local volunteers, the Trust has taken in hand the management of many of the old-established orchards in the locality, carrying out restorative pruning of the older fruit trees and planting over 500 new ones, mainly local varieties of cherry, apple, pear and plum. A small herd of Dexter cattle help maintain the meadows which are scattered in and around the Forest and provide a stable source of income for the Trust. The startling variety of wildlife in the Wyre Forest is greatly enhanced by these meadows and orchards, remnants of earlier farming activities. Natural England has carried out some enlightened woodland management, including the creation of wide forest rides and new coppice coups which provide important habitat for birds such as redstarts and hawfinches, and butterflies, notably the pearl-bordered fritillary and white admiral.

Through the winter just passed, working with volunteers from the Bewdley Apple Cooperative, we have completed the planting of a new orchard at St George's Farm. The orchard feels symbolic of the human and historical connections embedded in this place. The task has made me marvel at the contribution made by William Graham in the early years of Ruskin Land. It must have been backbreaking work to clear the land of oak-coppice stools before planting, single-handedly it seems, the 178 fruit trees on the plan of the orchard, beautifully drawn by his own hand. Even with the help of numerous volunteers and our modern tools, it has been challenging enough to plant the 151 trees that comprise the new orchard here, particularly during the very wet weather we experienced at the start of the year. The new orchard, which includes many of the original varieties planted by Graham, will stand we hope for many years as a monument to his work here.

His contribution will also be recognised in plans being developed to restore Graham's neglected grave, which he shares with his wife Eliza, at St Leonard's Church in nearby Ribbesford.

The new orchard is also a symbol of a new era for Ruskin Land. An era in which the values that underpinned its foundation will be explored and made relevant at a time when they resonate more than ever. A stronger sense of shared purpose will help overcome the inevitable challenges that arise often daily when dealing with pregnant cows, power cuts, uncooperative machinery or tracks blocked by trees brought down by high winds. There is a growing acceptance locally that effective management of woodland depends on partnerships which bring together public and private landowners across a wide area. This should help to address the challenges presented by the fallow and muntjac deer which roam through much of the Forest and prevent the regeneration of the trees. The Land Trust is also beginning to explore how it can best care for the woodland that it looks after for the Guild, along with a wider area it manages on behalf of other landowners. It has made a start in returning to coppice some of the stands of oak of uniform age, and by selective felling of some trees to provide a more diverse habitat for wildlife. At the same time we want the timber to spark, in some small way, the regeneration of the local woodland economy which was once so vibrant here.

As Edith Hope Scott wrote, in *Ruskin's Guild of St George* (1931), the early settlers from Liverpool:

> went down to Bewdley to try to turn a piece of the yet unreclaimed Wyre Forest into a fruit farm. They might have failed; it was work Ruskin had wished the Guild to do – to take the risk and expense of reclaiming yet uncultivated land – but for individuals the risk was double and dangerous … But they did more than add to the food-producing land of the country, they became the nucleus of Guild work which has had, and will yet have, far-reaching results.

Those words were written over eighty years ago. An element of personal risk remains, though nowhere near as great as that faced by William Graham. And while food production is now part of a much wider vision, aspirations for Ruskin Land remain as bold as they did in those early years. It is not difficult to feel inspired by the simple pleasures of this place, its sheer natural beauty which engages all the senses, and the ability quietly and closely to observe the changing seasons. There have been disagreements and distractions in the intervening decades and these will no doubt continue. But with effective collaboration, careful stewardship and a clear vision, it now feels like this magical place has a bright future with potential to improve the lives of many people in these difficult times. Every time we return to Ruskin Land, it is hard to believe our good fortune at being part of the next chapter in its story.

Heartwood

WINDSOR HILL WOOD, SOMERSET

Tobias Jones

I n July, I was walking in a mature woodland on the steep valleys
outside Hebden Bridge. You could hear the River Calder as it
smashed through the rocky gullies and under cobbled bridges. I
was walking to ponder the impending death of someone very close to
me. As I shuffled amongst the giant beeches and oaks, I saw a small,
neat sign which explained the importance of leaving fallen timber
in place: 'In a healthy woodland,' it said, 'you should be able to see
deadwood from wherever you're standing.'

It was one of those strange moments in which unrelated words
seemed to speak precisely to my own situation. I was considering the
demise of my mother, far too young and fit to be buried; and there,
in a neutral, educational rectangle, was advice that, in sylvan spaces,
health depends not on taking away the dead, but allowing them to be
seen from where they fall, leaving them to release vital spores for the
invigoration of their descendants.

Those strange moments of sudden insight and understanding
happen more often, it seems, under the canopy of trees. John Stewart
Collis, in his lyrical collection of essays, *The Worm Forgives the Plough*,
advised those young men and women who were 'ambitious only for
peace and sanity' to 'learn the craft of forestry, enter the woods, and
happiness may yet be yours.' What we nowadays call mental illness
has, in the past, been given other names: shell-shock, melancholy,

hysteria or insanity, amongst many others. But throughout mental turmoil in human history, woodlands have always been offered as a place of succour and serenity, providing what Edward Thomas called 'simply an uplifting of the heart'.

Within mental health circles, some scoff at the sudden appearance of endless new disorders which categorise unease and disease, but one of the most convincing (and also obvious) of recent times is 'Nature Deficit Disorder'. It's the idea that our alienation from the natural world creates everything from depression to behavioural disorders. Many would argue that such healing happens anywhere within nature or, as those of a religious bent have it, within Creation. But those of us who make a part of our living through working a woodland believe that it's particularly trees which soothe, heal and make whole. It's telling, for example, that Richard Louv, who coined the label Nature Deficit Disorder, spoke of woods in his title: *Last Child in the Woods*. It's woodlands, more than moors or mountains, which offer us mortals repose and rapture.

It's hard to know why that's the case. Certainly there's a primeval pull towards the shelter they offer: shaded in summer, protected (albeit dangerous) in high winds, they absorb if not solve flood issues, they're surprisingly dry in rain and, of course, warm us when cut and burned. Within myth, the wild woodland has been a place of outlaws and adventurers, the place where outsiders gathered because they were well-hidden or simply exiled: think Iron Hans, Grimms' most intriguing man of the dark forests. There's something counter-cultural amongst trees, however cultural you are.

Until the frantic enclosures of the sixteenth, seventeenth and eighteenth centuries, the English forests provided commoners with immediate access to their 'bote': the timber necessary to repair houses or ploughs. Some of the loveliest lost words of the English language – 'affuage' and 'estovers' – described rights we used to have to forage for firewood. Take away that connection to such ancient and extraordinarily generous woodlands, and it's not surprising an epidemic of depression ensues. We're now self-congratulatory about the access commoners have to forests and woodlands; we proudly boast about the great walks the public can enjoy within sylvan glades. But the vast majority of us still have to go to Travis Perkins or Mole Valley for our timber and that isn't, I suspect, so good for the soul.

The age and longevity of woodlands also put into perspective our mundane concerns. They encourage a certain phlegmatism about the worries of today. We're diminished in woodlands by the might of the trunks, examples of both rigidity and flexibility. They're not places of quick returns. The length of time between planting and productivity – of fruit, or firewood, lumber, syrup or nuts – is long, and means that the woodland is bound to be 'semi-permanent', a place you can keep coming back to. If you have set aside some firewood, the value of your stock is safe: for nobody can really steal it, the stock prices won't crash, or make you rich. It's simply a solid, reliable investment of your muscles, and there are ever fewer of those in our slippery, virtual world. Help someone plant a hundred whips in a day and it's simply inevitable that they'll feel a whole lot better about themselves, discovering in their own way the truism that the meaning of life is to plant trees under whose shade you will never sit.

The aesthetics of sylvan spaces, too, are breathtaking: the minute red scrotum of the spindle tree which drops ecstatic orange seeds; the scarlet elf cups which speckle the woodland floor in January if you've left sufficient deadwood visible; that brown rice on the beech trees before the leaves unfold; the witch's claws of the ash, the winter catkins on the hazel – it's hardly surprising that we should be uplifted here. Which isn't to say the woodland is a serene or always relaxing place: part of the attraction is that it's sometimes frightening. There are loud noises, especially after dark. Branches creak and groan. A woodpecker will machine-gun a trunk, a fox will appear and slay your flock. It's unsettling, as well as warming, here in Windsor Hill Wood. Unnerving, perhaps, because it's a brownfield site, and there are long, dripping railway tunnels, abandoned buildings and rubble. There's a sense of the post-apocalyptic out here, as if civilisation has really retreated. But it's also unnerving because our subconscious associates woodlands with danger. Many fairy tales begin with the command not to leave the safe path, and when innocents lose themselves in this dark space they meet strangers and deep lakes which change their lives.

So part of the curative effect of being in a woodland isn't that it's a safe place of succour, but actually that it brings to the surface our innermost fears. At Windsor Hill Wood we've worked with a lot of troubled teenagers: often those going through psychosis, post-traumatic stress disorder, homelessness and addiction. They're not surprisingly spooked when they find themselves in the middle of nowhere, with not a house or smartphone in sight. This is a place where they have to rediscover trust, not just in you who's taken them here, but in themselves.

And that's the key: in a woodland we all become survivalists. Not in the sense of gun-toters, ready for the apocalypse. But we rediscover how easy it is to do simple things: to make a walking stick for someone, to carve a spoon, to keep warm, to source food. Most of the young men and women I've worked with respond instinctively to the call of the woodland. They might be nervous, but with the smallest of instruction, they discover that they're able to meet their own needs through brute strength and subtle thought. They feel the allure of the woods because it allows them to do what comes naturally: to be themselves, to look after themselves, to offer themselves. Bushcraft is achingly trendy at the moment, but there are other elements to this enjoyment of survivalism which go deeper: it's something to do with personal resilience, with emotional robustness and, even, voluntary simplicity.

At Windsor Hill Wood we work with a lot of people in early-stage recovery, and have seen first-hand how substance abuse subsides when someone is sourcing more healthy victuals. Every day we spend hours, as a community, tending our livestock, working in the polytunnel, planting trees and so on. Much of what we need just comes by itself: hazelnuts, birch bark, willow for baskets. For carnivores there are squirrels, rabbits and wood pigeons. The dried canes of wild raspberries still bend amongst the coppice like four-foot parentheses. Brittle cow parsley from last summer makes immaculate kindling. The chicken manure will power the tomatoes. When you're that busy meeting elementary needs, it's not surprising that mental weariness is repaired and compulsive appetites are calmed. And because our attempt at permaculture emphasises integration rather than segregation, people feel included. They realise that nothing goes to waste and slowly, in the months they live with us, discover they are an integral part of a great whole.

There's nothing like a story of a comeback kid, getting up again after terrible setbacks. And that's the narrative every year in most well-managed woodlands. Each winter we coppice a small cant, leaving a few standards, but mainly being pretty aggressive in cutting back the hazel, willow and ash and leaving just those beige 'stools' like naked ovals. Every winter is the same: the members of our small community lament that I've turned our woodland into a brashy field. And every spring, the older hands here watch for the shoots. By summer, they can be two or three metres high, defiantly bouncing back from the dead. And not just one, but twenty or thirty from one stool. It's a magnificent metaphor for those in crisis who live here with us: that something written off can rise again, can defy all expectation and be resurrected.

Which is why, presumably, the Japanese practise *shinrin yoku*, literally 'forest bathing'. What might have seemed faddish thirty years ago (or, sorry, blindingly obvious further back) is now such a widespread health initiative that Japan has almost fifty accredited forests in which citizens can 'bathe'. The beneficial effects on insomnia, anxiety, anger and so forth are well-documented. Something similar is happening across the United Kingdom now with the creation of hundreds of both formal and informal 'care farms', a notion imported from Holland in which farming practices double as therapy for vulnerable people.

One can't imagine such ethereal social work being high up the agenda of a Westminster policymaker or, even, of a lobbying group. The notion that woodlands should be part of the health provision of this country seems, to most, slightly eccentric. And yet a growing body of Forest School leaders, bushcrafters, clergymen and conservationists are convinced that we will be more whole if we hang out with and in the trees.

We're now setting up another, this time non-residential, woodland. A 10-acre site again, it will be run solely for the benefit of the local townspeople and nearby villages. Thanks to the generosity of the donor, this site has negligible capital costs. We will need to improve footpaths and site safety, but the majority of the work will be human-centred, spending time alongside those who already appreciate the woodlands: the teenage partygoers, the BMXers, the dog walkers, the firewood poachers, the cavers, rock climbers and deerstalkers. At the moment it's an informal free-for-all anyway, a de facto commons which is, perhaps, why the donor asked us to take it on in the first place.

But such initiatives are extremely rare because the cost of land seems to rise exponentially. Politics is too urban-centric to notice how alienated children are from the countryside, even in rural areas (one of our Forest School children, a ten-year-old born and bred in Somerset, recently expressed horror at the idea that an egg comes from a chicken's vent). The solution, I believe, is the agrarian radicalism taught by Henry George and now given the regalish label of Georgism: the notion that land should be equally owned amongst the whole community, and that the basis of taxation should not be income, but land-holding. Comparable to Geoism, it's a movement with a noble tradition running through Locke, Spinoza and Paine, and recommends progressive rather than regressive taxation: those who hold the most land pay the most tax. Were there – as there was a hundred years ago – a political party offering a return to the commons through Georgism, many would sign up immediately. It would nudge society away from the iniquities of enclosure and privatisation, compelling patricians to become philanthropists and donors if only to diminish their tax bill. As well as addressing financial inequality, such a measure would also begin to address the mental-health crisis, because it would end the melancholy so many feel at not being able to work within a wood; and the melancholy so many feel at not being able to live in them.

Cusop Dingle

DULAS BROOK, ENGLAND-WALES BORDERLAND

Nina Lyon

Until late in the nineteenth century, Cusop Dingle was regarded as being haunted by fairies, will-o'-the-wisps and unnatural spirits of one sort or another. People were fearful about it. I had always found this counterintuitive, although I also found the idea that small children would make their way alone through the wood to get to the now-ruined schoolhouse near the top of the hill counterintuitive, but there is nothing geographically menacing about it, at least if you are minded to like woodland.

Tall ashes climb from its steep sides towards the light, and the edges are dotted with hazels and silver birch. Despite its location, deep in a north-facing crook of the valley, the light is always plentiful: silvery in the winter, marking out the smooth trunks of the bare trees, softly green with the first growth of the spring, warm and long and gold, throwing mottled shapes across the floor in the summer, and marked out in a carpet of coloured leaves in the autumn.

It is small but, carved out by two waterfalls which meet in a steep bowl in the middle, has a complex enough shape to feel like it might go on further into unknown territory. It forms a fragment of the western edge of Herefordshire, and that unknown territory, the impassably steep bank to the other side of the brook: the beginning of Wales.

From Hay Bluff, whose monolithic slope looms over the top of the Dingle, you can see the demarcated geographies of English rolling hills and patchwork fields and wild Welsh mountains as they meet around the Wye. Herefordshire has a good claim to being the most archetypal of English counties, excelling at oaks, orchards and endless sunlit swathes of long grass. But this part of it was Welsh in culture and character for most of recorded history, and the upland places retain their Welsh names.

The names of the waterfalls are not official names, but those adopted by my children. The High Waterfall runs down from the fields adjoining Cefn and Cusop Hill and, a little way after the broken tree, drops sharply down from a flat rocky ledge. Near the bottom of the longest part of the fall, it is joined by the Big Waterfall, which is the Dulas Brook, the ancient border between England and Wales. The redness of the Hereford stone is exposed in the waterfalls, as though the rush of water has eroded it to the quick; the Big Waterfall pours out of a wide red crescent of rock into a broad pool. You can only get there between November and March, when the undergrowth in the wood has died back, but the wet ground can get you then: you need to be on your guard when scrambling down the hill.

Near the top of the Dingle, where the wood clears to the steep upward incline of Cusop Hill, there is a lime kiln. It is still in good shape, although the chimney is partly obscured by grass and leaves and foliage, and if you scramble down you can see the furnace arch intact. The lime kiln marks the point where the track becomes a narrow path; it is the point where it is possible to get lost. The lime kiln marks an incarnation of the wood as a place of industry, long before the waymarked walking trails on the hills above brought in earnest droves of tourists.

Richard Booth, the self-proclaimed King of Hay responsible for the town's proliferation of antiquarian bookshops and concomitant visitors, was fond of writing pamphlets. These tend towards a vituperative quality – Booth has never been shy of a spat – and *Bureaucracy in Brecon and Radnor*, with reference to a horse ride through Cusop Dingle is aimed squarely at Margaret Thatcher, the Forestry Commission, the National Parks Authority, the Welsh Tourist Board and a number of lesser quangos. It is also a prescient piece of psychogeography, a photographic essay tracking the deserted bridleways up the valley past the ghosts of past industry: the cider orchards and hillside smallholdings, and quarries and kilns and brickworks that once dotted the Dingle with life.

Old Victorian maps show springs and tracks that, with a little detective work, can soon be uncovered. Networks of drover tracks cross the land at this height, working their way along the flatter, lower slopes of the hills, some indented deep into the ground with centuries of footfall and some grown over with brambles, bracken and grass. It is a parallel world separated by space as well as time, hundreds of metres up above the valleys we populate now.

As you ascend the Dingle, you emerge into a no-man's-land at the place where the lower slopes of Cusop Hill and Cefn Hill join. This is the treeline, and also the snowline. Above it, there is a commercial forest of tall pines and the broadleaved trees become scarcer, with field edges marked out in hawthorns and crab apples contorted by the wind. Nestling in the last trees in the crooks of the hill are storm-blown crumbling bothies and piles of stone where walls once were. They form a broken contour as you work your way around the edge of the wood at this height: once upon a time, it made more sense to live up here, so that you could avoid the dangers of the wood and graze animals on the steep meadows.

The flat top of Cusop Hill was once extensively quarried, like all the hilltops along that western stretch of the Black Mountains. Hereford stone is an Old Red Sandstone that forms flat slabs perfect for construction and roofing, and when freshly quarried it often has a purplish colour which weathers to the flinty greenish-grey of the ruined bothies and collapsed walls.

Booth's pamphlet was written over thirty years ago, in the early 1980s, and is a critique of a then-new order of affairs in which big concerns ate up the small, and where the last edges of an older, wilder world were within living memory. Booth laments the passing of the hillside smallholdings where cider, eggs and home-cured bacon far superior to their industrial replacements were produced, and the impositions of distant and artificial layers of political management to places that had always managed perfectly well on their own, and rails at the new breed of publishers and writers invading the old farmsteads.

The oddity of reading it now is that the bleak descriptive passages of deserted slopes and crumbling bothies and the accompanying midwinter photographs taken by Booth's partner, Hope, are exactly the sort of thing that gets published on psychogeographic rambles today, except we are now inclined to revel in it. Ruins signal lostness, and there are few lost places left. What could be more romantic than a hillside empty of human endeavour?

Thirty-odd years on and my children play in what was one of those lamented empty barns at the top of the Dingle, which was hastily developed into a home around the time of their conception. Booth's angry brand of localism avenged itself soon enough. He was largely responsible for the mechanism of its action, too, although perhaps not quite in the way he had intended – the bookshops attracted more of those bookish townies, who found the hills and bought the dilapidated farmhouses on them, and every lane is dotted with hand-painted signs offering chicken and duck eggs and surplus fruit, and the Thursday market, which has become a tourist attraction of sorts, is not short of artisan bacon or craft cider. The houses at the bottom of the Dingle, where Booth still lives, are a smart leafy suburb of a prosperous market town. It all feels dangerously civilised.

But Cusop Dingle manages to protect itself by becoming strategically impassable. At some point early in the year, a huge tree fell across the top of the High Waterfall, its trunk semi-snapped. If you did not know the place well, you might find the broken tree intimidating, lain at the only crossing point before a steep ravine.

In order to cross the waterfall, which runs down from Cefn Hill and which you can usually ford unless it has been very wet, it became necessary to duck beneath the snapped tree-trunk, and a gust of wind could move other broken branches, somewhere nearby, to make the sort of creaking noise one imagines preceding a tree-based fatality. After doing this a few times, though, it is part of the experience of the wood. The children find it amusing, ducking beneath it and along rocks that are no longer visible beneath new swells of water. Exhortations to be careful get swept away like twigs in a fast brook. It is similarly impassable from the bottom for much of the year, with a stretch of deep mud as the wood opens out towards the end that removes boots, quicksand-like, and obstructs vehicular access.

I have spent many anxious nights waiting for my small son and his father to come home for dinner, at least an hour late and well after dark. On one occasion the lateness was merited by a tumble into the ravine which resulted in a severely torn thigh and, miraculously, an unscathed child. And once, on the way back from the waterfall, we came across a woman who had slipped off the path and broken her ankle. It is my only recollection of meeting anyone there. We scrambled uphill to call an ambulance and waited while they arrived, realised that they needed a vehicle able to navigate the mud, drove as high up the track as they could, sent in some extra manpower on foot and stretchered her back down to civilisation. The sirens, dampened by the high-sided valley, and then the flashing lights when they came in half-darkness, and the paramedics, entertained by the unlikely location, were a strange thing to happen there.

I have never seen anyone else in the Dingle, but from time-to-time there have been marks indicating activity which I would track proprietorially: a tree felled, tyre marks in the track lower down, fallen branches and brush stacked to one side. Sometimes, in the late spring or summer when you can hide in full foliage, I heard voices or a saw nearby, and slowed to peer through the trees to see if I could identify who and where they came from, without success. It was like one of those fairy tales where the elves come out at night to work when they think that nobody is looking.

There was something unsettling about each change in the place, the unseen agency of it. It disrupted the pleasing assumption that the wood was a stable and dependable thing, a backdrop to walks with certain predictable seasonal variations, a place of big-N Nature unsullied by human hands. That's the way we think about the woods now – they have an ornamental quality, so that Cusop Dingle, with its archetypally perfect name, tucked away in the furthest reach of England, carries all the expectations of a living museum of what the woods were like.

As with all tourist attractions, the labour behind the image must be invisible, lest the illusion be shattered. When storms felled the tree at the High Waterfall, the Dingle was lined with rows of neat stumps and stacked logpiles. This did not seem right – it didn't fit the imagined domain of wild nature – and I experienced a Booth-like disdain for the notion of management, as though some ghoulish sylvan quango had assembled to produce guidelines for the correct stacking of severed branches to which the branch-stacking sylphs had rigidly adhered.

It was more than the neatness of the stacks, though. The high edge where the path ascends was where the winds blew hardest, and was worst hit. The bank looked thin, as though the hill might encroach on it. The illusion of the wood's continuity into the otherness of Wales was undermined by long stacks of felled logs, marking out a system of measurement in which the whole place looked smaller, like it had shrunk.

My children, arguing in the car one wet afternoon about the existence of fairies, concluded that they either represented a parallel dimension with its own set of natural laws or were real, visible creatures driven away to the last dark corners by technology. They were insistent, whatever, that you could still find them in the mossy banks between the two waterfalls.

A few Sundays later I went the long way to collect them. Beyond the bare trees, the waterfalls roared their months of rainfall. In the thick of a scramble from tree to tree, logpile to logpile, the old folk tales felt a little more real, as though the sense of jeopardy involved in impulsively heading down a steep slope, one you couldn't necessarily climb up again, might elicit malign supernatural forces. The crashing water had its own fearsome power, and I desisted from getting up close in the moss.

It was dark when I made it to the top of the hill. I nearly lost my phone, which I was using as a torch, at the top of the High Waterfall as I ducked under the broken tree. I found the children curled up with their father on the sofa in the half of the old schoolhouse that he had rebuilt. They were dismissive of my adventures, and said that it was always like that, and that the fairies chose that place for a reason.

The Gypsy Stone

EPPING FOREST, LONDON

Will Ashon

Very little is known about the early life of Adam Smith, the philosopher whose *Wealth of Nations* could be said to have invented classical economics. His first biographer, John Rae, could dig up only one story about his infancy: when Smith was just four years old he was stolen by Gypsies. Luckily or unfortunately, depending on where you stand on the baleful influence Smith's work has come to have – and in particular the free-trade 'think' tank which bears his name – a local Scot saw him 'crying piteously', raised some kind of posse and chased the Gypsy woman in question, who abandoned the child and fled. Smith was returned to his mother. 'He would have made, I fear,' his biographer states, 'a poor gipsy.'

The Gypsy Stone is a contradiction, and for more reasons than one. A large, solid lump of granite, fake-rough all over, carved with a caravan and a plaque for the inscription, it marks the birthplace of a man who grew up in a social group committed to nomadism, to being *of no fixed abode*. A dandelion would've made a more fitting tribute. But then Rodney 'Gipsy' Smith, as he was known professionally, wasn't a typical Gypsy.

The only way to write about Gypsies is to focus on the atypical. The typical ones don't want to be pinned down. The ones who are pinned – who pin themselves – are aware of their singularity. Cornelius Smith, Rodney's father, remembered his own parents: 'It was their custom to travel from place-to-place; thus rambling to fairs, feasts, and races, I was dragged up in darkness, misery, and sin, and became very daring and wicked, and loved the roaming life intensely.'

The Gypsy Stone can be found in a scrubby bit of woodland not that far from the North Circular orbital road on the north-eastern outskirts of London. You can hear the cars from the deep cut of the road as you stand there. If you're coming from the south, you either cross that thoroughfare from above, on a narrow bridge over six lanes or, a little further west, hurry through a small, subterranean tunnel which, if the smell is anything to go by, has been graffitied predominantly with human excrement. And yet somehow, when you reach the Stone, you don't feel as if you're squeezed between major roads on two sides and suburban housing on the others. Somehow, you feel like you're deep in the woods. The trees deaden and mask the sound, adding the hum of a million moving leaves to whatever comes from beyond them. The light is so green that your own skin seems tinted with chlorophyll. Birds bubble coded messages. Something is moving in the undergrowth and it's probably a rat. The truth is, though, that the fact of finding the Gypsy Stone is what most strongly gives this place its atmosphere.

Epping Forest as it exists today can be divided into two parts. The southern half of the Forest narrows from the playing fields and parks at its base into a thin corridor of trees, a kind of interstitial woodland beset on all sides by the ramshackle outer-city housing developments of London. The northern half broadens into what feels like a proper forest and is bordered by the fields and market towns of West Essex. The Gypsy Stone sits in the southern sector, and four miles north, Lippits Hill Lodge crouches behind a high wall on the edge of the Forest proper. It was here that John Clare, the 'peasant poet', was held at the private asylum of Dr Matthew Allen from 1837 until his escape in 1841, when he followed a Gypsy route north and walked a hundred miles home.

Clare had an intense and somewhat complicated relationship with the Gypsies which dated back to his childhood. Although a

wanderer on one level, he was also absolutely wedded to the specific
landscape around Helpston in Northamptonshire where he grew up.
He admired the Gypsies' *no-placeness* while himself being thoroughly
placed. His interest intensified when he was at the asylum, both
trapped and separated from the landscape which defined him. One
of the best poems he wrote while he was there is called 'The Gipsy
Camp' (1841). It's a very simple, very stark little piece – muted,
somehow, shot through with that woodland thrum of expectancy, as
if the whole consciousness of the place is waiting, anticipating some
violent rupture which never quite comes. A boy is gathering wood
and then returns to his snow-covered, 'squalid camp'. The Gypsies
are cooking 'stinking mutton' on the fire, but there's none to spare for
the dog. And that's it, that's your lot: 'Tis thus they live, a picture to
the place; / A quiet, pilfering, unprotected race.' Most commentators
take the phrase 'a picture to the place' to mean 'picturesque'. If it's
interpreted more literally, we see the camp as an embodiment of the
space it occupies, a human representation of nature. There's a tendency
to skip over it, though, as our discomfort focuses us in on that last line,
that 'pilfering ... race'. Interestingly, Gipsy Rodney Smith concurs
with Clare in his booklet, *From Gipsy Tent to Pulpit*: 'The gipsy does
not commit big robberies, he only pilfers.' As for stealing babies, he's
quick to put an end to that particular libel, and 'for a very good reason
– they have enough of their own.'

Gipsy Rodney Smith was one of the most famous evangelists of the
early twentieth century. He travelled from England to America and
South Africa, he preached to the soldiers near to the Western Front
in the Great War. He sold out the Royal Albert Hall three nights
straight, preached to open-air crowds of 10,000 on more than one
continent and led a march of up to 50,000 into Chicago's red-light
district, the Levee. He didn't much like drinking or dancing but he
had a lovely voice for a hymn. Despite the unbending nature of his
beliefs, he had a gentle, oddly likeable writing style which hints at
what made him so successful as a saver of souls. He even ended up
in a short story by Tennessee Williams. And throughout his career

he was known as Gipsy Smith, his ethnicity also his selling point, as if to suggest that if a Gypsy could be saved, then who on earth couldn't?

But to achieve this salvation Rodney Smith had to stop being a Gypsy. Having been picked out at a meeting of the East London Christian Mission in 1876 by none other than William Booth, who two years later would re-brand his organisation the Salvation Army, Smith bought himself a conventional suit, moved into a Mission house on the Whitechapel Road, and was taught the finer points of cutlery use, sleeping in beds and so on. He went to work for the Salvation Army in Whitby, then Chatham, then Hull, then Hanley, before being dismissed for his acceptance of a gold watch, a gift from the Christian folk of that town. After that, the rest of his career until his death in 1947 was spent as a freelance evangelist, going where God – or the bookings – took him, but based back at Romany Tan, his house in Cambridge. This was in marked contrast to his father and uncles, Cornelius, Bartholomew and Woodlock, who all converted in 1869, but continued to live as gypsies as well as travelling preachers. But then, life for the gypsies was changing fast by the end of the nineteenth century.

There's another Gypsy Smith to deal with here, one with a clearer grasp of economics than his evangelising relative. George 'Lazzy' Smith's cousin, Justinia Buckley, was married to Woodlock Smith, Gipsy Rodney Smith's uncle. Though there is no monument to him in Epping Forest, like Rodney Smith he did allow his thoughts to be written down. In 1886, Lazzy led his band of gypsies, under the name the Royal Epping Forest Gipsies, to the Liverpool International Exhibition. Here they 'exhibited' their encampment, charging entry, apparently so successfully that the Liverpool Review claimed 'the poor Laplanders are now having to play second fiddle'. As Smith was to outline in the pamphlet he authored for sale at the exhibition, his band had been working this particular stunt ('to charge a fee to those wishing to gratify their oft-times instrusive curiosity') up and down the country for a good few years, even claiming that Queen

Victoria stopped to talk to them while they were up near Balmoral (and doing little to quell the rumour that she had asked to have her fortune told). I can't help thinking – and the 'Royal' in their title reinforces the possibility – that the title of the group was chosen for much the same reason. Royal Epping Forest came into existence in 1878 as the result of a long-running campaign by the Commons Preservation Society, who saved it from being fenced for fields and housing. It's good marketing to tie your brand to an exciting new venture and Epping Forest had recently become, in effect, Britain's first national park, a Cockney Paradise. 'My ancestors recognised the Forest of Epping as their headquarters,' Lazzy claimed, possibly to drive home the point, 'and to this day at intervals we visit the spot, a sort of pilgrimage to Mecca as it were.'

Lazzy Smith was part of the most famous Gypsy family of the nineteenth century. He was the nephew of Ambrose Smith, who became better known as Jasper Petulengro, one of the key protagonists in the series of fictionalised memoirs that George Borrow pumped out between 1851 and 1874. Borrow's strange, unwieldy books – anti-Catholic propaganda crossed with philological bragging – were hugely popular in the middle years of the nineteenth century. He's perhaps best understood as the Patrick Leigh Fermor of his day, offering a vision of escape and social mutability while remaining essentially conservative in outlook. Only without the same quality of prose. Or the charm, for that matter. You could even see in his books a seed of the current obsession with fit young men yomping through the countryside armed with the deadly weapon of enthusiasm, spraying words as ammunition, as if the natural world were something to be occupied. (If the public school system in the UK was largely built to provide a cadre of administrators to run the colonies, perhaps this colonisation of nature is what they are forced into by the absence of the territories they were trained for.)

Strangely, considering that Borrow dealt with the same Smith family that Lazzy came from, he makes little mention of the Mecca at Epping, at least not until his short piece 'Kirk Yetholm'.

The story follows a standard Borrovian pattern, in that it involves him pretending to be an ignorant *gorgio* before revealing himself to know more about Gypsy language and culture than the Gypsies do themselves. If there were a literary prize given for bumptiousness they would have to retire it after Borrow. 'As for Romany-chals there is not such a place for them in the whole world as the Forest. Thems that wants to see Romany-chals should go to the Forest, especially to the Bald-faced Hind on the hill above Fairlop, on the day of the Fairlop Fair. It is their trysting-place, as you would say, and there they musters from all parts of England, and there they whoops, dances, and plays.'

The Bald Hind Inn was finally knocked down some time after 2011 so that flats could be built in its place. If you imagine the Lego blocks from a model of the Death Star blown up to human size and then used to construct luxury apartments in the Essex/London suburbs, you have a pretty good idea how Silver Hind Court looks. It has a fancy 'SHC' logo at the entrance to its underground car park and it's not hard to picture the meeting in which it was decided to drop any mention of baldness from the name. The view from the road is stunning, though. You can just about make out the snake of the Thames in the distance, the wind turbines down in Dagenham. Everything is held in a kind of translucent shimmer, as if standing here has instantly transformed you into Turner.

Of course, Borrow's celebration of the Gypsy as exotic Other could easily tip into its binary opposite – fascination replaced by revulsion, attraction by fear. It's time to welcome yet another Smith. George Smith of Coalville spent much of the late-nineteenth century trying to legislate the Gypsies out of existence. He had managed to get a Canal Boats Bill passed and introduced by 1878 – the same year as the Epping Forest Act – and then turned his attention to the vans of travelling people. He thought he meant well but, despite his claims to a scientific method, that meaning was built on the assumptions he began with: 'the Gipsies were neither more nor less, before they set out upon their pilgrimage, than a pell-mell gathering of many thousands of low-caste, good-for-nothing, idle Indians from Hindustan.' Just in case the implications of this belief aren't clear enough, Smith expands: 'In no country in the world is there so much caste feeling, devilish jealousy, and diabolical revenge manifested as in India ... Anyone observing the Gipsies closely ... will soon discover their Indian character.' Commenting on the way they have interbred and mixed with local populations, he goes on to say that 'the muddy stream of Gipsyism has been winding its way for ages through various parts of the world; and, I am sorry to say, this dark little stream has been casting forth an unpleasant odour and a horrible stench in our midst.' In England, an island nation, the situation is even worse, with interbreeding rife, but 'notwithstanding this mixture of blood and races, the diabolical Indian elements are easily recognised.' His solution is simple – assimilation through education of the children.

In his *Gypsy Children* (1889), Smith travelled to an encampment near Loughton on the edge of Epping Forest. In contrast to the Liverpool Courier's description of Lazzy Smith's 'scrupulously neat and tidy' tent, Smith of Coalville finds 'wretched dwellings, which were nothing better than horribly, stinking, sickening, muddy wigwams.' He stops a small boy and asks him his name. The boy replies 'sometimes they call me Smith, sometimes Brown.' He goes on to tell the – presumably terrifying – stranger that he has never washed, sometimes says prayers with his sister which he can't remember and has never been to school. Finally, he is asked if he's heard of Jesus. 'I never heard of such a man,' the boy responds. 'He does not live upon this forest.'

Lazzy Smith, on the other hand, claims in his pamphlet that 'Jesus Christ ... was a gipsy, and on Christmas day we burn an ash tree in honour of Him, because He lived and died one of us.' In this, his take on his people is very similar to that of his namesake, Gipsy Rodney Smith, both of them – though for different reasons – keen to talk up the respectability of the Gypsies: 'For morals, for purity of thinking and acting, the Gipsies come out at the top.' Indeed, Lazzy Smith claimed to have spoken against the other Smith's Moveable

Dwellings Bill at a committee meeting in the Houses of Parliament in May 1891: 'I took all as Smith said about us, and POUNDED it … I telled 'em what rale gypsies was – the particalarest an' cleanliest people there is.'

Lazzy also remembers Fairlop Fair – or remembers hearing about it, anyway. It was, he recalls, 'a little gold mine to the members of our tribe.' According to Smith's great-great-grandmother, the Fairlop Oak, around which the fair took place, was so huge that 'the shadow of its branches covered an acre of ground' (in actual fact, this 'recollection' is included in every one of the various pamphlets that were issued and sold at the fair from 1796 onward, so there's reason to doubt Smith's source). The fair was one of the biggest revels of its day, with people pouring out of East London so that at its height over 200,000 visitors would attend on the first Friday in July to get drunk, feast, gamble, have their fortunes told and so on. The fair ran every year from 1725 until 1851, surviving thirty years longer than the oak itself, which was first set alight in 1805 (John Hoyland blamed the gypsies but in fact it appears to have been day trippers from the metropolis) and then blown down in 1820.

Fairlop Waters Country Park is an industrial/entertainment estate built roughly where the great Fairlop Oak used to stand. There is a permanent marquee for weddings and so on; a soft play centre; a high ropes experience of some sort; a golf driving range; a visitors' centre and café currently undergoing transformation and obscured by a chrysalis of crowd-control barriers; a run-down looking windsurfing club; a small sailing club backing on to what must be the tiniest monster truck circuit in the world. You could be anywhere in Britain and yet, at the same time, you could only be in Essex. The lake is scrappy, small and strangely threatening, the aggressive drunk whose eye you avoid catching at the pub.

What finally finished the Fairlop Fair off was enclosure. In 1851 – the same year that George Borrow was publishing his first 'Romani' work, *Lavengro* – an Act was passed in Parliament to disafforest and sell off the common woodland round Hainault. While Epping Forest eventually ended up being saved, Hainault Forest was destroyed in a few short weeks, the trees being ripped out of over six square miles and new fields being ploughed in their place. Rental income leapt and the owners of the manors within Epping Forest began enclosing that land, too. The attack on the forests was the last hurrah of enclosure in England, though the techniques developed and the impetus it provided had already been exported to Scotland and then the rest of the world.

In a very real sense, then, by 1851 Borrow was already writing about the past, a lost world. Enclosure did far more harm to the Gypsies than any amount of legislation, because enclosure removed the wastelands and commons on which these people had traditionally made their temporary home. 'I think and often dream of the many well-loved spots on this beautiful land I have visited in my boyhood days,' claims Lazzy Smith, 'when all was health, glee and happiness. Now, alas! where are they? Gone! The busy work of the builders has covered those places once so dear to me.' Finding himself paying for the land he stayed on, Lazzy innovated and began charging the *gorgios* who wanted to visit him.

Cornelius Smith, travelling from Cambridge to Baldock in Hertfordshire in the early 1870s, where he and his brothers had been invited to evangelise, was arrested at four o'clock in the morning. The policeman who woke him told him, 'There is a law made that if any gipsies are found stopping by the roadside for 12 miles round they are to be taken up without a summons or a warrant.' They spent the night praying loudly in their cell and it was only after a whip-round among local believers that their fine was paid and they were released. Cornelius' son avoided this fate, these daily hassles, by renouncing the Gypsy way of life and becoming, in effect, a *gorgio*. Religion, like business, worked as an escape route in a shrinking world.

In the summer of 1897, the last Gypsies were finally cleared from Epping Forest. Local councils had first tried to pass by-laws prohibiting anyone from using the Forest as a dwelling place under canvas or in a caravan, but this move was blocked by the Home Office. Instead, it was decided to enforce laws that dwelling places should have proper sanitation and effective water supply, knowing that to obtain these in the bounds of the Forest would break other by-laws – an example of using 'protective' laws as a form of aggression. As Haydon Perry reported in socialist newspaper, *The Clarion*: 'A body of police, forest keepers and local residents proceeded to evict "the offenders." The result was a foregone conclusion. The gipsies were forced to pack their caravans and were slowly driven beyond the edges of the Forest.'

On the face of it, Rodney Smith wasn't driven from the forest. He walked out. And he was denounced for this escape. According to David Lazell's biography of the evangelist, Gordon Boswell, a distant relative, harangued him at the Cambridge Midsummer Fair in 1937: 'You know you've done a terrible thing after you was uplifted by the name of Gypsy ... In our estimation you made a fortune. You've come back for a holiday. And the Gypsy people that was old enough to know what you was doing at the time – they thought it was a shameful thing. You must have been money-crazed to do it.'

I'm going to say something which makes me feel uncomfortable, which I'm not even sure I'm allowed to say. There is no such thing as a Gypsy race, because scientifically speaking, there is no such thing as race. As Ta-Nehisi Coates puts it in his remarkable essay on race and America, *Between the World and Me*, 'race is the child of racism, not the father.' None of us is the member of any race beyond our common humanity. This is not to deride difference or belittle cultural specifity, just to point out that it isn't based on blood. If to be a Gypsy is anything, it is to follow certain norms and patterns of behaviour.

I intend now to make us still more uncomfortable by drawing on John Clare's taxonomy for a definition: 'quiet, pilfering, unprotected' (though we will follow Gipsy Smith's definition of pilfering as an *absence* of large-scale or systematic thieving, something to which he brings an almost Marxian edge when he says that gypsies take 'what they need, no more'). Gipsy Rodney Smith had abandoned all of this particular trinity and that, I believe, is the underlying thrust of Gordon Boswell's criticism. By leaving the Gypsy way of life,

Rodney Smith had ceased to be a Gypsy at all.

Then again, the space to be a Gypsy was shrinking. As Adam Smith points out in *Wealth of Nations*: 'Civil government, so far as it is instituted for the security of property, is in reality instituted for the defence of the rich against the poor, or of those who have some property against those who have none at all.' The privatisation of land demanded a growth of civil government and this meant less room to be quiet (i.e. uncommunicative with the *gorgios*), less tolerance of pilfering (seen as a kind of blurring of the borders of private property) and less chance of remaining unprotected (George Smith of Coalville's Moveable Dwellings Bill was presented as an attempt to 'protect' gypsy children).

One of the key forms of protection offered by the Moveable Dwellings Bill was compulsory education for Gypsy children. Yet there is no word in Romani for writing – a different kind of silence. Borrow claims *por-engri-pen* for penmanship, literally 'feather-thing-speak'. I wonder if that's what they told him to avoid offence. Isabel Fonseca, in her book about Gypsies in Europe, *Bury Me Standing*, points to another commonly used word: chin – to cut, or to carve, usually in relation to wood, though it would do for a Gypsy Stone, too. They agree, however, on the verb 'to read', offering versions of *del-oprey* or *dav opre*. It translates, literally, as 'to give up'.

The Gypsy Stone is a contradiction. Where you can choose to see a symbol of some lost, sylvan age if you so wish, it's also in the nature of forests to present an opposite image: dark, sulphurous, terrifying. In 1991, the Old Bailey heard evidence from a ten-year-old girl who claimed that she and her sister had been raped at the Stone up to three times a week as part of Satanic rituals culminating each time with their godfather, 'a Christian and a true gipsy', killing a baby: 'Sometimes he would cut the arm or the leg off, and sometimes he would make us take a bite off it.' Five people were put on trial, including her parents and the godfather. The girl claimed, furthermore, that 'my mum said that if we told, all the gypsies would come and cut us up and hang us. I was scared. I believed it.'

While it would be foolhardy with what we know now to ever discount or belittle a child's account of sexual abuse, it's also impossible to imagine that the linkage of the figure of the Gypsy with the spectre of the stolen baby (here transformed into a kind of blood libel) didn't act as an engine for the prosecution. After all, the police searched and dug all around the Gypsy Stone, but not one of the bodies the girls claimed were buried there – or indeed any other physical evidence – was ever found. After five days the case collapsed, the testimony from the younger sister being deemed by the judge to be 'uncertain, inconsistent and improbable'. The godfather, found not guilty on all charges, was George 'Sonnie' Gibbard, the grandson of Rodney 'Gipsy' Smith.

The Green Stuff

Ali Smith

I t was midwinter. The sun was glinting and low. The boy was in his father's woods when he met another child.

The other child, sitting on a stump with its legs crossed and its chin in its hand, was bright green.

Who are you? the boy said.

Who are *you*? the green child said.

It had such bright green hair, such bright green skin and clothes so green that greenness came off it like a halo and seemed to be leaching out of its feet into the mud they both stood in. If the boy had dipped himself under the curtain of algae in a summer pond and stood up, risen dripping in it, this is what he'd have looked like. The green child's skin was alive. Tiny segments of greenness shifted under and over each other like CGI in a PC game except more real. Tiny wet actual real leaves shifted and shimmered, merrily on the crawl, all over the green child.

I live here. Over there. These are my father's woods, the boy said.

Oh yeah, your father, the green child said. And your grandfather. And his father and grandfather and the ones before them and before them all the way back to the very first.

Then it laughed. Its laughter sounded very like the boy's own laughter. The boy stared. He felt himself become very polite.

These are our woods, he said. They've belonged to us for centuries.

The green child gave a little snort.

You can't own woods, it said.

Well, that's what the authenticated historic certificates we've got up at the house all say, the documents signed by kings and historic people, with the wax seals and ribbons still on them, the boy said. Certificates that go back nearly to the beginning of records.

Oh, *records,* the green child said.

Proving, the boy said, that for centuries our family has not just owned these woods but everything in them.

A twig snapped under his foot as he shifted his weight.

Yeah, and I bet you think you own that twig, the green child laughed. I bet you think you own that blackbird.

It pointed at a bird flying low over their heads. The boy felt himself grow pale.

I bet you think you own all the living things you can shoot and eat, and the things that are too small to, like the squirrels, the green child said, and the things too inedible to be eaten, they're yours too, are they? I bet you think you own the deer and the hares and the foxes and the badgers and the rabbits and the snakes and the birds and the bees and wasps, and the butterflies and the moths and all the insects. You think you own the dragonflies, don't you? You think you own that tree, and that one. And that one.

This is, yes, officially all ours, the whitening boy said.

The green child began to laugh. It laughed so much that wet green stuff came out of its eyes and ran down its face. It lay down on the ground and rolled about laughing in the dead leaves. It picked one up and held it out, brown in its green hand.

And every single leaf every single tree makes, the green child said. I bet you've got a certificate that says you own its whole life. From when it starts to form inside the tree then becomes a bud, all the way to when it falls off. And the fallen leaf when it gets thin and is just veins of vegetation on the ground. And the memory of the summer that the dead leaf has, and the memory of all the summers in every one of these winter trees.

We own it all, the paler and paler boy said in what was very nearly a shout. All of it.

And the grasses, the green child said, and the sounds that the leaves make in the summer when they're on the trees and the wind lifts them. And the creaking noises that the trees make when the wind knocks them into each other in the winter. You own it, do you?

The woods belong to my father, the pale boy said, and eventually, they'll belong to –

And the mud that comes in the thaw of the winter, the green child said. And the water that gathers in the tracks in the mud. The water in that hoofprint there. And the microbes that live in the mud and the water. You own the microbes. And the microbes on the microbes. All the spores. All the germs.

Both children looked at the deerprint in the mud between them. Then the boy looked the green child straight in its green eyes.

Do you live in this wood? he said.

You don't own anything, the green child said.

If you live in this wood then we own you too, the boy said. And if we don't, get out. You're trespassing.

The green child sat at the boy's feet in the mud and the wetness on the green of him winked like he was covered in Christmas lights.

You think I should go? it said.

The boy made his mouth a firm line.

Really? the green child said. Are you sure?

The boy stood his ground in the winter mud and the green child vanished.

The boy stood in the nothing for a bit. Then he went home. He was cold. Plus, it was frozen pizza night.

In the early hours of the next morning, the water all through the woods froze solid. That next day the boy didn't come down for breakfast.

Then he didn't come down for lunch.

At four in the afternoon, when it was dark out, his sister began to wonder where he was.

At half past seven she went upstairs. She stood outside his bedroom door and felt the unnatural cold in the hall. The handle turned in the door, which meant the door wasn't locked. But it wouldn't open.

She called their parents up the stairs.

At the top of the stairs the parents exchanged a look. The father put his shoulder to the door. The mother shoved hard. When they finally opened it enough to see into the room, they saw they'd been shoving against a substantial little wall of snow.

The room was full of snow. The boy was in the bed under some inches of snow.

They brushed it away from his face. They pushed the melting snow off his chest. His mother used her little finger to dig the frost out of his mouth and nose. He gave off coldness. His eyes were shut. His eyelashes were frosted.

Is he dead? his sister said.

Their mother sighed a no. She went back downstairs to watch the rest of *Antiques Roadshow*. The father pushed past, carrying her brother down the stairs. Well, given that he wasn't dead, then, maybe it was okay to take some photos on her phone for the family history etc. So she took some images.

The snow on the carpet on the landing. The snow on the inside windowsill of his room. The snow several inches high in a ridge on top of the books on the bookcase. The snow wedge on the laptop. The crust of melt close to the radiator.

She went downstairs herself.

The rasp of snow still stuck on the cotton on the shoulder of her now fully conscious brother's dressing gown.

He was looking at them all as if from a great distance away.

Do trees have memories? he said.

Don't be silly, his mother said.

On *Antiques Roadshow* an expert, pointing to carvings on a large cupboard made of walnut, was talking about mannerism and the sixteenth century. The cupboard, he was saying, was a forgery or a reproduction, made 300 years later than it was pretending to have been made, and therefore worth a lot less.

The boy's eyes were on his father, who stood at the window looking out at the blackness. He had his hands behind his back.

Does water in winter remember what it's like to be water in summer? the boy said.

The sister remembered that people who've been frozen should be wrapped in stuff that looks like tinfoil. She went to the kitchen and came back with a box. She pulled a long noisy swath of light out of the box and tore it loose on the serrated edge of the packaging. She wrapped it round her brother's chest.

How did you make it snow inside the house? she said in his ear.

Her brother closed his eyes.

Their father had his phone out and was calling the people who did the garden for them.

They came and dealt with the situation. They opened the boy's bedroom window and tipped shovelfuls out. They hung themselves out of the window and shook and banged the books and things together in the night air to dislodge what melting snow had stuck to them. They plugged little heaters in and placed them in strategic positions to dry the carpets.

The sister took some phone photos of how much snow was piled up against the side of the house after they'd finished. There was a surprisingly large amount. But somehow she managed, by mistake, to delete all the pictures she'd taken on her phone. That night it happened to snow out in the world anyway. This made it impossible, next morning, to differentiate her brother's snow from the general snow all around the house.

Snow fell all night. It fell all the next day and all the next night again. It fell silently. It gloved everything with itself.

So much of it fell that in the muted nearby town when people opened their front doors in the morning they couldn't see their cars in their drives anymore.

In the woods snow formed tall unstable walls along each branch and bank and surface. Birds shook snow off their heads, backs, tails and wings, and sheltered under branches where snowfall itself formed for them little shelters from the snow. Snow piled up on the backs and snouts and foreheads of the deer that lived in the woods. The one white deer in the herd disappeared except for its black eyes. When it closed its eyes, they disappeared too.

The aconites waited underneath everything. Above them was earth, mud that had frozen hard, layers of dead stuff from the year and all the years, and a good lagging of snow. Their leaves would eventually be green and their flowers vibrant yellow. They'd be both poisonous and healing. They'd produce themselves out of the ground when the time was right in the woods, as ever.

Forest Fear

WOOD OF CREE, DUMFRIES AND GALLOWAY

Sara Maitland

The Cree is a small river that drains off the western side of the Galloway Hills; it is joined by the Water of Minnoch and most of its relatively short course runs through Dumfries and Galloway. Below Newton Stewart the land flattens out into merse (or more locally 'inks') – tidal grass flats, famously home to over-wintering geese – and the river officially ends at Creetown where it flows into Wigtown Bay and thence into the Solway. The valley of the Cree above Newton Stewart is to me one of the prettiest places in Britain (not beautiful or sublime or spectacular, but very, very pretty). Green and sweet and sheltered, climbing steadily into wilder country with the profile of the big hills above. On the east bank of the river, half a dozen or so miles above Newton Stewart and hanging on to the steep valley sides is Wood of Cree, the largest extent of ancient woodland in southern Scotland. A series of burns flow down from the high moor, cutting through the wood – fast, always noisy, rocks and water, white with foam and golden brown with peat; there are several impressive waterfalls.

Wood of Cree delivers almost everything you would anticipate from ancient northern oakwood – oak trees of course and birch and rowan and hazel and crab apple; erratic boulders shoved into position by glaciers as well as the rocks pushed down more recently by the burns; an understorey carpeted with thick green mosses and draped with honeysuckle and lichens; and in season bluebells of course, but also some of the most flourishing, delicate, yellow cow wheat I have ever encountered.

But, at the same time, and like every other bit of ancient woodland, Wood of Cree is not like every other bit of ancient woodland because it, like them, has a long and complex relationship with people. Wood of Cree has been heavily managed, mainly for oak coppice, since at least the seventeenth century; probably because of its steepness very few oaks were grown on as maidens for timber – clear-felling was the traditional method of managing this wood. In the early 1920s it was clear-felled for the last time; but it was never grubbed up or replanted extensively with larch or spruce. This means that almost all the oak trees are the same height and age; but growing on much older roots; many of them are multi-trunked and they are very thin and tall – and close together, except where granite outcrops prevent them growing at all. This gives the place a rather different atmosphere from more usual oakwood, and in particular it feels more fairy-tale than ancient; more frolicsome than awe-inspiring. It also has an unusual 'soundscape'; not only is the sound of running water very loud and coming from all directions, but in addition the tall, thin trees are very 'creaky', even moaning.

Wood of Cree is now an RSPB reserve. Fairly obviously this is because it has a particularly rich avian taxa including a healthy summer breeding population of pied flycatchers – along with many other delights, and is blessed by an extraordinary, notable dawn chorus. The point about this here is that it all means it is still managed woodland; the paths are good, there are car parks and the whole place is littered with nesting boxes, interpretation boards, signposts and convenient benches. Although it is very pretty, it is not actually very wild. It is not a place where I anticipate feeling overwhelmed by deep fear. But I was.

Last January I went for a walk in Wood of Cree. The Cree, which only a couple of weeks before had broken through the flood wall in Newton Stewart and inundated the High Street, was still huge and fast and dark and threatening and the burns coming down were roaring more ferociously than ever. But the sun, for once, at last, was shining and, although it was muddy underfoot, it seemed sweet and agreeable to be out and the winter wood appeared gentle and welcoming.

I have a small golden-coloured dog – her vet who loves her describes her as a 'stretched border terrier': border-terrier size but all shaggy and elongated. She has an exceptionally joyous and ebullient character; nervy, timorous or servile are not words that come to mind in describing her! Like many terriers she likes to be The Leader and, when not distracted by wonderful woodland smells after too little walking in the previous weeks, she barges past me and heads out up the path. I follow her, wondering somewhat at the signs of preposterously early spring – there are green leaves on the honeysuckle and the hazel catkins are stretching themselves out and down, already turning from purple nubs towards golden rain. The moss seems denser and more luxuriously green than I have ever seen it, ramping over the rocks and up the tree trunks. The wind drops abruptly. And I hear her howl, above the crashing sound of the burns; a long howl followed by a strange, loud whimper. I start to run up the path, but it is very muddy and steep and I am unfit from the long spell of wet-confining winter. I stumble. Suddenly, she comes hurtling down the slope, throws herself against my legs and I can feel that she is trembling. I bend down to her and realise she is half wild with fear.

And then I am too. I am consumed, abruptly, breathtakingly, totally, by terror. Some atavistic bitter flavour that I cannot identify rises in the back of my throat. I am unable to move – this is something way beyond the adrenalin rush of 'flight or fight'; this is something very dark and primitive; above the sound of running water I can feel my heart thumping; the taste of the fear is itself fearful.

It does not last long, moments rather than minutes. Then the dog relaxes, looks at me almost slyly, shakes herself vigorously and turns and trots off up the path again. I straighten up; wilfully unknot all my clenched muscles with a sort of shudder rather closely akin to her shaking; take a deep breath. Think, 'What was that?'

And indeed, what was it?

I have felt it before, this forest fear. Older sections of the great Caledonian Forest have produced a very similar sensation, with a background awareness of the ghosts of long-gone wolves; and coming down from a long, high hill walk, through plantation forestry and realising that it will be dark before I reach my car has had the same effect. I have never (I am glad to say) been seriously lost in the woods, but I would take all possible care not to be. I have however been frightened on numerous occasions – once on the very final cusp of dusk and dark a barn owl, white as a ghost, flew almost into my face and I screamed and it made its loud wheezy-sounding alarm cry. Once I walked into a gang of robbers – who were I am sure in retrospect just a group of local youths having an alcohol-fuelled good time. Once someone hidden in the trees whom I could not see let off a rifle that felt very near. And more, I have been frightened in woodland. But on most of these occasions I happened to be in a wood when something frightened me. In Wood of Cree, and years ago in Glen Affric, and once in the birch woods above Loch Hope in the very farthest north, usually in winter and usually at dark-fall and always when I have been alone, I have been frightened by the wood itself. Forest fear. And yet Wood of Cree is such a very pretty wood.

I am not alone. Not by any means. One of the best descriptions of this fear is in Kenneth Grahame's *Wind in the Willows*:

> Everything was very still now. The dusk advanced on him steadily, rapidly gathering in behind and before; and the light seemed to be draining away like flood-water. Then the faces began … Then the whistling began … They were up and alert and ready, evidently, whoever they were. And he – he was alone …

> Then the pattering began … As he lay there panting and trembling and listened to the whistlings and the patterings outside, he knew it at last, in all its fullness, that dread thing which other[s]. . . had encountered here and known as their darkest moment – the Terror of the Wild Wood.

Poor Mole. Poor me too – except there is also something viscerally thrilling about this fear, something both uncanny and exciting.

When I encounter something mysterious and profound in the forest I go back to the Grimms' collection of stories; I have argued elsewhere that these stories took shape from and emerged out of forest cultures – northern European forests; instinctively one thinks that fear and the forest are closely entwined; that the stories are driven by the Terror of the Wild Wood and the deep magic of dusk and the long, green shadows that move and stir, the strange pattering hush which is never truly silent, but still hard to hear properly. Surely the fairy stories will lay bare the source of my fear.

Yes, here is Snow White, terrified in the woods:

> The poor child was all alone in the huge forest. When she looked at all the leaves on the trees she was petrified and did not know what to do. Then she began to run, and she ran over sharp stones and through thorn bushes. Wild beasts darted by her at times, but they did not harm her. She ran as long as her legs would carry her.

Excellent. Except – except that it is not the forest itself that has frightened her into this wild flight. As it happens, she has something very concrete and not remotely connected to the forest to be frightened about: someone has just tried to kill her. Not just 'someone' but someone she knows, someone who loves her, someone who is acting on the orders of her stepmother. Putting physical distance between herself and the cause of this fear as fast as possible is not crazed at all, it is very sensible. This is not a response to the uncanny, it is proper reaction to the much commoner, much simpler domestic fear. The most dangerous place for children in terms of both accidents (including fatal ones) and abuse (including sexual abuse) was and still is in their own homes. The moral of Snow White's story is not 'stay out of the forest', but precisely the reverse – 'get away as quickly as you can and the forest will protect you.'

And so it is throughout the stories. Of course, frightening things happen to the characters in the forest, but they are all social, human bad things: witches, robbers, stepmothers, human cruelty. And interestingly, they are people who should not be in the forest;

wherever a hunter or – particularly – a woodsman of any kind (a forester, a woodcutter) appears in a fairy story of this type, it is as a good character. No one gets mauled by a wild animal, crushed by a falling tree, bitten by a snake, stung by a bee or other insect (not even by a nettle now I think about it), poisoned by a fungus or drowned in a bog or pond. (All fairy story drownings take place at sea.) Even the wolf in *Little Red Riding Hood* slips into Granny's pyjamas and becomes a farcical character: the forests and woods of the fairy tales are not dangerous and they are not frightening.

There is a telling, though nowadays less told, story in the original Grimms' collection called 'The Boy Who Went Forth to Learn What Fear Was'. The protagonist of this tale is a slightly goofy but entirely fearless youth whose exasperated family send him off to discover what being frightened feels like. In his endeavours to learn he encounters a variety of people who send him off to supposedly scary places – for example, he spends a night under a gibbet, visits a haunted castle full of demons and ghosts of assorted horrible kinds, and eventually defeats the Devil himself playing bowls with dead men's skulls. His general insouciance ultimately wins him a fortune and a loving princess bride. It is a silly, funny story. But it is noticeable that although he often has to go through the forest to get to these spooky places no one suggests that the woods themselves are frightening. No one says: go and spend a winter's night alone in the forest. The overall message of the tales is exactly the opposite: run away into the woods when things scare you at home; the forest will set you free, make you rich, give you wisdom and love and prepare you to be happy ever after.

If I am right that these stories grew out of forest cultures, shaped themselves within small rural societies that needed the forests – for food (both wild game and for grazing), for warmth, for building materials, for protection (Julius Caesar expresses his irritation at the Gauls sneaking off into 'impenetrable forests', making it impossible for his army to demolish them) and particularly as the route to anywhere else – then, I increasingly feel, one of their didactic ends may well be to allay the Terror of the Wild Wood, to be an antidote to the deep forest fear. Because any such gripping alarm as Mole or

I experienced would be – to put it mildly – extremely inconvenient. Better for everyone to have stories that teach that there are worse things to fear; that the terror of the woods can be managed, can be indeed outmanoeuvred, dealt with, disempowered by human intelligence and courage.

Because the true forest fear, the Terror of the Wild Wood, comes from somewhere lower and deeper than the fairy stories. It is a darker, more chthonic, horror than any ghosts or demons we want to play at being frightened by, or that we use to make children behave. There is a revealing name for this fear – what I felt in Wood of Cree was 'panic'. The word panic has a very simple derivation – it is the fear induced by Pan, the Greek god of wild places, of mountainside, high moor and above all of woods and forests.

Pan is a strange god who sits uneasily alongside the golden Olympian gods of classical Greek mythology. He is seldom to be found in the bright courts of Olympus. He does not even have a proper divine genealogy or pedigree: he may be a child of Zeus with one of any number of nymphs, or of Hermes, or have some altogether less glorious father. Some of the Greek poets maintained that Penelope, Odysseus' wife, was not the chaste and faithful queen that Homer made her – she had sex with all those suitors and gave birth to Pan – named after his convoluted paternity. But, though perhaps not an Olympian – and often in competition with both Apollo and Bacchus – Pan is definitely a god, not (like the nymphs, Satyrs and Fauns) merely an 'immortal'. He has all the powers of god and was worshipped extensively, especially in Asia Minor.

So even his classical status is liminal – part god, part goat, fecund, priapic, powerful, dangerous. Deformed, hybrid but very sexy: even Silene, chaste goddess of the white moon, came down to his wooded mountainside to fuck him. He made his seven-note reed pipes out of the metamorphosed body of one of his would-be rape victims. And when he cries out, shouts or yells, deep in the ancient woods, he will still drive even the innocent-hearted to irrational, senseless, panicked fear. Morally ambivalent, instinctual, transcendental, he is as Aldous Huxley describes him, 'the dark presence of the otherness that lies beyond the boundaries of [our] conscious mind.'

Pan used to inhabit the open hillside, deep-cut ravines in the mountains, high moors and rough pasture land as well as woods and groves in very rural places. But sharp modernity has banished him from anywhere that he might be fully visible. Now he must live in the woods where it is possible to lurk – to hide with intent – and where one cannot see what is coming towards one.

Woods are very beautiful, they are embedded deep within our imaginations and our hearts – and we should walk in them with delight and preserve them with a passionate tenderness, but we should never forget that they hold terrors too. They contain a dark indifference and a dispassionate contempt for all the forces of so-called civilisation. There is no escape from that deep uncanny terror. Let yourself be afraid, very afraid.

Thwaite (a clearing, from the Old Norse '*þveit*')

ULPHA FELL, CUMBRIA

Richard Skelton

```
                        A S E L
            H Æ S E L        H Æ S E L
            H Æ S L          H Æ S L
            H A I S E L        H A I S E L
            H A S A L A        H A S A L A
            H A S A L Ô        H A S A L Ô
            H A S E L        H A S E L
            H Ā S E L        H Ā S E L
          H A S E L L E        H A S E L L E
          H A S E L O        H A S E L O
            H A S L              H A S L
            H A S L A          H A S L A
          H A S L E        H A S L E
        H A S S I L L E      H A S S I L L E
          H A Z E L        H A Z E L
          H A Z Z E L        H A Z Z E L
            H E S E L          H E S E L
          H E S E L L E        H E S E L L E
          H E S L I          H E S L I
        H E Z Z I L        H E Z Z I L
          H E Z Z L E      H E Z Z L E
          H I Z Z E L    H I Z Z E L
            K O S E L O
```

hazel-thwaite

```
                ÆSC
        ÆSCAS          ÆSCAS
          AICH           AICH
           AIS             AIS
            AISSE           AISSE
          AISSH           AISSH
          AISSHE          AISSHE
          ASCH            ASCH
            ASH             ASH
       ASKA             ASKA
    ASKIZ               ASKIZ
           ASKR       ASKR
           ASSE       ASSE
             ASSH             ASSH
              ASSHE           ASSHE
             EISCH           EISCH
            EISSE           EISSE
            ESH             ESH
               ESK             ESK
            ESSH            ESSH
              ESSHE             ESSHE
              EX              EX
            HAIS            HAIS
              HAS          HAS
              HESS       HESS
                         OS
```

ash-thwaite

```
                    VALIGA
          VELIGÔ        VIÐ
            VIÐIR         VIÐJA
            VILOU         WALLER
            WEL           WELEU
        WELI              WELIG
        WELIG             WELIGE
            WELO      WELOGH
              WELOU




                    WELOWE
              WELU        WELUE
              WELWE         WETHE
          WHILUH          WIDDY
        WIÐEN             WIÐI
    WIÐIG           WILE        WILGE
    WILGHE          WILH          WILIG
    WILLE           WILLO       WILLOW
    WILLOWE     WILLU         WILLUGH
        WILO                WILOGH
        WILOU           WILOUGH
        WILOW         WILOWE
          WILU      WILUG
          WILUGH    WILWE
            WITH




                    WITHE
          WITHEN        WITHTH
          WITHTHE         WITHY
            WIÞÞE       WUDDY
              WYTHINS
```

willow-thwaite

```
        BEORC
        BERC  BERC
    BERK-JÕN  BERK-JÕN
      BERKIÔ            BERKIÔ
       BERKIÔN              BERKIÔN
        BERKÔ             BERKÔ
         BHERƎG
         BIRCE
            BIRCH
              BIRCHE
              BIRCHEN
                BIRK
            BIRK-TREE
              BIRKE              BIRKE
              BIRKI              BIRKI
          BIRTH              BIRTH
          BJÖRK              BJÖRK
        BÖRK              BÖRK
      BRECHE            BRECHE
          BURK-TREE
          BYRC
```

birch-thwaite

On the 7.46

SHREWSBURY TO CREWE

Paul Evans

Memories growing
Ring on ring
A series of weddings
SYLVIA PLATH, *Winter Trees*

They materialise from violet edges of sunrise and are brought to stand before the scarlet by a speeding train. Heading north, I watch the east from carriage windows as they flash before my eye like the blood vessels inside it and for a moment they are etched black on red so clearly, so emblematically horned, forked, fractal – the geometry of winter trees.

A kestrel appears above the lineside fringe of young birches – a blur of white poles and purple mist framing the margin between fence and track. Behind the fence are fields, gauzy with frost where the old trees are. Along the track, the train I'm in is doing 74 mph. As the kestrel hovers, tethered by its forensic gaze to a mouse heartbeat in the birch roots, the world slows to a standstill. With barely perceptible wing and tail adjustments, the bird's silhouette holds against a Technicolor dawn and the trees reveal themselves.

The stretch of track the kestrel stills is three and a half miles long on the line from Shrewsbury North to Crewe. Aboard the blue and yellow, 175-feet-long, 36.9-tonne Arriva Trains Wales' car with a Cummins N14 engine developing 450 bhp, the view is only a couple of miles deep towards a little wooded ridge beyond which the sun begins to haul itself from the North European Plain, across land and sea where the highest point east is in the Ural Mountains of Russia.

I watch from the train as the window's cinema screen fills with the English lowlands and its trees come into focus. Galleries of wine-dark alders holding the brooks in procession; little pond-swamps of willow, upswept leaning till they crack; thickets of hawthorn growing from old sandpits like hairs from an earhole; ash trees gangling, their bent staves nailed to the sky. Hedges slide between trees with whispering lines of dialogue. Some hedges are so flailed each shaved quickset lets light through; some are so fiercely resurgent they form palisades strong enough to stop a train. If not for the kestrel I would be propelled through this scene in less than three minutes of rapid eye movements, enough time to fall under the spell of the black, beatific oaks.

Anything from the trolley? Anything from the trolley? Anything from the trolley? She pulls her refreshments up the aisle like a pram with paper-cup chimneys – cheesy crisps, regular tea, regular coffee, spit-sized bottles of wine – searching through the passengers, the desperate panic in her eyes replaced long ago by a quizzical resignation, and in her best jackdaw voice she asks: *Anything from the trolley?*

Remain vigilant at all times ... If you see anything suspicious please report it to onboard staff ... Unidentified articles will be removed from the train. Thank you.

Two men talk football; one of them punctuates with loud coughs as if suppressing terrace obscenities. A young woman eating a bacon roll the size of her head makes tiny kitten noises. Another bites into an apple, at first it sounds like a horse munching in a tunnel but builds with repetition into a dustbin being thrown down a lift shaft. Passengers not sleeping are fixed in a phone-face: *Ask Rachel in Accounts, no ... no ... ask Rachel in Accounts! Please tidy up a bit, darling, someone may come round. Yeah, mate, brilliant. Tar-rah, mate. Ta, mate. Tar-rah.*

I imagine the zombies turning on me, identifying me as suspicious and jettisoning me from the train the way postal workers once threw satchels of mail onto trackside hooks.

Emergency information is displayed on this train. For your safety please take the time to read it. I read the emergency instructions in English and Welsh in the vestibule beside the door about how to smash the glass, pull the green lever, open the door, sit on the ledge and drop down onto the track; penalties for improper use. Door opens in this direction. Morning opens in that direction. Feel the scrunch of lineside ballast; the sting of whippy birch twigs; the barbed wire snag of the fence. Don't turn around to look at the train, don't glance up at the kestrel or, like Orpheus, all will be lost. Head for the oaks in the field. Any oak. That oak.

A monster tree: massive, craggy and dark, of all those here it is the most abandoned yet oddly prominent, hiding in a scrubby corner like a giant in a school playground. Before I enter its orbit, I turn to look across a scattering of oaks: some hundred paces, some five paces apart, rising through dawn light from short frosted pasture. They are a similar size and age: 30 to 50 feet high, domed crowns 40 feet across, trunks with a four-foot girth, 300 years old, planted by the squire when his Georgian country house was built in imitation of the Grand Manner during the Parliamentary Enclosures – oaks to build a proud nation and its navy, oaks to shelter prized cattle and a ragged swain at noon, oaks for an eternal midsummer night's dream. This is an English Arcadia the squire's line bequeaths to the future. They were not expecting winter, me, and the world that fills my pockets and my head.

The oaks appear to move slightly as the psychedelic sky brightens, sliding into place, occupying their daytime positions. There are those manoeuvring into parkland tableaux, actors on a grassy stage; others once in hedgerows that have been grubbed out now stand in awkward gap-tooth grins; others sink slowly into the slough of fields put down to maize – churned-up, claggy, flooded tractor ruts frosted over with ice thin as kitchen film. Each of these trees is unique. Some are stag-headed, dead upper branches, bone-hard antlers; some lost limbs to gales; all have been sculpted by droughts, storms, floods. The oaks have reached an age where their crowns are retreating; they are turning in on themselves. It is said that oaks take 300 years to grow, 300 years to mature and 300 years to die. However, this does not count the thousands of years of oak afterlife when they become soil microbes, fungi, mosses, grasses, wildflowers, worms, beetles, birds, bats and other oaks which also become roof beams, floorboards, tables, doors, ships. The soils left here by glaciers have become *āc erthe* – Old English for oak earth – a land made from oak for oak.

The slow ruination of many of these older trees shows their roots are withdrawing because the *āc erthe*, with its living underground that trees depend on, is just collateral damage in the agricultural wars waged with ploughs and poisons against Nature. The *āc erthe* haemorrhages history, secrets, lifeblood. Today this is stopped by the freeze.

I turn to the monster oak. It is such a significant tree and must have been an important landmark for centuries. It is possible that the oaks the squire planted came from Germany or Holland, as was the fashion in those days. This one is older, bigger and although the same species, *Quercus robor*, looks different and more likely to be indigenous. It must surely have a name. A boundary marker, a meeting place, a preaching tree, a tree for rites and rituals, weddings, wakes and waits, fairs and festivals, a gallows? It looms above other trees in a scrubby corner of the field. It must have been visible from all cardinal points and is far larger than trees in surrounding fields and woods – 80 feet in height, crown breadth the same, girth wider than a span – its longest boughs touch the ground; an open-grown tree that has known six centuries. It survives because each of its winters fixed its architecture, stopping each annual growth ring in a kind of death. I imagine travelling back through the tree's dendrochronology to when it was hatching from an acorn a jay had stashed and forgotten or else planted by some other magician 500 years ago. Inside the trunk's dark hollow there was a growth ring around the pith which held the year of an event which suggests a name: Queen Mary. The daughter of Henry VIII and Catherine of Aragon, Bloody Mary tortured and burned Protestants at the stake when she came to the throne, she gave birth to phantoms, spent much of her youth at Ludlow Castle – four stops back on this railway line – and was born this day, 18 February, 1516. However inviolable the tree appears after all those years, this Queen Mary's infamy is forgotten. Now her space is jostled by upstart ash, elder and hawthorn in the hedge concealing an old air-raid shelter and derelict sheds. The Tudor countryside and the people it mattered to have all but vanished.

Her low branches are evidence that she was never browsed, that the ground surrounding her was protected. Queen Mary's buttresses, an inner sanctum concealed under her sweeping skirts, is where the hares, hinds, foxes and martens hid from hunters and where the heathens met to drink cider, hatch plots, hold secret assignations, lovers' trysts; they were drawn to her shade like filings to a magnet. No one comes now. The ground is littered with her own debris caught in a rug of bramble. Now Queen Mary is stuck in a ghostly *rigor* and like the abandoned village that once surrounded her, she awaits the storm, lightning, fire or bulldozers that will finally do her in. And yet, in the manner of great trees, she is full of life even in death. Tree rings, as Sylvia Plath wrote, are made of memories, 'a series of weddings'. They advance annually from the tree's core and hold an archive of years in as basic a molecular form as a parish register. In the names and dates of that list of marriages lies a history of family trees, many of which are lost. Who remembers the weddings of cuckoos and turtle doves? Queen Mary has been the chapel of love for so many: tawny owls, chiffchaffs, mouse-eared bats, oak eggar moths, gall wasps, white admiral butterflies, lesser stag beetles, greater spotted woodpeckers – all that animal handfasting, the singing and dancing, all that frantic coupling! People too. In secret or in celebration, most of the families who held their weddings here are atomised, gone from this country to towns and cities – places connected by railways not blood. Way back, Mary married the King of Spain in rings rotted into silence at the tree's heart. Bloody Mary left only a frightful story of her life, her bloody deeds and a nursery rhyme. Now, cut off by the railway line, quarantined against trespassers, exiled in her own realm, the tree endures as a monster from history with the stature of an ocean liner and a decaying heart: *Mary, Mary, quite contrary …*

But as Bob Dylan sang, 'Queen Mary, she's my friend. Yes, I believe I'll go see her again'. If I were to bore into her trunk to extract a core of annual rings, I would only have to drill an inch or so to reach the year of my own wedding and yet it is a lifetime away. We look so young in the photograph, wearing clothes we never wore before or since, wearing the expressions of lovers the world is happening to. You in a wedding dress still makes me gasp. We placed the Lovers card from the Tarot pack on the vestry table. The card shows two trees: the Tree of Knowledge entwined by a snake has a naked woman standing in front of it; the Tree of Life bearing golden fruits has a naked man in front of it. The man looks at the woman. The woman looks above the trees to where a winged figure, an angel, a kestrel, hovers in the fiery dawn.

Head on window, I watch the geometry of winter trees flicker against a brightening sky. Each one is a character; each leafless crown tells its own story. Every bifurcation, branch and twig division, splits from one meristematic thing into two things and each thing ending in a bud finds its own future to unfold, fall and divide again. And a similar thing is happening in the soil. The questing roots have their own marriages with lives of the *āc erthe* surviving in the patina of enclosed fields, open fields, wood pasture and wild forest stretching back millennia into the memory of the land.

Into my memory, aluminium light comes through the carriage window from behind a mesh of branches overhanging the track. There is a slight flow from the lake, along a path used by fishermen and kids where a man with a fighter's face and the quiet voice of my own people tells me about the safety line unspooled on the bank, how a baby drowned in that pool, crawled into the water, where were the parents? He is suspicious about how water has changed and won't let his son into the sea anymore. Once it was warm like bathwater, now the currents are too strong and, he gestures, a wave can come from nowhere and sweep you away. From the train, the pool is still, the willows dark, malevolent. The sun rising, lights up between things, revealing gardens, grassy mounds, people walking around, gulls, sparrows and the enamelling of spaces. Grey wood pigeons in a green field, sitting together in silence like a Quaker meeting discerning the light of God. Twenty swans, dark against the sun, veer over pools as anglers and a string of sheep walk into the day. The sun's a thumb's width above the east and still the frost hasn't lifted from the stubble field where a lone fox crouches as the train goes by. Rising ash-sprung, quick yet unhurried, she is full of watchfulness, as living as the light.

Each image becomes a memory: a little psychic snatch from the railway-carriage cinema of the weird wood of winter trees. On this half-hour train journey from dark through dawn, through town, village and farm, the trees in their dreaming state hold the land. The ridge woods, copses and plantations, the brook alders and pond osiers, the hedge hawthorns and blackthorns, the park beeches and sycamores, the garden cypresses and cedars, the street limes, the slum elder, the rubble birches, the black beatific oaks – they're all putting the final touches to the last ring. The circle closes when the year ends. Winter night hardens under the bark before the first cambium cells of the new year are laid. Whatever size or species the trees are they all share the same radiocarbon date, the same molecular register, but each tree writes its own signature. This is their land and they are its wood. Come morning, in a few minutes, the trees will appear dormant, anaesthetised. The next warm day will change all that. Come the green: leaf, blossom, the swell of life through phloem and xylem, the song thrush in the branches and the space between trees floods with spring. Until then, the wood of winter trees stretches as far as the eye can see, cold and dark as a kind of death made glorious in the sunrise.

On the edge of morning: frost under a clear sky across the flat land, all its cunning and clag painted over with hyacinth emulsion. I have not noticed the train stopping at a station until it slows down unexpectedly just beyond it. I am watching a charm of goldfinch fly down the line. They're travelling one way at 30 mph and the train is travelling the other at 30 mph. So, at a combined speed of 60 mph, each bird is a tiny collision of visibility. Perhaps that makes the train stop just as light seeps through pine trees behind new houses built in a poor, puddled field. Then the train reverses back to stop at the platform. There is a long pause. The conductor appears, lurching awkwardly down the aisle even though the train is stationary. He looks shaken. His ticket equipment, his uniform, the flesh about his bones, are all askew. He speaks to a couple of passengers and tells them the driver left him at the station and drove off, against the signal. There may be bad blood between them. Abandonment is a crime on the railways; this driver must now be taken off the train to face an investigation. A replacement driver will have to be fetched by road from Crewe. The train is already late and we are now castaways. Passengers persuade the conductor to make an announcement explaining the situation; he agrees reluctantly: *Ladies and Gentlemen, I apologise for the delay, this is due to operating difficulties in the Nantwich area* ... The birds, like little black shooting stars, leave a trail of what they are and what they mean along the railway line where fields and farms look ruined in this derelict light and the oaks stand darkly against the sky – neurons of the winter trees, remembering. Then over the public address system on the still-delayed train, the conductor sighs, *oh dear ... oh, dear ...*

Alison

WEST SUSSEX DOWNS

Madeleine Bunting

It was one of March's bleak days when the land seemed exhausted by the chill. There was no relief in the old Sussex barn with its high-pitched tiled roof supported by crooked timbers where the artist Alison Crowther worked. The cold, I was to discover, was important. The studio was unheated and draughts whistled through the barn doors and windows. My fingers turned yellow, Crowther was dressed in thick layers, but could only manage an hour or so of carving before she retreated to a small heated office to thaw out with hot tea.

This cold is good weather for carving green oak, slowing the process of drying and cracking. The barn was dominated by the trunk of an oak tree swollen by a huge burr which had been roughly cut into a massive sphere, 1.8 metres in diameter. An equally large piece had just left the studio to be installed. These are bold monuments which speak powerfully of the material's astonishing capacities for endurance. The timber comes from trees which have survived centuries of disease, storms and the vagaries of English weather.

For all the solidity of the forms, the material has its own volatility. The tree's history of growth, moisture and how it fed and supported its own colossal weight is still reverberating in the timber, and as the wood slowly dries and splits, it shapes itself into fissures and cracks which can pucker the surfaces Crowther so carefully carves.

As soon as the sapwood has been stripped off, carving commences before the heartwood dries out and grows brittle. Too much heat in the studio – a hot summer for example – accelerates the process so that Crowther can find herself in a relationship of friendly rivalry with the wood to shape the final piece. The cold of this bitter March gives Crowther her best chance.

This is a part of the intimacy of the relationship between this artist and her material; the way she has accumulated knowledge of the particular properties and characteristics of green oak. It is in this close working of the material that the magnificent oak trees of the English countryside are finally knowable to the hand and the eye. It's a knowledge which sits in a long tradition of wood-working whose legacy is still evident in countless buildings and furniture across England. The oak tree in leaf has been a symbol of England, but even more importantly, its timber has been used to meet so many of our basic human needs – for shelter, for rest, for comfort and for convenience.

Crowther carves grooves across the surface, following the annual rings and the medullary rays, to cover these large forms with sensuous lines. When oiled multiple times with linseed, the rich tawny yellows, creams and pale oranges of the wood emerge and glow in the dusty barn. Crowther rolls back the protective blankets as if the finished pieces are sleeping. They are deeply seductive, begging to be felt with the stroke of a hand, the tracing of a finger along the grooves which pattern the silky surfaces. This is wood at its most lovable, rich with the history of its own struggle with the elements of earth, wind, air and water.

By way of explanation, she showed me how the annual rings can suddenly kink, marking a moment in the tree's history, or the rings swirl around where there was a branch. The challenge lies in how to acknowledge these and create the patterns which fully express the truth of the material, she explains.

The immense ball of the oak burr was fiendishly complex to carve; its surface was riven by deep crevices bulging with the boiling mass of wood nodules characteristic of burr. In some places, the wood had rotted and had to be dug out. Through these diseased sections, the grooves she planned to carve will swirl and unspool round the surface so that the vast mass of material will almost appear to spin.

Much of Crowther's material comes from the Sussex countryside where she lives between Midhurst and Petersfield. Magnificent trees are still part of the hedgerows and copses which patch this farmland and its carefully manicured villages. Nearby estates such as Cowdray are a precious source of old timber which may have been blighted by disease or is too awkwardly shaped for commercial buyers. Crowther has built up relationships with specialist timber merchants across the country so that they turn to her when a particularly unusual piece of timber becomes available. The old hands in the trade, she said, can tell from a piece of oak the soil it grew in and read its origins to a particular part of the country, even to a specific estate. It's this kind of deep knowledge of oak, past and present, built up over a lifetime which is a powerful inspiration for her work.

Crowther started in furniture design – in a great English centre of the craft in High Wycombe amongst the woods of the Chilterns – and the keen interest in the techniques and engineering with wood have persisted. But she moved away from the functional, and the pieces now serve as bold punctuation in a landscape. The metaphor is apt because her pieces are often not upright but like a full stop or a parenthesis, and relate to the lay of the land. They can sit or sometimes even squat: they are rounded forms like eggs, kidneys and soft-nosed torpedoes. They have the modesty of comment rather than making an assertive statement as monuments are wont to do.

Their power often comes from the sense of inner force bulging beneath the patterned surface. Seeds are an inspiration for both their patterns and their forms; and some pieces are resonant of the dramatic curve of a full-term pregnancy. There is a generative force concealed in the work, and which the cracking expresses. Just as some seeds scatter through explosion, so these recumbent massive seeds hint at this natural history of reproduction and forceful expulsion.

David Nash and Peter Randall Page have been key influences, and the resonances are not hard to find in the forms, and the interest in charring which marks some of her smaller pieces. The burnt surface grid speaks simultaneously of pineapples and hand grenades: those echoes of fruitfulness and explosion.

The biggest influence has been the theory of the 'workmanship of risk' of David Pye, the famous theorist. 'Workmanship … in which the quality of the result is not predetermined but depends on the judgment, dexterity and care which the maker exercises as he works ... and the quality of the result is continually at risk during the process of making.'

For all the hours and days of carving and oiling the pieces to fulfill her vision, there is always the risk of her work being disrupted by the wood as it responds itself to the elements: the heat of an indoor space or the wind and rain in the case of an outside installation. It can crack, split in unexpected ways, still working out the huge tensions which were stored in its growth.

It's this combination of monumental strength with delicate sensuality which has ensured that the work has found its way all over the world. The enormous round ball of oak burr on the studio floor is destined for Barcelona. Major pieces have been installed in the glass palaces of corporate headquarters from Hong Kong to Canary Wharf where they strike a dramatic contrast with the shine of steel, marble and glass. In the Shard, London's new skyscraper, a piece bulging with curves serves to support a glass top as a table for diners. The gorgeous extravagance of these pieces is a far cry from Crowther's chilly barn.

The tractors of the working farm are parked up outside next to piles of timber offcuts and new massive trunks awaiting their metamorphosis. This Sussex farmyard is a place of hard labour; of precarious livings from the land. Yet the work produced here is now part of a global currency of style and status. Crowther acknowledges the multiple paradoxes encapsulated by her work: an old tradition of English oak-wood carving being appropriated by new centres of power for its associations of longevity and stability.

More important even than either of these great symbolic values, to my mind, is the intimacy of touch which these carved pieces both express and demand. A recent photographer caught a poignant image of Crowther's hand stroking a carving. Against the gleaming wood, her small fingers seem worn, a little grubby, the nails short. It's a comment on human vulnerability, and of how human lives are both shorter and so much more fragile in many ways than this oak timber. In the gleaming offices, Crowther's work is a quiet but powerful comment on such truths.

Yggdrasil in Shetland

LEA GARDENS, SHETLAND

Jen Hadfield

*for James Mackenzie & the Shetland Amenity
Trust Woodlands Team and volunteers*

My aunt owns a cabin by a river in British Columbia. It's
wrapped in temperate rainforest, dense and protean:
pockets of old-growth cedar and maple, the glittering
autumnal coins of quaking aspen. In the 1950s, a car broke down here.
Twin maples grew up around it, cracking its bonnet like a nut. The new
growth and rotting wood are webbed with bandages of sopping moss,
hung with old man's beard, like an aerial seaweed. Trunks utter smooth
bracket fungus: toad-throats and harelips. The fallen trunks, drilled
by sapsuckers and downy woodpeckers, melt down into a deep bed
of humus. Up, 20 metres up, ferns garner moss, manufacturing their
own soil, in which showers of seeds, like a golden rain, can germinate.
And everywhere, nests – from the ospreys' splatter of twigs and fouled
traps to the moss thumb-pots welded into the joints of branches by
hummingbirds. This is bush that gets hold of you. The bramble vines
are laced with claws that hook backwards into your skin. You get free
by tearing out small chunks of flesh. The logs are glassy with greasy
algae; massive, fallen trunks criss-cross in impassable mats over your
head. When a twig cracks, or the salal begins purposefully to wag,
your heart pounds in your throat. Bleeding lightly, you escape onto the
riverbank. In the baked clay between the rocks grow cottonwoods by
the thousand. In BC, where such a phenomenon is conceivable, these
are weed trees: seeding on poor ground, their reptilian leaves flashing.
In spring, the Lower Mainland reeks of them, a constant simmer of

honey. For my family and me, the cabin – and what surrounds it – is one of those places that are sacred in a domestic, familiar kind of way.

In my Shetland garden grows a single, precious cottonwood. Scorched and tattered by salty winds, the leaves sometimes seem to shrink back as fast as they grow. In 2005, I nearly moved to Canada for good, but then I was offered a residency in Shetland, and could not bear to leave. The contrast between the two places is extreme and I'm often asked why I chose Shetland over Canada. This morning, in Cheshire, I went into a Ryman's. 'It must be terribly bleak,' insisted the stationer. 'No,' I said, 'it's beautiful.' 'I didn't say it wasn't beautiful,' he interrupted cleverly, 'but isn't it terribly bleak? And remote?' *Whatever evaluation we finally make of a stretch of land*, pitches in Barry Lopez, *no matter how profound or accurate, we will find it inadequate. The land retains an identity of its own, still deeper and more subtle than we can know.*

Like many northern landscapes, Shetland is far too often defined by people who don't live here. But while its comparative treelessness is undeniable (Shetlanders themselves dub the islands 'Da Aald Rock'), I've met few Shetland or Orkney folk who feel that trees are something they lack. 'They get in the way of the view,' says Mary. 'When I visited my English grandmother,' said Amy, 'the tree and hedge-lined roads seemed dark and narrow.' In *60 Degrees North*, Shetlander Malachy Tallack talks about his relief on reaching a vantage point in Fort Smith, a town 'islanded' by trees, and is able to relax his eyes, looking into the horizon.

So, what primal buttons is the idea of 'treelessness' pressing?

I asked James Mackenzie, the Woodlands Officer at the Shetland Amenity Trust, what he thought. His answer was beguiling. 'Trees are branchlets of the life-lungs of the world, breathing in CO_2 and exhaling oxygen.' But he also enjoys the apparently bare hillsides, the contours – like muscle and bone – of rock visible under *djub* and *julk*; peat and sphagnum and heath. He and Rosa Steppanova – whose book *The Impossible Garden* is about establishing Lea Gardens on two acres of open hill at Tresta – are two of Shetland's defiant gardeners. Her specialism is the herbaceous border; his – first a shelter belt, then a thicket, then a wood – of exotic and native tree and shrub species.

When they go out into the garden, says James, pulling on his boots, he looks up and she looks down.

I notice a rare quality of light in James and Rosa's porch: an autumnal light. The smoky sun is as small as an aspirin, now; it dapples through leaves and hazy glass. It's almost as if there *is* no autumn in Shetland – though I've hardly missed it. There is instead the slow, golden *hairst* at the summer's close, vegetables after a late spring finally coming to ripeness, roses blooming right into November; then a week of indigo shadows. A scant leaf-fall from willow and *Rosa rugosa*. Then the fright of the first winter storm. Here, heavy violet petals spout and sag from colchichums. James leads me through a plantation of larch; a heron barks and lifts from a pond. Agapanthus and red-hot pokers are going off like fireworks. A wall of pallets retains, just, a mighty compost heap. The Lea Gardens trees are a quantum thing, changing, if not the nature of time, the nature of the Shetland seasons.

I too loved at first sight the deep, broad views, which came to me like a relief. You could relax your gaze across the sea. To snooze on the cropped grass of the banks in summer, amongst over-stuffed tussocks of *banksflooer*, or in a streaming mirage of spring squill, is to rest upon the hide of a huge, tolerant, sweet-smelling mammal. You can look far and wide, and close and deep, right down to the glittering eyelashes of the round-leaved sundew. Walking the headlands, I visit rocks, rest on and with rocks, learn from rocks. There is, for example, in the scree and shatter north of Virda, a smooth blade of glittering schist with a raised spine, aligned east–west like a compass needle. Like a tiger on a branch, I rub my cheek against it. At Gössigarth, thick veins of pure quartz run through the rock like coconut meat. Either side of South Voe stands a menhir big enough to dwarf me:

Everything juicy –
August night of rain –
the succulent ancient
cactus of the stone

Who knows how deeply rooted they are, how long they've yielded to the battering flanns of wind that roll off Mid Field? Is there, in standing stones' deep-rootedness and resilience, some likeness to trees? What is it that they're giving us?

A friend in Orkney is enraged by the tourist habit of piling flat beach stones into towers. They're soon dismantled by wind and sea – but I'm interested in what leads folk to build them. I wonder if these columnar cairns are, like the Inuit's *inuksuit*, a way of leaving part of yourself on the beach, a kind of stony avatar. As another friend offered: after we pile, soaked, frozen, elated and exhausted, into the car after a winter walk, the big stones stay out there on the hill, mitigating our regret at leaving. They also predate and succeed us. James tells me he remembers reading *The Lord of the Rings* and visiting a stand of stately beeches in Surrey. The beeches, with their smooth grey boles, he said, were more Ent-like than the Ents in the film. In the taxonomic forest of our relationships, we've parents, and grandparents, then, somewhere between grandparents and gods, trees and stones. Losing our reverence for ancestors, and our families becoming more and more dispersed, we lack them especially.

I asked James if he thought he'd surrogated anything else for trees, and this set him off on sphagnum moss. A rootless plant, sphagnum is over 90 per cent water. Jelly-like, it knits the delicate bog together, staunching it after heavy rain. As its subterranean layers rot, they turn into peat. Forming at a rate of a millimetre a year, peat two metres deep with a crown of living sphagnum could easily represent an organism 2,000 years old. Its antibiotic qualities are well-documented. The Vikings used to preserve fish in it. The peat is important too, as a 'carbon sink', sequestering carbon dioxide from the atmosphere. Perhaps, proposes James, in the absence of trees to absorb CO_2, Nature finds ways to compensate. At present, an experimental conservation project is underway in the fragile and much maligned valleys and hills of the Lang Kames. It involves sowing bog-cotton and sphagnum, blocking the gullies of damaged peat, sandbagging its leaking pools. At the mouth of the same valley is the Halfway Hoose, an old whitewashed pile where cattle auctions used to be held, and latterly, epic parties. Pulling out plaster and lathe, its present householder discovered the walls were packed with sphagnum. The moss would've acted as both insulant and, with its prodigal thirst, a damp course. A resilient, useful and delicate organism, but can sphagnum moss fill the spiritual need that trees seem to? What does James see when he considers it? His face shines with a deep pleasure. 'I think it's like living jewels.'

We are climbing a boulevard of balsam poplars, past the sheathed blades and tarry pods of a huge New Zealand flax. It's as big as those I saw on Kapiti Island, where thickets of the saw-like leaves were beset with hungry, green *kakariki*, prising seeds from the greasy, black husks. At the house, the fierce gaze of the Inuit spirit Talelayu, made of whelks, violet mussel shells and bottle-ends pressed into the *gaevel's* rendering; then, after a fork in the path, the South American garden. Fuchsia species, *Lomatia*, *Chiliotrichum* (a relative of the daisy bush that grows in Patagonia, Southern Chile, Southern Argentina and the Falkland Islands), *Drimys winteri* and *Crinodendron* flourish in a waxy, green gloom. All along, James sings the song-line of the garden. 'This is *Crinodendron*, which has little lovely crimson bell flowers on it ... but the best of the lot is this one here, *Embothrium coccineum* [Chilean Fire Bush] which has red spider flowers on it of scarlet intensity ... they just come out in these tentacles.'

James has been experimenting with these species at Lea Gardens since a visit to the Faroe Islands in 1993. Rationalising that the far-South American climate had much in common with the North Atlantic, being windy, salty and cloudy, the Faroese forestry service had made collection and research trips to Tierra del Fuego. On a similar trip to the Norwegian Arboretum, James and Rosa filled their Berlingo with Southern Chilean species. Nothing could be more typical of Shetland than this dispersal of seed across the oceans, this global web of horticultural correspondences: throughout the winter, Shetlanders search the beaches for drift seeds – plump, polished tokens of dimpled leather – from the rainforests of South America.

'That's another of my favourite trees,' James says, pausing at a lissom ash, '*Yggdrasil*, the tree that supported the universe ... Some people think it was maybe a yew tree because it was actually supposed to be evergreen, which of course an ash isn't … And they actually grow here just as well as sycamore. They can have female flowers one year and male flowers the next: they can kind of change sex, which is clever, and you can also burn the wood green … if you had a sickly child, there was an old belief that if you cleft an ash tree in the middle and slipped the child through … if the tree healed itself it would mean the child would heal.' Now he reaches for the cone of a noble fir, as big as a hedgehog, with a pineapple's bloated spines. I'm dizzy with light and lore and the strong linctus scent of the garden. The surrounding hills are gold and russet, the bay of Tresta brilliantly corrugated by a south-westerly. The world-tree is growing in a hidden garden in the centre of Shetland.

A Sunday in December. Big, new, polished cars seem to cross the bridge almost constantly. Under it, the Burn of Crookadale, as black as sump oil, pours noisily into a gully. The rocks are ice-glazed, the mounds of water-hoarding sphagnum frozen solid, and dark red, like rumpsteak. I lie on my belly at the overhang. The relict hazel, and a true wild rose, its hips ice-blown, jut from the rockface on stems as thick as plumbing. A rowan wand yearns skyward. Like a pencil, it's been whittled and scraped against the rock until all that remains is a flat, living wound, like a scab peeled from skin, but somehow still growing. The curved twigs are like bolts of frozen iron. It's hard to imagine life in them. The stems are so wrinkled they look like they're wincing. But the tree is aureoled in buds like flames, like statues of the Hindu Lord of Dance, Shiva Nataraja. The *Rosa canina* is a slow kindling across the rockface. Surrounded by a stock-proof fence, the hazel is about to broach the safety of the gulley. This is the work of the Woodlands Team.

This hazel, the rose and rowan are, with a scattering of other trees, what remains of the isles' native woodland. They're referred to as Shetland's relict trees, and each one is recorded in S.C. Jay's report, *Shetland's Native Trees* of 1995. One of the two last *Malus sylvestris*, or wild crab apple, hangs, in this report, at the literal brink of local extinction, on a cliff face subject to rockfalls and pounded by winter seas and winds. The ecology of these cliffs, ravines, holms on lochs may look desperate, but they can also be fantastical and perversely lush. I've wandered the frost-shattered fellfield of Ronas Hill, with its tiny arctic species, such as Alpine Ladies' Mantle and Mountain Azalea, in an underlit haze of fog, looking for *Boletus edulis*. Also known as pennybuns, ceps, and porcini mushrooms, these grow, like lumps of Wonderland furniture, wildly out of proportion with their hosts, the vein-thin roots of *Salix herbacea*, the least willow. At Beorgs of Housetter, a bonsai rowan grows thickly from a sheltering fissure, tangled with wild honeysuckle. Halfway up an inland cliff at Too Brekk, its roots apparently drinking the rock itself, hovers a kind of arboreal Yoda: a wrinkled, twisted aspen with multiple stout, silvery leaders and unstinting buds. Like Yoda, it's almost impossible to hazard a guess at its age.

What became of these aspens and crab apples, the many species of willow, the rowans, junipers, hazels and birches? Traces of fossilised pollen suggest up to a third of Shetland might once have been covered in such species. In addition to a marked deterioration in climate, the main culprit may have been the advent of agriculture. Some survived only because they were sited on holms in lochs too deep for sheep to cross. In species that reproduce sexually, the sexes are estranged, or too stunted to produce seed. I don't think I'm imagining a current of emotion in Jay's report under the latinate names, co-ordinates and scientific patter. 'This is a very important site [that is] very vulnerable to sheep gaining access in the winter, as proved the case in early 1994 when a sheep was stranded for some weeks on the holm. It was removed on 4.5.94 after committing severe damage to the willows.'

But recently, it's been possible to propagate plant material from some of Shetland's relict trees using tissue-culture techniques. In a greenhouse in the Staneyhill Industrial Estate, December strawberries are ripening very, very slowly. A nugget of sphagnum establishes itself in a cup of agar in a sterile cabinet. It looks like one of the exotic shots that will give you a ruinous hangover in any of Shetland's pubs. Outside, blueish junipers scramble across each other in raised beds. Suckers probe James' thick white hair and beard, as he reaches to show me plant labels: after hundreds of hours of propagation, the benches, coldframes and cabinets proliferate with the children of Shetland's ghost forest. James draws my attention to a tray of healthy young ginkgos too. Twenty-five seeds from a tree that survived the atomic blast at Hiroshima were gifted to the Shetland Islands Council, a member of Mayors for Peace. Ginkgos, James tells me, may do well in Shetland, given the right soil and shelter conditions.

Shetland's 'treelessness' is inseparable from the pervasive conception of the isles as 'bleak', 'lonely', 'remote' and 'impoverished' – a sort of *Edge of Darkness*. Does it matter? If places of the mind are projected over the true topography like holograms, can't they be dispelled? If we know a highly creative community of outward-looking, well-travelled folk, cliffs shimmering with squill and tormentil, fields of gentian and ragged robin, bogs of butterwort, grass of parnassus, luckie-minnie's oo and orchid, does it matter, really, if others, suffering from what Robert Macfarlane usefully terms 'attention deficit', imagine a depopulated rock, denuded of vegetation, in the middle of the North Sea? Writing about Pingok Island, Barry Lopez warned, 'It is in a place like this that we would unthinkingly store poisons or test weapons, land like the deserts to which we once banished our heretics and where we once loosed scapegoats with the burden of our transgressions.'

Almost exactly this paradigm is explored by Macfarlane in *Landmarks*. AMEC proposed to build Europe's biggest windfarm on The Brindled Moor in Lewis, which was perceived to be, and promoted as, 'barren' and 'remote'; a 'wasteland', a 'wilderness'. Capitalism creates and then exploits this perverse kind of commodification, where places are marketed in terms of their proposed worthlessness. After a campaign of creative protest challenging how the moor was perceived, and taking into account its protective designations, the Scottish Government rejected AMEC's application. They did not, though, reject Viking Energy's application to erect 103 turbines of 145 metres on and around the Lang Kames in Shetland, with just as much attendant and largely permanent infrastructure. The land on which Viking proposes to excavate its quarries, to build roads the width of runways and install the windmills' massive, permanent concrete founds, is fragile. The 'development', visible from most of Shetland, includes a high-voltage subsea cable to export energy to mainland Scotland, making further such projects financially compelling. The Viking Project is opposed by Sustainable Shetland, which raised nearly £200,000 to appeal the Scottish Government's decision in the courts. Public opinion on the project is characteristically (for Shetland) polarised, but there has never been a referendum seeking the community's views, despite Viking describing the windfarm as a 'community' project.

With Sustainable Shetland, I believe in the right alternative energies in the right place. Few of us are opposed to the use of wind turbines in Shetland, if they're scaled down to benefit the communities that live with them and, ideally, own them. In this context I'm content to be accused of nimbyism: though I hope this pejorative term may become outdated in the growing hunger for devolution on all levels. We must cherish the world-tree in our back yards, be it an ash, a yew, a rash of ancient crab apple on a cliff face, or a bed of sphagnum two metres deep.

What is a Tree?

STUMP CROSS, ESSEX

Germaine Greer

W hat is a tree, exactly? We all know a tree when we see one (providing we don't get it mixed up with a palm or a fern or a cycad, all of which are likely to be called trees by people who should know better).

A tree is a woody plant. It is not the only kind of woody plant. There are woody vines and woody shrubs. And there is even a woody grass, namely bamboo. According to the usual websites, 'a woody plant is a plant that produces wood as its structural tissue. Woody plants are usually either trees, shrubs, or lianas. [Or bamboo.] These are usually perennial plants whose stems and larger roots are reinforced with wood produced from secondary xylem.'

The element of pleonasm in all such descriptions will continue to bedevil our attempt to unscramble the mystery that is a tree, a mystery as familiar to us as the mystery of the blueness of the sky and as unfathomable. It is hardly helpful to be told that a tree is a plant made of wood that makes wood. For rather more than a century, scientists have been struggling to identify the mechanisms of wood biosynthesis, which reveals itself to be more complex than anyone had imagined. This is the more disappointing because for many conservationists wood is seen to be the energy source of the future and the race is on to find or to engineer trees that can be farmed to produce wood faster and more cheaply.

The definition of a tree that most tree scholars recognise is 'a woody plant with a single erect perennial trunk that reaches at least three inches in diameter at breast height (DBH) when mature.' This would deny tree status to the mallees of Australia, multi-stemmed eucalypts that grow from a lignotuber to a height of ten metres or so. Mallees comprise nearly half of the known eucalyptus species, and Victoria's vast Murray-Sunset National Park does not in the least resemble a shrubbery. Single-stemmed trees might be the loggers' preference but they are by no means the norm: in the wild, trees are very likely to end up multi-stemmed because of insect or other damage to the apical cells of the leaders which has caused them to split.

The dwarf willow of Greenland (*Salix herbacea*) is generally held to be the world's smallest tree but, if you believe that a tree that is worth the name achieves three inches in DBH, then a dwarf willow doesn't make it, because it can never grow taller than two and a half inches. The world's smallest trees are probably bonsai, true tree species kept small by perverse human ingenuity. Basically, trees aren't small, let alone tiny. When it comes to trees, size does matter.

Trees come in two kinds, gymnosperms and angiosperms. The gymnosperms, or naked seed bearers, come in fourteen families and eighty-eight genera, most of them conifers, which account for seven-eighths of the gymnosperm total. These are often, and for no good reason, referred to as softwoods. The tallest trees in the world, the redwoods of the west coast of the USA, are conifers. The tallest known at present is 'Hyperion', a coast redwood (*Sequoia sempervirens*) at 115.72 metres, which is about as tall as any tree will ever be. The largest trunk volume however is to be found in a related species, *Sequoiadendron giganteum*, in the Sierra Nevada. The oldest of these trees is thought to be more than 3,000 years old.

The world's tallest angiosperm or flowering plant is an Australian mountain ash (*Eucalyptus regnans*), at 99.6 metres tall, only discovered by Forestry Tasmania as recently as 2009.

Trees will attain their full size only if they have room. Many (even, one suspects, most) tree species have ways of limiting or distancing competition, even from their own progeny. A seed that falls within the drip line of its parent is already in trouble. First of all trees cast shade, and seedlings need light. Leaves drip, and drips bruise young foliage. Many leaves are adapted to carry out this function, having drip tips that turn accumulating rain into heavier drops. This would be enough to discourage most trees' own seedlings from competing with their parents, but trees have other strategies for discouraging competition, strategies that, like so much about trees, we do not fully understand. The collective name for such strategies is allelopathy. Allelopathy includes the exuding by roots, or fallen foliage, or by transpiration, of toxins that inhibit growth and development of surrounding plants; an obvious case is the power of eucalypts to eliminate competition by a combination of soil allelopathy, allelochemical volatilisation and foliage litter decomposition.

Some dendrologists believe that there are trees that function as nurse trees for seedlings and saplings of other species; in reforestation these are sometimes referred to as pioneers. Pioneers are called that because they are the first tree species to colonise cleared areas, only to be overshaded by the seedlings and saplings of taller, longer-lived species that they are thought to have been protecting. When this relationship was put to the test in regenerating forest, and the so-called nurse trees, in this case blackwoods (*Acacia melanoxylon*), were poisoned, the red cedar saplings beneath them grew away at a greatly increased rate. We now know that phytotoxic leachates from the decomposing foliage of blackwoods inhibit the growth of surrounding plants.

When the competing plants are the tree's own progeny the process is called auto-allelopathy. Many tree species need assistance to get their seeds removed to a safe distance; this can be provided by birds or by mammals like squirrels and bats that physically carry the seeds, nuts and fruits away in paws, in beaks, or in guts. Once the seed disperser goes extinct such trees cannot protect themselves from becoming scrub. Scrubland will not revert to woodland unless the seed dispersers return or are replaced by new ones. When the balance of woodland is disturbed, or trees are grown in unnatural proximity in plantations, the allelopathic mechanism can turn lethal for the trees themselves. This may be what has happened in the case of ash dieback and the worldwide proliferation of phytophthoras. So, a tree has bigness as an essential element in its character. A creeping shrub is not a tree. A seedling is not a tree either. A sapling is not a tree. A bush is not a tree. Neither bush nor shrub will become a tree, but the seedling and sapling could, if they are lucky.

Trees are gregarious; to plant them as specimens in parkland or as street trees is to deny them the realisation of their potential as governing organisms in rich ecosystems. As the tree is programmed to achieve its optimum size, the tree communities called forests too need to cover a minimum extent before they can function adequately as tree habitat. When an area of forest is reduced below a certain optimum, it becomes vulnerable to 'edge effects' which change the microclimate. Wind and frost penetrate under the canopy; water retention becomes a problem. Weeds invade. It is only forty-one years since pine forests in the Sierra Madre de Oriente in central Mexico were found to be the place where millions of monarch butterflies overwintered, but indiscriminate felling of the pines has already destroyed the integrity of the forest and with it the welcoming microclimate that the butterflies used to find there.

For optimum development most tree species need the option of growing into a canopy with other tree species. This is as mysterious as everything else about trees. To watch a forest developing is to see the gradual elimination of unfit species, as the faster growers grab all the light. The process is so ineluctable, so merciless that it feels as if the forest has a will of its own, an agenda even. The aim is not apparently to become a monoculture; to grow a tree species as a monoculture is to increase its vulnerability to all kinds of fungal, bacterial and invertebrate infestations. Forests are mosaics, aggregations of niches for a variety of species that can keep each other in check.

Canopy science is so new that it has still to formulate its basic questions. Allometry is the name we now give to studies of forest formation, in which the attempt is made to define the systems by which fast-growing and slower-growing, longer-lived and less long-lived species come together in canopy formation. Trees both have canopies and are part of a canopy (pleonasm again). Trees in a closed canopy do not seem to vie for space; they do not grow into each other's crowns or struggle to out-top each other. They will grow to a genetically determined maximum height and then continue to grow radially, expanding the girth of their trunks. Some of the most impressive trees in the world, such as *Tāne mahuta* (Maori for 'Lord of the Forest') in New Zealand's Waipoua Forest, have huge boles and comparatively diminutive canopies. Nevertheless, it would be a mistake to think that competition has somehow ceased in mature woodland; what seems to have been arrived at is a truce, that will be renegotiated with every tree-fall, as new routes are opened by which the saplings can grow into the light of the sun. This is a stasis that has been arrived at over millennia; to clear a forest is to lose thousands of years of natural selection and to destroy a galaxy of microclimates that cannot easily be reproduced.

The grown tree is an individual that supports and is part of a colony of other creatures, from beneath the ground to the summit of its crown. To synthesise nutrients its roots require the assistance of root fungi called mycorrhizas. These specialised fungi colonise plant roots, increasing their surface area a hundred to a thousand times, and so enabling them to absorb nutrients and water more efficiently. Several miles of such fungal filaments have been found in less than a thimbleful of soil. Mycorrhizal fungi release into the soil powerful enzymes that dissolve nutrients such as organic nitrogen, phosphorus and iron that are otherwise unavailable to the tree. Specimen trees, planted in streets, parks and alongside ploughland would appear to be condemned to do without the beneficial contribution of mycorrhizas; for them life is a struggle even without the effects of agrichemical spray and run off, draughts and vehicle fumes.

A tree's life begins when it germinates; one shoot will turn downwards and begin to develop as roots; another will turn upwards and begin to develop as leaves. The tree seedling is pretty much the same as other plant seedlings. Like them, it consists of vascular bundles of xylem that transport water from the roots to the leaves, and of phloem which transports nutrients to all parts of the plant. Xylem is to be found in non-woody plants, so to differentiate the potential woodiness of tree seedlings we identify something called secondary xylem, which will be laid down by a meristem called the vascular cambium. Wood is produced from secondary xylem. We are not helped to understand this by the fact that word xylem itself is derived from the Greek word 'xylon' which means wood; wood comes from secondary wood, as it were.

All vascular plants have primary xylem and phloem. These are produced by the vascular cambium, which is said to originate 'from procambium that has not completely differentiated during the formation of primary xylem and primary phloem'. This sounds more circular than ever. Procambium produces vascular cambium produces xylem and phloem. The missing term here is 'meristem'; the vascular cambium is a meristem and it is that which lays down secondary xylem. The *Oxford English Dictionary* explains the word 'meristem' as 'the unformed growing cellular tissue of the younger parts of plants'. The word comes into use in the scientific literature of the 1870s, before any clear idea of what it meant. A rather grumpy comment in Kerner's *Natural History* of 1894 refers to 'the groups of constructive, dividing and enlarging cells, the so-called "meristematic tissue"'. Current understanding of the role of the meristem is still rather tentative. This account by Susan T. Rouse is less baffling than most:

> Meristematic cells are fully developed and functional at maturity, but unlike other cells in the plant, they remain totipotent. This means that when induced, they can develop into any specific plant tissue at any point during the life of the plant. Other cells in the plant are fully differentiated (meaning that they are specialised in both form and function) and do not divide. Cells in the meristem, however, divide and produce all of the new cells in a plant.

Meristematic cells would seem to be the vegetable counterpart of the animal stem cell. Plants have meristematic tissue in several locations. Both roots and shoots have apical meristems at their tips that are responsible for their lengthening. The shoot apical meristem is formed during embryonic development, and after germination will give rise to the stem, leaves, and flowers. The root apical meristem is likewise formed during development, but during germination gives rise to the root system. Cell division and cell elongation in the apical meristem are called primary growth and result in an increase in plant height and root length.

Lateral or secondary meristem is what allows woody plants to increase the diameter of their roots and stems throughout their lifetime. The main stems of plants that do not have secondary xylem, as palms and bamboos do not, grow as cylinders, because they cannot increase their girth as they mature. Secondary growth gives a plant a broader base and hence added stability, allowing it to grow taller – and turn into a tree. At a certain stage in their life cycle, trees cease to grow in length and begin to add to the girth of their trunks. This is accomplished not by the addition of more primary tissue but by the growth of secondary vascular tissue around the entire circumference of the primary plant body. Meristem tissue is not self-regulating. Throughout the life of the plant, the rate of cell division and cell elongation in the meristems is regulated by plant hormones.

In vascular plants, phloem is the living tissue that carries the products of photosynthesis, or photosynthate, in particular, sucrose, to all parts of the plant. In trees, the phloem is the innermost layer of the bark. Phloem consists of columns of living cells while xylem vessels consist of dead cells with thick, strengthened cellulose walls round a hollow lumen. The 'cambial initials' produce the daughter cells which produce in turn a variety of wood cells which expand, laying down the multilayered secondary cell wall, which hardens or 'lignifies'. When that process is complete, the xylem undergoes programmed cell death involving 'cell autonomous, active and ordered suicide'. Many attempts have been made to replicate lignin biosynthesis, but it seems that current models of the pathway are either incomplete or incorrect.

The process by which water is drawn up to all parts of the tree seems less biological than mechanical. As the website BBC Bitesize has it:

Water on the surface of spongy and palisade cells (inside the leaf) evaporates and then diffuses out of the leaf. This is called transpiration. More water is drawn out of the xylem cells inside the leaf to replace what's lost. As the xylem cells make a continuous tube from the leaf, down the stem to the roots, this acts like a drinking straw, producing a flow of water and dissolved minerals from roots to leaves.

This explanation may seem clear and simple, maybe even a little bit too simple. Both conifers and broadleaf trees transpire, but conifers, which generally grow in colder, drier conditions, transpire much less. Their reduced leaves are coated with wax and have smaller, recessed stomata. BBC Bitesize describes the process of transpiration as it can be observed in broadleaf species, but a clever child would still ask why the tree wastes the water it has harvested so carefully. Why does the water that has been drawn up through the vessels of the xylem evaporate out of the leaf? The process of which transpiration is a part is called gas exchange; the stomata or pores in the surface of the leaf open to allow air into the plant. From the air the carbon dioxide necessary for photosynthesis will be harvested, while the surplus oxygen escapes along with the water vapour. Water rises in the hollow vessels of the xylem as it does in a straw, by capillary action or the 'transpiration-cohesion-tension mechanism', providing that the column of water from root to leaf surface is continuous.

The cut surface of a tree trunk or limb will show both 'sapwood' and 'heartwood'. Sapwood is the younger wood surrounding the older heartwood, which is drier and less permeable. The outer ring of the sapwood is called 'early wood' and the outermost 'late wood'. Surrounding the sapwood is the cambium, through which the vessels of xylem and phloem pass. In young trees all the wood is sapwood; as the tree grows the proportion of inner heartwood increases. Extractives such as resins, phenols and terpenes, residues of the once-living cells with additional chemical compounds garnered from elsewhere in the plant, accumulate in the heartwood, which becomes darker in colour. Sapwood contains more water, but it no longer transports water from root to crown. The idea that sap rises in a tree in the spring and stops rising in the autumn is simply wrong. Both the upward action of the dead cells of the xylem and downward transport by the living cells of the phloem slow down when shorter days signal that it is time for entry into dormancy, but they never stop altogether.

In the growing season a tree is a powerhouse, driving transpiration one way and absorption the other. Clearly leaves play an essential part in this process; the only way to stop it is to shed the leaves. Trees that shed their leaves slow down the traffic of water and nutrients and enter into a period of dormancy, which is essential if they are to survive drought or freezing temperatures. Evergreen trees that do not deciduate shed leaves in response to different triggers, to water shortage for example, curtailing new growth until the conditions change. In rainforest trees can flush with new growth in any season. When unusual weather conditions mean that trees do not enter into dormancy at the right time, but continue developing buds, the sudden arrival of frost can kill them outright. If normally deciduous trees are prevented from deciduating by artificial light and warmth, they may grow on for a year or two but they cannot survive the disruption for very long.

Trees are the armature supporting thousands of other species, from the humblest algae, moulds and fungi, through the bryophyte assemblages, to epiphytes and vines, creepers, lianes and mistletoes. Then come the armies of invertebrates, mites, moths, hoverflies, bees, ladybirds, snails, spiders, weevils, katydids, crickets and beetles. The older the tree the greater the number of organisms that depend upon it and the more varied their ways of doing so. Even when its heartwood is eaten out, the tree continues to support a vast ecosystem. We are losing animal and bird species all over the world because of a shortage of hollow trees. Plantations that are felled regularly will not solve this problem. Even the dead tree continues to support an array of other creatures, animal and vegetable.

Most of the trees growing on this planet in the twenty-first century will not live out their potential life career as habitat trees. An ever-growing number will be destined to be turned into toilet paper. In a single lifetime a user of toilet paper will consume 384 trees, and the number of people joining the ranks of paper users increases every year. The purveyors of this entirely unnecessary commodity tell us that for every tree that is felled to make it, three more will be planted. That means that three more trees, most of them Monterey pines, will live nasty, short lives in gloomy plantations where no bird sings. The Monterey pine is now all but extinct in its homeland of southern California and the community of creatures that depended on it no longer exists. This is just one of the ways in which the vast treasure house of the primordial forest has been trashed for human convenience.

Laburnum Time

B13

Zaffar Kunial

A dendrite is a branch in a neuron, a branch that quickens, receiving sparks of life across infinitesimally small distances. A dendrite is also anything with a tree-like structure – moss comes to mind, which has a canopy look about it from above, close-up. Christian hermits who withdrew into the branches of trees were also known as dendrites, like the sainted holy fool of Thessalonica, David the Dendrite, who lived for three years nested in an almond tree. Likewise, those ascetics who perched on a column, near the sky, were known as stylites, from the Greek *stylos*, 'pillar'.

I wasn't quite a dendrite when I was a kid, but the laburnum tree at the far-end of our little back garden in Birmingham was known as 'my tree' for as long as I can remember. This was partly because I could often be found (or not) sitting about halfway up it. And also because its yellow flowers arrived – like a bright envelope from someone who always remembered – during the week of my birthday. The way early birthdays are hazily memorable and exist in their own candle-measured time, so that old laburnum can be made present again in my head, with its Y-shaped forked trunk – a first rung that was easy enough to step into, from the age of about seven onwards. Whenever I did, my eyes would swell and blur if I touched my face after handling the poisonous powder on the laburnum's bark. Sometimes, like the cats I was also allergic to, my tree would shorten the intervals of my breath, the disturbed dust making the dendritic tubes in my small asthmatic lungs contract and wheeze.

But to what purpose
Disturbing the dust on a bowl of rose-leaves
I do not know.
               Other echoes
Inhabit the garden. Shall we follow?

Looking back now, seeing myself climbing again into the odd space of the laburnum's green-grey branches, it feels like it was *time* I was sitting in, and absent-mindedly rubbing my eyes in, as much as a particular tree.

The half-echoing endings of Eliot's first two lines, up above, seem hazily unpunctuated. The way things looked from inside the laburnum.

The tree would punctuate my year – and, from the outside, teach me about time. Before I knew about punctuation, the story goes that while my father was away for months, 'back home', visiting his mother, I asked my mother when he'd be back. My English mum was a primary school teacher and my Kashmiri dad was away for the whole of her summer holidays, and even beyond. And, with me not understanding when exactly 'October', or 'autumn' would be – as long as the answer wasn't 'today' or 'tomorrow', she may as well have said 'till forever' – Mum pointed through the window:

When all the leaves fall from your tree.

This was my language – the tree, and the absence or presence of its yellow pea-like flowers, was how my mum would answer one of my other questions – showing (not telling) me that it wasn't about to be my birthday any time soon. Or, at the end of May, how she would point out, literally, that it was. The 'laburnum-candles' on my birthday were like the clock hands that I was beginning to get the hang of, or like the calendar in the kitchen, with its columns and illegible months that were more of a mystery than the ticking clock. The next day, after explaining 'autumn' to me in this tree-language I could understand, Mum says that she saw, through the kitchen window, at the far-end of the garden, a strange breeze shaking the laburnum. And then, beneath the tree, she saw a child, his eyes staring up at the branches, his palms on the trunk.

Time on my small hands, I was pushing as hard as I could.

Mum wrote a letter in black ink on pale-blue airmail paper, that summer, posting it – I imagine in a red pillar box – to my dad, telling him this story of me trying to get the leaves off the laburnum, that he knew was my tree, my birthday tree. And how I wanted the tree to bring the day of his return to me, because the tree told the time and could make things arrive. Like presents.

And the story goes that in the added heat of the other side of the world, receiving the letter, weeks later, my father – who couldn't read English letters when he first took flight to Britain for a job in the factories – cried on to the thin blue page.

And at this point in the story, which was often told in our house, I picture the words blurring into a cloud. An English cloud. A grey smudge on a faint blue leaf. The story first penned in my mother's hand, that I only see because I was told it. And in the telling I started to imagine it, unfolding again, as if it were my own memory.

The sky then becomes a thin blue-grey page, held in my father's hands. One sky like tracing paper, held above another. Held above a laburnum.

★

Acocks Green (B27), a district of Birmingham which perhaps sounds a lot greener than it is these days, was just down the road from our house in College Road (B13). In a book called *Folklore of Warwickshire* Roy Palmer writes:

> People living at Acocks Green in Birmingham believe that an oak tree in Arden Road marks the heart of the ancient Forest of Arden, which formerly covered northern Warwickshire so well that a squirrel, or so we are told, could travel from one side of the country to the other without once setting foot on the ground.

It wouldn't take too many leaps by a squirrel to get to the oak tree in Arden Road – from the laburnum in Moseley, B13 – though it would definitely run out of branches and touch tarmac and have to brave a fair bit of the traffic on the way.

A proverbial million miles away from my laburnum, and our back garden – and up the road, rather than down – was a fenced-in area of suburban woodland called Moseley Bog. It seemed a kind of primordial place and I can't say I liked being there. I associated it with unwanted 'cross-country' sessions in PE that began in September at my comprehensive school, snaked through the gates on Wake Green Road, and left me asthmatically wheezing through a muddy place somewhere in the Dark Ages. And all this in the same square mile where I grew up, in the one double-session of a school timetable.

My school was on the same road as the house I lived in for my first nineteen years, on 58 College Road. Its other entrance was on the adjoining Wake Green Road, where you'd also find Moseley Bog.

Before I ever wore a black, red and white Moseley School tie, Moseley Bog was a forbidding area I connected with *age* – somewhere older kids hung out, leaving crushed and corroding beer cans behind them. The older boys sometimes hung out literally, on knotted tree-ropes – dangling over streams and ravines in the earth – that I wasn't gutsy enough to jump up and swing on, or tall enough to reach on my own.

The woodland in Moseley Bog is mentioned in the Domesday Book. In a different way, the old forest there throws its various shades on another book too – Tolkien's *The Lord of the Rings*. As a small boy Tolkien lived at an address which I would have known as 264 Wake Green Road, in Moseley, Birmingham, but which he would have called 5 Gracewell, in the hamlet of Sarehole, Worcestershire. Either way, the Moseley Bog we both knew was apparently an inspiration for his 'Old Forest'. The old county boundaries ring a bell for me as I remember an explanation for them given to me when I started playing for a cricket club as a boy on Wake Green Road, called Pickwick; in winter I played hockey for the same club and went on to play for the county, Worcestershire – whose ground was a long drive away. My school meanwhile – across the road – sent me to have a trial at Edgbaston, three miles away, to play cricket for Warwickshire.

One of Tolkien's biographers, Daniel Grotta, writes of this old woody district of Birmingham:

> Sarehole was Tolkien's vision of a 'kind of lost paradise' … Sarehole had 'good waterstones and elm trees and small quiet rivers'. It

was surrounded by open fields and farmlands, though in the distance one could see the grimy smoke of nearby Birmingham. Shakespeare was said to have visited Sarehole as a youth and it had not appreciably changed since his day.

It's a stretch for me to see this as the same area I grew up in – my father walked back home at dawn, along the Stratford Road, from his nightshift at one of the factories that would spring up in Tolkien's distance as Birmingham expanded.

One of the oaks in the protected area of Moseley Bog is a century short of stretching to Shakespeare's time, but is an impressive 300 years old.

I googled the year 1716. It was when Bach began composing *Jesu, Joy of Man's Desiring* – which was played by the organist in a village church in Bodenham, Herefordshire, at my mum's funeral, on a fugue-like day of falling leaves, one October. And meanwhile, on the other side of the world, 1716 (in the Japanese Edo period) was the year that the *hokku* poet Buson died.

That three-century-old oak tree in Moseley Bog might perhaps have been an acorn when Buson wrote (translated by Robert Hass):

> White blossoms of the pear
> and a woman in moonlight
> reading a letter.

★

The laburnum my mum wrote the airmail to my father about can't have been much more than two or three decades old. It certainly didn't then have roots in another century. Although it does have now, if it's still there today in the garden.

There are no laburnums in Shakespeare's plays or poetry. Knotted within the tunnel of the Knot Garden at New Place in Stratford, you can now find laburnums and apple trees. The folk name of the laburnum, 'the Golden Chain Tree', seems a name Shakespeare might have riffed on, regarding time and the seasons, but no, apparently not.

It makes sense he didn't mention the laburnum because the tree's introduction to Britain – from the mountains of southern Europe –

only happened in his time, in the Elizabethan era. So the laburnum's introduction to this island coincides with a time when the country was in transition from being an oral culture to being a print culture. But the laburnum didn't really catch on until the mid-1800s, when a hybrid species was created with the more thickly clustering flowers that made it popular in British gardens, despite the fact that all parts of the tree are poisonous.

'God made the country, and man made the town', wrote William Cowper in his long poem *The Task*, published in 1785. As the year goes round, he noted each 'family and tribe' that would re-appear, and 'publish' after winter:

> Then, each in its peculiar honours clad,
> Shall publish even to the distant eye
> Its family and tribe. Laburnum rich
> In streaming gold; syringa ivory pure

Jane Austen was an early adopter of the laburnum trend – partially because of this poem. In an 1807 letter about the new plants in her garden border, she refers to the above lines of Cowper (who I've just learnt is pronounced 'Cooper' and not 'Cow-per'):

> I could not do without Syringa for the sake of Cowper's Line. We also talk of a Laburnam.

I know that spellings were less standardised in the past, but I like how she has her own spelling of laburnum – *Laburnam* – different from Cowper's more usual spelling.

The point I'm trying to make is that the laburnum is a relatively young tree on this island. Despite its youth, *my tree*, my birthday tree, was to me at least, a kind of elder. And to me our garden felt like the beginning of everything. So the laburnum – the tree that stubbornly taught me about time and my own birthday – was always going to feel like the most rooted thing possible.

That scheme of things broke down in the woods up the road, past the comprehensive school that loomed in more ways than one. The ornamental laburnum belonged to a different but parallel world from the gnarled trees that ganged up in Moseley Bog and kept the murk beneath them, their own muddy atmosphere. Later, a school student, I'd trip on sudden, half-sodden roots – the trees in the bog sticking out their collective feet. When they put their heads together, the sky (and the time of day – perhaps even the year, or century, or era) was obscured. The leaf-light's densely layered unreadable page.

More interested in trying to be a leg spinner for Warwickshire, I'd go through school largely untouched by books and literature, and never read a novel until I was nineteen – so I was far from catching up with Tolkien's

> It was not called the Old Forest without reason, for it was indeed ancient, a survivor of vast forgotten woods; and in it there lived yet, ageing no quicker than the hills, the fathers of the fathers of trees, remembering times when they were lords.

And although we 'did' *Macbeth* at school, I paid little attention, so wouldn't have known that it contained a wood called Birnam which fulfilled the witches' prophecy. Neither was I aware that this was based on an old story Shakespeare heard about the branches of trees from great Birnam Wood nearly a thousand years ago camouflaging the advancing army against Macbeth. And I wouldn't have known that Shakespeare's version annoyed and inspired Tolkien to write a scene where trees could become an army in the actual sense, and lift up their roots and march – a scene I now know from the film, rather than the page.

And what's more, I wouldn't have heard a distant (and doubtless unrelated) 'Birnum' in a word my mum had taught me before I could consciously remember learning anything; *laburnum*.

What I did know, or dumbly feel, was that the oldest area of the woodland in Moseley Bog kept a more compressed version of time, a million echoes packed inside, darkly, like an impossible envelope.

★

I've just moved to Hebden Bridge in West Yorkshire, to be nearer to my seven-year-old son, and was struck by 'The huge clock of the laburnum'

as I sat in a local café, leafing through their yellowing copy of Ted
Hughes' *Birthday Letters*.

>... Yes, yes. Tell me
>We shall sit together this summer
>Under the laburnum. Yes, he said, yes yes yes.
>The laburnum draped deathly in the blue dusk.
>The laburnum like a dressed corpse in full yellow.
>The huge clock of the laburnum stuck at noon,
>Striking noon noon noon –

This is from a poem called 'The Inscription' about a last conversation
with Sylvia Plath and her ripping up his inscribed red *Oxford Shakespeare*.
The poem shares some lines with another called 'The Laburnum' which
was included in the proof of *Birthday Letters* but was eventually left out.

Anyway, I'm still puzzling over why I associate trees with time and
beginnings – and with learning about calendars and letters. Perhaps
it's something to do with some forgotten picture book, that made 'A'
into an acorn, or a gleaming red apple.

Hughes, who spent his early years until seven in Mytholmroyd,
near my son's school in Cragg Vale, might have passed me his copy of
The White Goddess by Graves:

> in all Celtic languages *trees* means *letters* ... the most ancient Irish
> alphabet, the Beth-Luis-Nion ('Birch-Rowan-Ash') takes its
> name from the first three of a series of trees whose initials form the
> sequence of its letters.

And then he'd have flicked through to another chapter.

> I noticed all at once that the consonants of this alphabet form a
> calendar ... Since there are thirteen consonants in the alphabet, it
> is reasonable to regard the tree month as the British common-law
> lunar month of twenty-eight days ...

And, losing me slightly, he would have flicked through to another.

> For *Ura* is the next letter of the alphabet, the midsummer letter
> ... The authors of the Irish *Hearings of the Scholars* connected the
> midsummer-letter *Ur* with *ur*, 'earth'; and we are reminded that

this is found in the Latin words area, 'a plot of earth', *arvum*, 'a ploughed field', and *uvare*, which means 'to drive a plough ceremoniously around the proposed site of a city' – a sense also found in the Homeric Greek *ouron*, 'a boundary marked by the plough'. Grammarians assume a primitive Greek word *era* …

★

I'm staring at that *Ur* above, across the border of the last section, and thinking of how this 'midsummer-letter', *Ur* also sits somehow inside a laburnum. Apparently the Latin suffix *urnum* usually means 'belonging to'. Another possibility is that the tree's name comes from the Laburni people, an ancient tribe from within the old borders of Illyria. Which makes me think of that shipwrecked scene in Shakespeare:

What country, friends, is this?
This is Illyria, lady.

Again I feel lost in the woods / words.

I suppose, going back to *Ur*, and to *era*, the seasons mark a boundary – at least those times when one season becomes another – and some trees stand out as 'boundary markers' in this regard. And the laburnum blossomed at the border – if there is one – between spring and summer. And perhaps that's why I associate climbing the laburnum with climbing into time. And the tree was at the back of our garden, in the narrow border between the lawn and the fence.

And. And. And. And time seemed to border on much more distant times in Moseley Bog, in the old wood up the road, behind the school fence on Wake Green Road. And deep under the border of old forest ground, we now know that fungi send out fine filaments that penetrate into the furthest fingertips of tree roots. This ancient relationship, between fungi and tree roots, goes back a long way (over four hundred millions years). It's become known as the 'wood-wide-web'. Perhaps it's a bit like the dendrites in a neuron, at the thinnest end of communication. The nearest thing to correspondence or letters between trees in a wood.

And talking of letters, because I wasn't much of a reader, the whole of old literature felt like a dark wood at school – like Moseley Bog, behind the fence – that half crowded out the sky of the present when you entered into it. A wood I wasn't sure was part of my territory or, in Shakespeare's case, a language that seemed almost foreign to me, even in its spellings. Something foreboding with a boundary around it, or perhaps the whole thing a kind of border where you can't see the wood for the trees.

Pressed between yellow leaves of a book that has never been opened.
And the way up is the way down, the way forward is the way back.

Literature still feels like a big wood to me, a wood with a more complicated pattern of time.

Even down the Stratford Road, and in the streets that were concreted over for shops and factories, I wonder if the presence of the old woods wasn't far away – or at least a feeling I was half afraid of – of the deep, dark past mixed shadily with the future. An expansive place that might lose me, like the woods in Moseley Bog. And so with literature. Even when I'm encountering something very contemporary, if I'm engaged in what I'm reading, I don't feel I'm far off much older beginnings. Perhaps even some kind of boundary between the verbal and the pre-verbal. But I can't put my finger on that feeling.

I'll end, even more tenuously, with a couple of poems that have something distantly to do with the district of this feeling. In the way that where I grew up includes a woodland that is mostly no longer there. Like the B13 I knew, where a squirrel would have to touch concrete as well as branches, pillars and posts – the poems are not obviously within the envelope of arboreal territory. There is only 'a fingernail of forest' within them. But the dendritic connections to the old woods /old words are there. Just about.

★

Fielder

If I had to put my finger on where this started,
I'd trace a circle round the one moment I came to, or the one
that placed me, a fielder – just past the field, over the rope,
having chased a lost cause, leathered for six …

when, bumbling about, obscured in the bushes,
I completely stopped looking for the ball –
perhaps irresponsibly – slowed by bracken, caught by light
that slipped the dark cordon of rhododendron hands,
a world hidden from the batsmen, the umpires and my team,
like the thing itself: that small, seamed planet, shined
on one half, having reached its stop, out of the sphere of sight.
And when I reflect, here, from this undiscovered city,
well north of those boyish ambitions – for the county,
maybe later, the country – I know something of that minute
holds something of me, there, beyond the boundary,
in that edgeland of central England. A shady fingernail
of forest. The pitch it points at, or past, a stopped clock.
Still, in the middle, the keeper's gloves
clap at the evening. Still, a train clicks
on far off tracks. And the stars are still to surface.
The whole field, meanwhile, waiting for me,
some astronaut, or lost explorer, to emerge with a wave
that brings the ball – like time itself – to hand. A world restored.
But what I'd come to find, in that late hour
was out of mind, and, the thing is, I didn't care.
And this is what's throwing me now.

★

Jane Austen: Selected Letters

I

Where shall I begin? she starts. *Which of all
my important nothings shall I tell you first?*
In her shortened sign-off, above, she'd *remain*

with Love,

    Yrs affec JA.

And into the absence I'm reading names;
Julia Ann… who helped shape my initial scribbles
and kept an old card with first words in my hand:

from Zaffar
         – that *ff* pointing backwards,

back to that consonant I couldn't then say;
stuck with my start, I was an Affer, or Faffer –
which proved true, Mum later said, of the latter.
Dawdler that I became. So here I am

taken aback by letters – their afterlife –
and how we draw together when they arrive.

II

We also talk of a Laburnam. – The Border
under the Terrace Wall is clearing away …

I go back, to that second, shadier *a*
in *Laburnam*. It's you, Mum, I remember
explaining to me how a soft Indian u
is equally an a. My dad taught me to say
'Mera nam Zaffar hai'. The first vowel
in my name like the last u in laburnum.

As a child I'd climb that tree, spend hours lost in
its grey-green limbs at the end of our garden.

Early days, at the registry, in Birmingham
Mum wrote out, in her own spelling … *Kunial*;
from Jat-Rajput-Kanyal – Dad's tribe or clan,
clearing those parts that talk of caste.
                    In *Austen*
that *A*, almost from the off, is a different sound –
more like the o in of, than the u in ground.

The Common Dean

Alan Garner

The alder bog was old and overstood. The last time it had been cropped was 1916, when travelling clog-makers camped in bothies by the brook and felled the trees for the men in the trenches of France. Since then, the coppice had grown unkempt and was a dark acre.

For the first year after he came to live in the house on the field above, he cleared the rotten trunks and branches, carrying them on his shoulder. The next year he began.

The coppice was nearly dead. If worked, it was everlasting, but now the stands of alder were too tall, too close. The underlife was choked. When he went into the bog he lost the world beyond. The stands were so thick that he could not see how far they reached. Although he knew the acre it felt to have no end, and the light gave him no direction and no time. The silence held ancient noise. Only by the patterns of lichen and moss, which were thickest on the north side of the bark, could he tell the way out.

The floor was leaves, black water and black mud, held by the surface roots that ran from the alder stools, the flat wide living base from which the stands grew. He had to place his feet and not linger. If he did, or if he misjudged a step, the crust would give and take his leg into the marsh. He had to pull himself free of the suck before his other leg was caught. When he rodded to prove the depth, he could not ground it. And it was not his weight alone he had to know. The crust told him what load of tree he might carry.

The ditch was hard. Coppices were shielded from the wild, and though the deer were gone, the ditch and bank that kept them out remained. Each load had to be thrown over and picked up again. Then the climb to the house.

The railway boundary was a relic line of ash, with hedges running from it to the brook, a corridor for predator and prey. Alder mixed with ash burnt hot.

He did not take the oaks along the bank, but when fungus killed the elms he wore out a bowsaw blade to get three trees and snapped the helve of a sledge in their rending. And the grain in the wood could drop its branches on him with no sound. The old saying has it well: 'Ellum mon hateth; and waiteth'.

The bog was safest in frost, when the leaves were stiff and stuck together. They let him carry two stone more. Snow was not safe. It blurred the feet to the feel of roots. And when the rain and February thaw came the crust was too wet to bear. Then, he left the coppice and went along the valley of the Common Dean, following the brook upstream by the old road through the tunnel under the railway, its arch curtained with a drape of ivy, to the trees of the marl pits.

Here the world was different. There was no guzzling bog, but a green causeway reclaimed by bramble and alder; sycamore, hazel, ash, and strays seeded by birds, with space and light to grow; and celandine in season, and the wild garlic smell.

And on either side of the causeway lay the pools of the pits, eyes of black water dug to get marl, the lime-rich clay beneath the silt, to fetch life to the hungry sands of the field. The waters hid their depth and were mirrors for the trees and sky, their surface still in every wind, and each a trap.

The sides went down 20 feet and gave no hold, swallowing any weight they caught. In childhood lore marl pits were bottomless. Here, once, a horse, a strong Shire, strayed and slipped; but its strength made it sink the faster in the ooze. Ropes and grapples could not get it out, and the farmer shot it as its head went under.

He could lift heavier loads from the marl pit wood, but it was further to the house; and after felling, trimming, cutting into lengths, he carried each hundredweight a quarter of a mile, along the causeway, through the tunnel, up the field and tipped over the hedge into the yard.

Next, whether from the bog or from the pits, there was the cleaving.

Alder and ash were sweet. He set the steel wedge at the end of the cut, tapped with the sledge until it bit, then swung. The short lengths from the bog split in one go. The lengths from the marl pits needed a second wedge along to help the first, to ripple open the trunk.

A tree had to be quartered, and the quarter sawn to 18 inches for the fire; then stacked into the house. An alder would last two weeks.

In the felling, elm could not be trusted to drop clean. The saw hit crossing grain, and jammed. The only way to save the twisted blade was to drive wedges in to ease the grip; and they must be hammered sideways to get free. And all the time the elm might kill.

'Elm's cold as corpse-light,' his grandfather had told him. 'It wants thorn to make it go.' And as he sweated he remembered other wisdom. 'Logs warm three times. Once to get; once to fettle; once to burn,' the old man said.

To fell the tree, he first chose the line of fall, so that it did not snag in other branches. If it did, and lodged, the next tree had to go as well, and that was danger. A leaning trunk could not be governed.

He set his feet where the roots were thickest as they left the stool. He made a level cut low on the side where the tree should drop, and then began the main cut higher, sloping a little downward, on the other side.

The blade swished back and to. He went at the saw's rate, not hurrying, not pausing. The trunk sat quiet, and he watched the line of the teeth in the wood. When the line opened, he stopped and listened. If the tree was still he began again, but now softly, careful, listening, until the wood spoke. He stopped, listened; began again; the line opened to a thin mouth. He took the saw out, and listened; put it back and moved with gentleness, until he heard the tree grieve. He stood off; and the mouth gaped and the top of the tree levered the weight so that it fell with grace, peeling the bark to the small cut; and came free.

A moment of silence in the air, then the crash, and the floor quaked.
A greater silence hushed all sound. The white sap turned red as blood.
   So he renewed the tamed wild. He cleared from the centre; and
with the light each year growth came, and flowers returned; and with
the flowers life. A robin disputed the saw.

> Fire on a wedge from a mis-hit sledge
> Hammers the dusk of another day
> In the yard hewing alder. The wood
> That grew splits, telling years
> Saw, cleave, and the spark dies in the air
> Alder reddens to logs.

> We were all the sun.
> Round and round the fire flies
> For ever in veins, the long ropes of blood
> Keep the same heat. And though it slept,
> The spark waits
> Somewhere between wits and the swung hammer
> And the steel in the wood that grew
> Memory promise or threat
> We are the same waiting
> In the dark yard.

   Archaeologists came and trowelled one of the Bronze Age barrows
near the house. With the burnt bone they found the turves that built
the burial mound, and in them the pollen of the plants that lived
then: willow, hazel, ivy, ash; alder, lime, elm, pine, and oak; moss,
fern, bracken, heather, sedge, and gorse; meadowsweet, vetch, daisy,
buttercup; spelt, grass, corn spurrey, wheat; dandelion, chickweed and
fat hen. Four thousand years ago the wild was cleared and gone. All
was fields, farms, ploughs, crops, cattle, order; rule: an open world.
   The dead men in the ground had worked the same land.

Stars 15
FOREST OF FONTAINEBLEAU, FRANCE, 2014
by Ellie Davies

The Dwelling 2
PUDDLETOWN FOREST, DORSET, 2012
by Ellie Davies

Ellie Davies began taking photographs in forests in 2008, inspired by childhood memories of playing in the woods with her twin sister. Woodland has since become her studio, especially in Dorset and Hampshire, where she works alone responding to the landscape by building small structures, creating pools of light, or using materials like paint and wool. These interventions can seem, at first, to be part of the natural wooded landscape. But as we look closer, noticing something unusual about the trees, we step into an imaginary forest, one that is both personal to Ellie and also able to challenge our own perceptions of nature, asking to what extent our relationship with trees and woods is personal or constructed by cultural history.

Half Light 11
NEW FOREST, HAMPSHIRE, 2016
by Ellie Davies

Smoke and Mirrors 2
NEW FOREST, HAMPSHIRE, 2010
by Ellie Davies

Searching for Natural Woodland

LADY PARK, WYE VALLEY

George Peterken

I grew up, as woodland ecologist, in a world defined by Sir Arthur Tansley, who, in the publication of *The British Islands and Their Vegetation* (1939) set out the prevailing view that 'of the great forests which at one time covered a large part of the British Islands only fragments remain, and most of these have been very much modified by human activity.' Indeed, most of the woodlands dominated by native trees 'are semi-natural communities, while a few may fairly be regarded as completely natural, either quite virgin or so little modified by human interference that they are essentially the same thing.' Moreover, woods were the stable end-point of successions. Described as the 'climax', it was easy to envisage natural forests as something wonderful, great trees towering over multiple layers of saplings and smaller trees of all sizes stretching unbroken into the distance.

When I joined the Nature Conservancy in 1967, the only places I knew well were the New Forest and the woods of north-west Middlesex around Ruislip. The latter was where I grew up, but the former was my mother's home district, the place where almost all our holidays were spent, where biologists from my school, Haberdashers' Aske's, went to learn ecology with Barry Goater, our enthusiastic botany teacher, and where I had just completed three years studying holly and the history of the woods for my doctorate. Hardly a balanced background for a career in woodland ecology and conservation, but at least it comprised representatives of both wood pastures and ancient coppice woods.

Most visitors, I imagine, accepted the New Forest as natural, but my research convinced me that its woods had been shaped more by people. Collaborating with Colin Tubbs, the Nature Conservancy's local officer, I was able to show how the age-structure of the open-forest woods had been largely determined by fluctuations in the numbers of deer, ponies and cattle, which in turn had been influenced by larger economic and political changes. Then, once installed at Monks Wood, I spent many days with Oliver Rackham and became ever more engrossed with the human aspects of eastern England's coppice woods; clearly, even these woods were at most 'semi-natural'. Within a few years, work had taken me all over the country and I had acquired what must then have been an unrivalled first-hand acquaintance with the full range of semi-natural woodlands from Caithness to Cumbria, Ceredigion, Cornwall and Kent. But, wherever I went, I found myself concentrating on how the woods had been managed, for this would define the possibilities for their future management. Natural aspects were not ignored, but they were recognised as the features 'left over' after other features of structure, composition and pattern had been explained by the actions of people.

Repeatedly describing woods as 'semi-natural' begged several questions. Would I recognise natural woodland if I saw it? Is it – or was it – an ideal state to which we should aspire on a woodland nature reserve? Could a wood become natural if we adopted a 'non-intervention' approach to management, and how soon? And, what does it mean to say a wood is natural, anyway?

It was then that I came across Eustace Jones' 1945 article, 'The structure and reproduction of the virgin forest of the north temperate zone'. Written in the Oxford University forestry department towards the end of the Second World War, at the request of editors who were evidently short of material, he drew on some pre-war lecture notes reviewing the literature on what Germans call *Urwälder* and Americans call 'Old Growth', most of which was evidently unknown to British ecologists. To me it was an eye-opener. Virgin forests were prone, sometimes literally, to a multiplicity of natural disturbances which shaped their structure and influenced their composition. Far from being stable, 'climax' stands, they were distinctly dynamic, even unstable. Moreover, the natural dynamics of many virgin forests were uncannily similar to silvicultural systems used by foresters to manage forests. Perhaps our managed forests were not as artificial as I had thought.

My first chance to see virgin forest was in 1968, when I was invited to tour Czechoslovakia. The month was August and I duly arrived in Prague, where I witnessed the 'Hyde Park Corner' speakers on the Charles Bridge, one harbinger of the Prague Spring. However, on the morning I was due to drive south to see the forest, the Russians invaded, and I spent three electrifying days roaming the city amongst the tanks and protesters before escaping by train into West Germany.

My chance came again in 1976 with a tour arranged through the British Council. Unfortunately, translation difficulties had classified me as a forester, so I spent many tedious days looking at plantations. But, late one afternoon in southern Bohemia, I persuaded my hosts to call at Boubínský Prales, the very *Urwald* that I had intended to visit in 1968. There, I dashed round the forest for an hour in a state of acute over-excitement, taking in the tall spruce, firs and beech and the giant standing dead trees. So this was natural woodland! Later, my eccentric interests now being recognised, I was taken to Mionší Prales and Lanžhot, and there I started to have doubts. Mionší was a wonderful ancient stand of beech, fir, spruce and sycamore, but it was mixed with oxlip-ridden hay meadows and contained a hunters' lodge, where we partied overnight. Lanžhot, on the floodplain of the Morava and Dyje rivers, was graced by gigantic spreading oak, ash, hornbeam and elms amongst younger growth, but its structure was just like the New Forest. How could these places be 'virgin' when one was so close to farmland and the other looked like any other former wood pasture?

Natural woodland remained on my back-burner until 1982, when we spent the royalties from my book, *Woodland Conservation and Management*, on a grand family tour of the western States. The circuit brought us to Yellowstone National Park, Wyoming, where we toured all the geysers, hot springs and other marvels, but I became increasingly conscious that they were set in a matrix of decrepit conifer forest composed of species I had got used to vilifying in Britain. If this was a top location for nature and its conservation, what did this say about my attitudes back home? We drove on to the redwoods, the sequoia groves and other magnificent West Coast forests, natural forests by any reasonable definition, but which, like Yellowstone, had certainly been shaped by the extermination of top predators, millennia of repeated fires, many caused by people, and latterly by decades of fire control.

By this time I had read most of the papers to which Eustace Jones had referred and had discovered many recent papers on US old-growth forests (many of which cited Eustace's review), including several dealing with mixed broadleaved forests which could be related to British woodlands. Developing an urge to see them for myself, I arranged to visit some of the researchers in the fall of 1985. The bargain was all on my side: I gave a lecture in their departments, they took me to see their study sites, and this enabled me to see old-growth stands in Massachusetts, New Jersey, Kentucky, Tennessee and South Carolina. All were impressive, and one cove forest, the Joyce Kilmer Memorial Forest in the North Carolina Great Smokies, embodied all that a virgin forest should be according to legend, with giant tulip trees towering over an amazing variety of other species, all mixed together, most regenerating. By then, however, I knew that even this stand originated after a major disturbance, a blow-down that had enabled the light-demanding tulip trees to regenerate, and much the same point emerged from the Hutcheson Memorial Forest, New Jersey, where the great oaks were magnificent, but all were old. Both stands were ecologically equivalent to a long-outgrown coppice wood in Britain, where we know the oaks are relics of former management.

Then in 1987, our son Andrew spent a summer as an intern in Corvallis, Oregon, helping the forest researchers with field observations in the Cascades and Coastal Ranges. Visiting, we seized the chance to see more old-growth forests, including remnants of the temperate rainforest in the Hoh and Queets valleys of the Olympic Peninsula, Washington, where one can see Douglas fir, Western hemlock and Sitka spruce growing in mixed 500-year-old stands, the very species that were blanketing British hills and replacing lowland broadleaves to a chorus of criticism from my colleagues in nature conservation. In the Pacific Northwest, these forests were revered. They were full of wildlife and carpeted with herbage, while natural rivers snaked through their bottom land, eroding the banks and depositing shoals on which fine cottonwood stands developed. Again, undisturbed though they had long been, they all contained a 450-year-old generation, indicating that they grew up after a region-wide, cataclysmic fire. Could they, perhaps, provide a vision of the forests we might develop in the equally oceanic western parts of Britain? Needless to say, a constructive approach to upland plantation forests in Britain was not in accordance with the conservation zeitgeist of the late 1980s.

By this time I had also seen supposedly virgin forests at Boatin in the Stara Planina, Bulgaria, the Bayerischerwald National Park in Bavaria and the La Tillaie reserve in Fontainebleau, France – in each case I emerged doubting the label 'virgin'. In Bulgaria, there was a suspicious lack of deadwood, and indeed it transpired that it was removed for forest health and firewood. In Fontainebleau, I was worried that the reserve was just one compartment in a managed forest, bounded by straight rides. Here, as elsewhere, I concluded that forests supposedly untouched by people were far from pristine; that, insofar as they were natural, they were far from stable; and that in many ways they were not completely distinguishable from managed forests. How should this influence our thinking on woodland nature conservation back home?

Eventually, it became possible to take a sabbatical, partly as a refresher, but mainly so that I could see more of natural forests. In 1989–90 I spent eighteen months away, first in Sweden, where a group of us spent a month surveying woods on the island of Lake Mälaren. These were former wood-meadows, but they had been left untouched for decades, and some had developed into stands that looked natural, complete with ancient limes and a variety of other species. Then, Harvard granted me a Bullard Fellowship that enabled me to spend ten months immersed in the American literature, learning from their forest ecologists and visiting old-growth forests throughout the eastern and western States. Returning home, a Leverhulme Fellowship enabled me to visit Bialoweiza Forest, a much wider range of Czechoslovak *prales* (their *Urwälder*) than I had seen in 1976, and equivalent forests in Slovenia, Croatia and Bosnia. Having survived the Russian invasion of Czechoslovakia in 1968, I found myself close to the opening shots of the Balkans wars of the 1990s: my train out of Croatia was held up for hours by a bomb threat and the car park at Ljubljana airport, where I had said my farewells, was strafed a few months later, killing four people.

Much of what I learned was eventually set down in my book *Natural Woodland* (1996). Virgin forest is best regarded as an over-literal translation of *Urwald* and related terms. Ecologists in mainland Europe have no illusions that such stands have always been pristine. When I said that Lanžhot, Krakovo and Prašnik Prales looked like former wood pastures, my hosts confirmed that that was so. I was even shown a twenty-year-old alder stand in an abandoned meander bed that was classified as a *prales*. Across the Atlantic, old growth means, in effect, untouched by Europeans: previous cultures had used and modified these stands a great deal. Like a now-ungrazed wood pasture in Britain, younger trees had filled all the gaps after European colonists had replaced Native Americans and their extensive forms of land use.

Eustace Jones' comparison with managed stands was abundantly justified. Take beech woods, the common types of *Urwald*. I saw beech 'coppice' high on the ridge between Slovakia, Poland and Belarus that was created by snow breakages. The group regeneration of mature beech woodland in the adjacent Stuzica Prales was like regeneration after small-group fellings in some Chiltern beech woods, and the structure of carefully managed selection forest in Switzerland was much like forests in the Balkans, such as Čorkova Uvala, Croatia, that I was assured were natural. Even-aged pine forest developing after fire in northern Sweden was almost as even-aged as pine plantations in the Highlands. So, too, the cottonwood (alias poplar) stands on the Queets valley floodplain in the Olympic National Park were just as even-aged as the modified poplar stands beside the Danube downstream of Vienna and indeed some poplar plantations in France. The shelterwood regeneration of pine in some New Forest enclosures matched the structure generated by large fires, which tend to kill the young trees but spare the old ones. And, as I have said, the restriction of oak to the oldest generation in most British former coppices is matched by a similar restriction in some American old-growth. Even the long-term surge of maples in the understorey in many old-growth stands looks uncannily like a sycamore invasion into a lowland English wood. And, the remarkable flattened and bleached forest around Mt St Helens, Washington, bore some resemblance to a felled, but not-yet-extracted conifer plantation in the British uplands.

In 1938, Eustace Jones was the only ecologist to react quickly and decisively enough to an invitation from the Forestry Commission to propose places on their estate where natural processes would be studied in perpetuity. After a wartime hiatus, Lady Park Wood became in 1944 the first and only research reserve to emerge from this initiative. Changes in the trees have been recorded ever since, so that now, seventy-two years later, we have a massive body of observations on what has happened and how the trees have responded. In some parts of the wood, where coppicing ceased in 1870 and only light thinning was undertaken in 1902 and the 1930s, we can even see the outcome of 145 years of almost-unfettered development. If there is any place where we can now witness British natural woodland, this is it.

It was the existence of the detailed record of trees that captured my interest. Reviewing the project in 1980, I could stand in the wood with the maps and measurements in my hand and see precisely how the wood had changed naturally in the previous thirty-five years. Sure, I had read many papers on natural-stand dynamics, but here was a real-life example where I could see the unpublishable detail. By continuing and expanding the record, I could appreciate the stand-changing events to which British woods are naturally subjected, notably the great drought of 1976; that within a century the volume of dead wood can climb to the same high values sustained in *Urwälder*; that woods become less stable as they become more natural; that natural disturbances may have lasting effects on the balance between species and the structure of the stands; that different stand structures can develop on shallow and deep soils, and on the steepest slopes; and that the supposedly natural soils of ancient woods have been artificially stabilised by centuries of coppicing. Eventually, we also discovered that, in some respects, the wood had become less diverse than it had been when it was managed: small-scale tree diversity, vascular plant diversity and butterfly diversity all declined, while probable compensating gains in fungal diversity and usage by bats were difficult to prove.

At the same time, events elsewhere have demonstrated that the woodland we see now is just one manifestation of what natural woodland might become on this site. If the great storms of 1987 and 1990 had taken a not-so-different course, Lady Park might have been blown flat, in which case it would now be, not the high forest of beech, ash, sessile oak, small-leaved lime and large-leaved lime that we see today, but a twenty-five-year-old thicket of mainly birch, sallow and ash. The drought killed vast numbers of thirty-year-old birch, but this could not have happened if the whole wood had been spared from wartime felling.

We have also learned that even non-intervention stands cannot be isolated from their surroundings. While drought is clearly natural, disturbances brought about by Dutch Elm Disease, grey squirrels, changes in the size of deer populations, nearby forestry operations and, shortly, Ash Disease are semi-natural: they may act naturally within the wood, but their arrival and the intensity of their impacts are determined by people. Put another way, however hard we try otherwise, the disturbance regimes which profoundly influence the structure of natural woods have become increasingly semi-natural. Absolute natural woodland is now unattainable.

Further, we find that we have to intervene to prevent naturalised introductions from entering the reserve and frustrating our aim at Lady Park, which has been to maintain what we assume is the pre-Neolithic, lime-dominated, mixed deciduous condition, or the 'original-natural' composition. The alternative would have been to allow naturalised species to colonise and thereby change stand composition to a 'future-natural' condition, which could well turn out to be an unprecedented mixture of western hemlock, western red cedar, sycamore and cherry laurel.

Lady Park had long been so heavily grazed by fallow deer that it was not regenerating, even in gaps, and the annual deer cull had steadfastly failed to lower the population. Debate on whether to fence the reserve was enlivened, if not challenged, by the promulgation of Frans Vera's view that large herbivores once maintained natural woodland as scrub, parkland and glades. Perhaps Lady Park would become more natural if we let the deer slowly convert it to wood pasture. Eventually, however, failing any prospect of re-introducing the large carnivores, we seized an opportunity to deer-fence the whole reserve, knowing that some deer would get in anyway. But the debate highlighted again the uncertainties of seeking natural woodland.

Natural woodland has become for me almost a mirage. I now see it as one end of a spectrum at the other end of which is, say, Lodgepole pine planted on drained mires in Caithness. But, just as the most forbiddingly artificial plantations have some wildlife, so natural woodland is never completely free of some human influence: the ends of the spectrum are unattainable reference points. Further, the nearest approaches to natural woodland take many forms and change, sometimes extremely rapidly. If natural woodland is adopted as a target in a nature reserve, we have to remember that there is no one composition and structure that is 'right' for that reserve. Nevertheless, the concept is useful in the sense that it gives a label to the natural end of a spectrum and defines a range of conditions that offer benefits, including a richness of some types of wildlife, reference points against which to assess our impacts on the environment, and the psychological benefits of wildness.

Mention of the benefits of relatively natural woodland brings us to the modern interest in re-wilding. The several schemes started and proposed mostly involve free-range grazing by semi-domestic stock and limited intervention in semi-domesticated woodland, all open to free-range public access. The questions are: how far dare we go, and what is the optimal degree of re-wilding? Re-introducing the lost fauna is logical and attractive, but discussions become febrile when they turn to wolves and bears. Protagonists should also be careful about allowing the woods complete freedom to develop naturally, for in the long run this will generate large, old and decrepit trees, the dangers of which have become increasingly obvious in Lady Park. Perhaps the New Forest is our best guide. Despite the press of residents and nearby urban sprawl, it is large and still wild enough for visitors who do not always recognise that it survives only with careful and largely unobtrusive management.

Woodcock

WICKEN FEN, CAMBRIDGESHIRE

Tim Dee

'He gives good wood'

My bag: thirty sightings in fifty years. One got up from my feet, one in off the sea, two above two motorways, one out of an island garden, and twenty-five separate craft on lonely summer orbits.

Lonely, it seems to me, is the woodcock's road. Its rode: a circuit required and undertaken in the sky after a life lived with all meaning on the ground. A figure followed in the air. A rode, up there, measured in falling light: love-flights or territorial anger-management, males mandated on summer dusks to perform slow-flapped crossings of the night's hearth in order to declare something to the earth. The rode: a word kept lonely for the bird and only for the bird: a dance otherwise no longer danced, some antic hay, and the dancer, dirty old man as reluctant old debutante and most probably a stranger to deodorant, like a badger forced to fly.

Such crepuscules witnessed twenty-five times. Or dreamt. At Wicken Fen along a line of trees at the edge of a reed-bed I have seen roding woodcocks during one dusk or more most springs for the last thirty years. They go round and come around again. Always old-timers, the children of the children of the children, and their rode is a ritual carried out with unthinking purpose. Every spring the woodcock takes the same path through the night air as it did last year or as its father did or as its father's father did. I have grown old under these flights.

Roding is more surprising for being so unlike a woodcock. The birds are earth's thing and hide in it until they are steered skywards by some seasonal worm in their heads towards the coming dark. Flying his *via dolorosa* the male repeats his course waiting for the shadows to endorse his downward return. Meanwhile he moves stiff with phantom gestures, ghosting a display, slowly and deliberately across the prickling low sky.

As he goes he speaks a kind of Linear A. 'To the present writer the sound seems to defy description' – Alfred Newton in his 1896 *Dictionary of Birds* – 'though some hearers have tried to syllable it.' Psst. Psst. And a piggy grunt. Tonight, above the fen, I felt I understood him. He was a businessman stepping awkwardly into a dance and not drunk enough to lose his inhibitions at the disco except for the accidental farts he let off as he went. My father in 1973. But the usher of dusk, I thought a woodcock once, or a shambling clerk with a heavy ledger making his way through pea-soup. You can look and have your visions, but everything summoned by the bird and its rode draws backwards and downwards and it is always old, gone, or going, and of dust or mud. Dreams and other night things shuffle the same tarot between them: bats, owls, goatsuckers, crakes mooncalfing, swifts lifting from the planet to sleep on the wing. But among them, darkly, the woodcock is dirtiest and oldest of all.

Woodcocks feed feelingly, seeking the movement of a worm through soil. They bend their beaks underground. And they live in this fashion, as night workers, something like a geophage or a turd-bird: long beak, lizard feet, streaked browns, and all their antiquity scored with brief squeals, snores, grunts, and methane blows. Old, far-off, unlovely things. And *only* old, it seems. The woodcock hides twice over from now in a double cloak of dark: the night's fleece and the soil's suit. I have never seen one on the ground yet there is no bird more grounded. It would prefer to do all of what it must do, to run its gamut, when close to the earth and at night. Only for minutes of its year will it show itself voluntarily upwards. And even then stiffness hobbles its dressage. Otherwise, it is a night-soil bird and it carries with it something of the dirt inside us all. It is old like shit is old. Or like a wormcast is old, being made from double-buried earth that has already moved through a body, from earth that has itself been buried within the earth.

At its home in the dirt the woodcock has long kept a wooden shield half-hidden in leaf-mould, its prize for the bird least resolved on modernity. At the tournament the jousting also-rans included corncrakes and stock doves and willow tits. But since the woodcock has for so long made his rounds and always looked the part, a macrocephalitic boy crowned Queen of the May every year, the half-masted bard permanently installed at the Eisteddfod, everyone else has given up imagining that they could ever win and it has been charitably decided the woodcock best keep the trophy for all time.

Is it any wonder that we struggle to configure them for today? What workshop could newfangle a woodcock? How would it look? A Kelmscott smock? A Leach pot splashed with telluric glaze? An artisan pie? Is there someone or something that will scan its barcode of browns and digitise a bird whose feet and beak are still stuck in the mud? Might you steampunk one from worms and wood-waste, a whittled stick for its hard bits, mud and leaf-rot for all else apart from a pair of ripe blackcurrants for eyes? 'Its plumage ... could not be briefly described' – Alfred Newton again. Take, if you will, instruction from the soil. Put out the light. Roll the bundle you have gathered beneath your blind fingers in the earth. Assemble the black back-story. Feel how you have made a snowman-bird in night-shades. And know, even as it shrugs into life, how ancient it is already, how the woodcock gathered words to it in the olden days and remains cock-shutt, trapped by them, like a dinosaur tarred and feathered in Latin. Learn how birds do not carry bags but nonetheless come with baggage.

I asked the British Trust for Ornithology, who promised to survey the bird for a year, to put me in touch with their woodcock-workers. Could I run a wire? Meanwhile, I was forced back to the old books. I stared at Thomas Bewick's *woodcut: a wod-wo* or cross-section of a dead tree with legs, eyes and a beak. I word-processed a feathered variorum. The brainless bird with the bending nose that lives by suction and winters on the moon. The 400 served at an archbishop's banquet in the autumn of 1465; the 470 drowned and picked up by a single fishing boat off Lowestoft in the autumn of 1928. Other stories of woodcocks ferrying or piloting tiny, enfeebled goldcrests across the North Sea. Wordsworth who, as a boy, stole trapped woodcocks from other hunters' 'springes'. Tolstoy giving lines to Levin's dog, Laska, in *Anna Karenina*, when the dog, Levin and Oblonsky go hunting snipe, and Levin blurts a question and receives news of Kitty, who he thought he had lost, at the very moment a woodcock flies towards them – 'What a time they have chosen to talk … And there it comes flying … Just so, here it is. They'll miss it …' And Gilbert White's notes on being sent a milk-white woodcock, plump and in good condition, and his worrying otherwise about worms – 'Many times have I had the curiosity to open the stomachs of woodcocks … but nothing ever occurred that helped to explain to me what their subsistence might be: all that I could ever find was a soft mucus, among which lay many pellucid small gravels.' Then I saw one flying over the M42, *towards* Birmingham in a way that made it inevitable that I would italicise its direction of travel. And I tried to remember how T.S. Eliot (was it?) said of *eldritch* that the word itself was what it meant, ghostly, weird, and out of date, and I thought the same of my *wode cucs*. I went on and ate one on toast in Lexington Street in Soho. Half of one: split in two, my friend Robin taking the right half, me the left. The sticks of the beak and the legs were like a scaffold lifting the flesh to our mouths. The toast was brown, the bird browner. It tasted so. There was bracken in it, and something of the soil around the leg of a mushroom. I set my heart on learning the sequence of the weave of dead browns that stripe a living woodcock's head, paler, darker, paler, darker, and I sought a paintbox of words for that earthenware that would do more than indicate one tone as a variant of another, but every time I started looking at the pictures (all I had to go on) something about the dome of the bird's head (a schoolteacher's head, or Philip Larkin's, or Moby Dick's) and its beaded eyes (those blackcurrants with a bit of stoat) fixed me in such a way that nothing new could go in beyond what was immediately yet bafflingly there. Thus I learned how camouflage messes with the mind as well as with the retina.

★

My new home county of Cambridgeshire has fewer woodcocks than almost anywhere else in Britain. In the fens a flight or two come in the winter on what Gilbert White called moonshiny nights from further east to crouch in ditches and drains. If the fields flood or freeze and if you are lucky you might see a woodcock trundle the wheeled wooden siege engine of itself out into the open. I never have. The bird really wants woods and wanting woods the county hardly holds more than a handful. Last winter my neighbour saw a pair hanging from the belt of a huntsman just outside our village. On a misty November morning, thirty years ago, I put one up from a tiny garden in the centre of Cambridge by opening my then front door. I remember the shock more than the bird, the fluster rather then the feathers, the rifled air.

At Wicken Fen, somewhere near the middle of the southern peat fens, there are trees growing out of the drying swamp and since the 1950s woodcocks have found them good enough to hide beneath. The fen is one of only two or three sites in the county where the birds now breed. Through the spring and early summer they rode above the trees and out over the reeds and sedge, their transects and commentaries cutting through the tossed rocket display-flights and the tribal drumming of snipe, the woodcocks' wetter cousins, equally surprised into the upper air but showing more buoyancy and spirit there.

Walking the flatness of the fen your thoughts travel further than your destination, just as the bird's rode turns upon itself in its journeys and knots the end of its flight to its beginning. Unravel that rope, then, feel fingered by the *scolopax*. The fens were forest once; the bog oaks that still occasionally rise like whale-backs through the wasting peat declare it. Read the woodcock as bog oak, a wet tree kept underground until it surfaces, old and intact though made of rot.

The great energy-gift of nature is that it arrives and is experienced in a permanent present. Sitting indoors we know autumn comes after summer and winter after that, but being in the autumn, indoors or out, we are always in the now. Its nowness and its thisness, its specifics, cap any sense we might have of the world ageing. It is the same for all the seasons and all their life. We die but the world renews. But we experience renewal as a permanently breaking wave. This follows this, now follows now. The flight of birds is an especially potent account of this: it is time suspended, hung in the air, and made visible. But every now and then we catch at something that carries more of the mulched life it is made from than the green life it is flying now. This tells us how much has happened before the moment of our meeting at the crossroad. And the brown woodcock, rotting forever, is a bird flying out of the past.

In the 1930s, the British Trust for Ornithology ran their first woodcock survey. A modernising zeal was abroad in British ornithology. The woodcock-surveyor-in-chief was W.B. Alexander. For £5, from a second-hand bookseller in Cambridge, I bought a bound reprint from the pages of *The Ibis* of Mr W.B.'s findings. A questionnaire had been devised and distributed seeking information on the birds' breeding, migration, and wintering status, on the 'chief enemies' of the woodcock and on noteworthy roding behaviour. It also queried the best of the woodcock myths – 'Have you ever seen parents carrying their young?'

Some birds are too known for their own good, too surrendered to the birdmen. On this list today we might put avocets, marsh harriers, and bitterns even. Special birds in Britain, birds you might go looking for purposefully, can seem owned, managed, and all but tethered in their reserves and guarded places. The woodcock is not. It is still more anomalous because it was once known better than it is now. Woodcocks are birds in retreat. They might be the last wild birds in Britain (perhaps with the red grouse) that are more familiar to those who want to kill them than to those who would love them if they could. All the records of American woodcock in Europe come from hunters' bags. No one who might love the living bird (and close relative of the European species) has seen them alive on our side of the Atlantic.

Imagine a sleeping woodcock lit by the sun on the floor of a wood. It is disappearing into the living light and the dead leaves in a drowsy doze. So cryptic is the incubating bird on the ground that its nest is hardly ever found. David Lack, the author of the first Cambridgeshire county avifauna published in 1934, knew of only one modern record. He describes its finding at Chippenham Fen with the social politesse of a man marking a dance card: 'The keeper, Mr Mercer, who knows the bird well, showed the nest to Mr Allen, the estate agent.' The finder, like a pointing dog, shows his master the bird, who authenticates the rustic's record. Via their lairds and lords, it is the keepers of Britain who supply Alexander with sightings of woodcocks carrying their young.

Alarmed adult birds are supposed to help their flightless downy chicks to safety by picking them up. As well as roding the skies in its limping sex dance, in extremis the woodcock will carry its own children aloft to escape the trappings of the down-there world that it otherwise loves. In this way the bird might show itself to us at the very moment it is fleeing from us. In this way the past and the present meet. Men on the ground have witnessed these flights, book writers are not so sure. Gilbert White, who was both, wondered if the injury-feigning distraction flight, where the bird depresses its tail between its legs, might make a woodcock look as if it were carrying the little bag of a baby. But Alexander reports on his reports: 'Keepers in Hampshire, Worcestershire, Glamorgan, Cheshire and Lancashire have sent particulars.' Some woodcocks dropped their young mid-air and these were watched falling or were found, lonely, on the ground, other chicks were seen lifted further by their parents: ninety-seven were held between the legs, or between the legs and breast; thirty-eight were carried in the adults' feet or claws; nineteen were partly supported by the adults' tail and thirteen partly supported by their bill; seven were seen riding on their parents' backs.

Taking Root

MOONSHINE WOOD, BATH

Piers Taylor

It is mid-May, and I am surrounded by iridescent lime-green beech trees, heavy after the rain with shimmering – even effervescent – wild garlic bursting into flower underneath. The trees, plants and sheer visceral actuality of the stuff around me – and its seasonal abundance – remind me that woodland is our natural state in the UK, and that everything here reverts to woodland if left alone. This makes it hard to remember that globally, we are living through the greatest rate of social change in the history of humankind, where, at an unprecedented rate, we are becoming urbanised, abandoning the countryside for the city, seemingly unconcerned with the bucolic.

Such is the dominance in the arts of the metropolitan, that for an early part of my working life I felt a kind of guilt that my own work was so focused around the rural – and questioned even the validity of making work that was concerned with matters that did not address the overriding architectural concern of our age: how to live sustainably in dense, urban environments. As an architect, I often find myself on the fringes as a reluctant agent of cultivation.

Although for periods of my life I have lived in the city, growing up, landscape and nature were woven into the fabric of my life, inseparable from the day-to-day – and this intrinsic and fundamental relationship with the natural world stemmed from my upbringing. As children, we grew up with a small woodland on my parents' land, and in our mid-teens, my brother and I would spend much of our time thinning the woodland, felling trees and splitting wood. In our later teens, my parents bought a remote Welsh house two miles from the nearest road and with no electricity, where we spent most weekends and much of our holidays.

My father would always know instinctively and precisely how the daylight patterns of sunrise and sunset differed from the day before and the day after. He'd be the first to spot the subtle changes in colour in winter as, way before there were any buds, branches would become slightly pinker in preparation for spring. He would always know when the first snowdrop appeared, and how it differed from all of the previous years, where the first nightingale would be singing, and how in spring the brightness of the green elm flowers differed from year to year.

My father was (is still, at eighty-seven) always an obsessive naturalist. He had grown up as part of a generation that made an exodus to the countryside during the Second World War, and as part of a family with a single working mother and four children, they ran semi-wild in the Cumbrian landscape to which they had escaped. As a teenager, he'd think nothing of cycling the full length of the country birdwatching, sleeping under hedges as he went. This desire to explore led him to become part of the British Antarctic Survey Expedition in the 1950s (immortalised in W. Ellery Anderson's 1957 book *Expedition South*), where, dressed in tweeds, he spent three years sledging with a pack of huskies, surveying glaciers and designing the first optimised dog diet.

Landscape, nature, the countryside – all of this, as a wider family, was part of who we were – but I'd never really made the connection with architecture until my first week of university. I'd been a wayward child and had been repeatedly expelled from school – being considered 'unteachable' (read energetic, curious and distrusting of authority) – and had wound up in Sydney (my mother's homeland) and entered university on the strength of a portfolio (I had no formal A-levels) to study design.

In the first semester, all design students were taught together alongside architecture students – and consequently shared lectures. The first lecture was by an architect – Glenn Murcutt – who gave me a road map for most things I've done in the twenty-five years since then, and I came out of the lecture reeling, my head spinning with the possibilities I'd been shown by Murcutt, and went immediately to the university office and transferred to architecture.

Murcutt talked of geomorphology, geology, hydrology, topography, flora, fauna and the imperatives of understanding weather patterns and climate as intrinsic to architecture. He talked of how farmers and rural dwellers knew characteristically how to orientate a building to keep the rain out, and how to maximise ventilation to moderate climate. He demonstrated how to use scarce resources effectively. He talked of the fragility of landscape and how to build without disturbing a site. And, he showed me how you could define an architecture by examining a place – critically, an architecture that was distinct from place, but was utterly defined by it.

Murcutt's work was also quintessentially and effortlessly Australian, and presented such an incredibly powerful narrative about place. His modest, frugal, delicate structures were so totally bound up in the specifics of site – and yet spoke of universal themes about climate, belonging and culture. Conventional modernism had banished regional concerns, but Murcutt showed how the particular, the regional and the local were themes that could have centre stage in a new architecture. As legendary British architect Alison Smithson said, 'Murcutt found an exquisite architectural poetry in sunlight and rainwater collection and harnessing the natural environment.'

Fast-forward ten years or so and back in the UK, I was practising in the south-west of the UK and teaching architecture at the universities of Bath and Cambridge. The divisive split in architecture between 'thinking' and 'making' was becoming apparent to me. What I hadn't understood at the time was how timber – or trees – would help me bridge the gap with my own practice and teaching work.

In 2002, I'd bought with my partner a 200-year-old tiny stone castellated building in the middle of a woodland (traditionally called Moonshine Wood) on a valley side five miles from Bath that was inaccessible except on foot via a 500-metre path. I'd fallen in love with the site when Sue was in hospital having our second child, and was gripped by a primeval need to be in that woodland. The old building was habitable (just) and came with about half an acre of land.

Immediately, woodland became a way of life for us – it completely surrounded us and the rhythms of the woodland became, to a degree, our own rhythms. The woodland rhythms were those of the bluebells, the goshawks, the fungi, the badgers, the wild garlic, the orchids and the gradual closing in of the woodland each May, which, living so immersed in the woods, threatened to envelop us completely. What we were so graphically exposed to was the way that woods work. Woodland ceased to become an abstract entity, and instead we saw – as Richard Mabey described in *Beechcombings* – 'symbiotic networks of carpenters, beetles, deer, land-thieves, lichens, pollards and toadstools' and, critically for us, our home.

A love affair with timber itself began when we built a new house on the site, next to the old stone folly. The house was conceived of as a structure that – using Murcutt's own phrase – touched the ground lightly. It was raised off the ground, leaving the highly shrinkable clay and the water table around the house undisturbed.

The house in Moonshine Wood was designed to maximise early morning and winter sunshine, and took its form from an analysis of wind and weather patterns in the valley. Having lived on the site for two years helped enormously. One of my teachers, Richard Leplastrier, described how he got to know a place, prior to designing:

> For many buildings I have camped on site, many days and nights, with a drawing board. It is the best way to feel a place out. The form of the terrain, its effect on climate, the path of animals and the sun. Where do you put your campfire?

Using Leplastrier's analogy, we felt ready to know where to put our campfire. The house had to be designed to be carried in components along the woodland track and so inevitably using timber made sense, as it is so ready a material that allows – encourages, even – on-site improvisation. Curiously, though, I'd had little experience of working with timber. It was a material that the architectural world had become suspicious of – given its relative unpredictability and its refusal to act submissively.

Working on my own house – physically constructing it myself – exposed to me my own naivety in terms of preconceptions about the idea and ideal of the drawing being a mechanism of control. In architecture, instead of drawing being a tool for thinking or discovery, it has become a 'command' whose purpose is to banish contingency, uncertainty, or on-site discovery.

Historically, it was drawing – as opposed to building – that affirmed the status and idea of the architect as an individual mostly concerned with immaterial ideas. The architect produces a set of instructions – drawings – which fixes outcomes and ensures that a singular vision is exactly realised by anonymous construction workers who are concerned with material (and subservient) ideas. Indeed, the prevailing condition in architecture is one where the hand – and judgment – of the maker is banished.

Building my house, and using timber, gave me a glimpse of the extraordinary richness of the material world, and how more than anything, I was missing out on a world of visceral and sensual feedback. Not just from the material itself, but also from the sheer potential and excitement that was exposed, once 'making' and the collaborative conversation with all involved in making was expanded to encompass designing, and the real time uncertainties were brought centre stage instead of being banished. Looking back now, the evolution of my way of thinking about making stemmed from this period of building my own house. It opened my eyes to a sense of what the process of construction and material exploration could offer.

What followed was an about turn in my method of teaching, and the same year that I built the house a group of us started something we called 'Studio in the Woods'. We didn't 'set it up' – I'm suspicious of things that are 'set up' or premeditated too much. Studio in the Woods just evolved out of friendships with other architects, and casual conversations about how it could be fun to organise a workshop with students in the woods around my house. Trusting we'd be agile enough to catch things as they happened, we just threw the cards up in the air to see where they landed.

Where they landed – or what came out of the first weekend of

Studio in the Woods ten years ago – set the pattern for subsequent years. We'd test ambitious ideas quickly, at 1:1, using timber felled and milled on site. For me, the giddy and heady freedom that came with being able to work directly, with materials to hand, and with the chaos and surprise of on-the-hoof, invention was amazing, and liberating.

This way of working allows the richness of discovery, conversation and contingency to be incorporated in real time into the architecture. The anthropologist Tim Ingold calls this 'a way of knowing from the inside – a correspondence between mindful attention and lively materials conducted by skilled hands at the [material's] edge.'

This is a way of working that I've been moving towards for fifteen years now. Underpinning this move towards a different way of working is a fascination with using full-scale making as a method of testing ideas, and using the process of consolidation or accumulation as a design tool. Rather than refining a prototype and then unveiling something perfectly formed and defect free, I am interested in allowing a prototype to be continually modified and adapted so that it is allowed to become the 'final' piece, with modifications and mistakes made manifest.

This thinking provided me with a way of working – one where new architectural forms and relationships could be discovered, rather than merely willed. One of the big questions many architects have is – if we don't merely want to use precedent or deterministic processes, how do we discover architectural form? For me, allowing construction, material exploration and full-scale making in real time went some way to answering this.

In addition, it provided a freedom from a world where only 'skilled' people could make things. The material relationships that are formed by alternatively-skilled (conventionally unskilled) people are often more interesting to me than those that are perfectly, and blindly, crafted. I'm a big fan of the 'bodged' joint where evidenced in it is the maker's journey of discovery. Of course the 'bodger', instead of being a cack-handed and clumsy labourer, was traditionally an itinerant worker who used green timber and found materials that led to unconventional timber joints and connections.

Architecture is, or was, full of concern with 'correct' detail and material expression. Mark E. Smith of The Fall called rock 'n' roll the 'mistreating of instruments to explore feelings'. In architecture, even at its most loose and improvised, there has conventionally been little room for mistreating of tools to explore ideas – or buildings made by 'amateurs' or 'bodgers' without due regard for technique. My buildings are often badly made in the received sense and often have little regard for technique. This doesn't mean I don't care about how they are made. On the contrary, I care enormously about how they are made and the elemental relationships between components, but these relationships differ from those held sacrosanct by high architecture.

What emerged was an invitation from the Architectural Association to get involved with establishing a new programme for students in a 400-acre woodland in rural Dorset, Hooke Park, which had been bequeathed to them by the furniture designer John Makepeace. He had established the woodland as a research facility which examined how low-grade forest thinnings could be used in construction. Several seminal structures had been built there, including Frei Otto's building that used young waste wood in the construction of a lightly skinned big workshop.

The Architectural Association's idea was to set up a new masters programme where, over sixteen months, architecture students would design and construct their own campus using timber sourced from Hooke Park. The first building that came out of the programme was a complex and unusual big-span workshop that used juvenile larch between twelve and eighteen years old. With the engineers Atelier One and carpenter extraordinaire Charley Brentnall, we developed a system of using standard 300 mm house-builders, fixings to connect the timbers – a low-tech, low-skill method that allowed students and volunteers to assemble the building alongside Brentnall's skilled team.

What followed was a series of buildings and structures forming the campus using almost exclusively materials sourced from the woodland at Hooke, with teams formed from a combination of those who were conventionally skilled alongside those who were unskilled in construction.

Inspired by an impromptu, ad hoc coming together of interesting people at Hooke Park and Studio in the Woods, I realised that there was no room in conventional practice for me. I resigned from the practice that I'd co-founded, and formed Invisible Studio to allow a method of practice that made more sense to me.

Invisible Studio took its template from Studio in the Woods where there was no institution, no one owned it, no organisation funded it, no one audited it, and it was beholden to no one. There was never any commitment to ever work together again. There was no hierarchy, no presumptions and certainly no succession planning. Studio in the Woods wasn't a charity, a company or a co-op – and nor is Invisible Studio. Like Studio in the Woods, Invisible Studio isn't a practice – it's a kind of anti-practice. It is just people, who work together with no labels, titles or expectation. It has no fixed workforce, no formal company – it is just a loose, unstructured collection of people who work together when the conditions are right, and don't when they aren't. The simple motivation is the creative work. Alongside this, the world of timber has become more and more fascinating to me. We've recently bought – with our neighbours – the 100-acre woodland around the house, which we manage alongside working and family life, and built our studio in it with timber from the woodland, using friends, neighbours and bodgers in its construction, and almost no drawings.

The studio was an exercise in harnessing the resourcefulness that many of my rural neighbours have. Few had any formal construction knowledge, and certainly none had ever built a building before. Free from the baggage of 'correct' ways of doing things, they all brought an extraordinary sensibility and energy to the project. The building was an exercise in frugality that is typical of many traditional rural buildings – we simply used local materials and resources to shape the project. In an era where most architecture is defined by its extravagance, the studio was an attempt to do the most with the least.

Working in this vein, we have now just finished delivering two buildings for Westonbirt, the National Arboretum, that forms their Tree Management Centre using a similar method, but with a completely different scale. The buildings are the first that the arboretum have built using their own timber – and use 20-metre-long hand-hewn Corsican pine in complete lengths, as well as oak, spruce, larch and Douglas fir. Many volunteers have worked on the project alongside skilled carpenters, and the Carpenter's Fellowship have used the buildings as vehicles for up-skilling their trainees.

Living in a woodland, working with timber in this manner and embracing contingency, chance and the glorious properties of green timber felled on site as part of a wider management plan meant that architecture, for me, has shifted immeasurably away from the idea of a lone designer, working on a static object of singular, finite and shallow beauty. Design has become a forum that allows the unexpected to emerge. The architectural academic Jeremy Till, who is highly critical of much contemporary practice, describes this way of working as a 'crucible for exchange between a mix of professionals, amateurs, dreamers and pragmatists', with the architect an 'open-minded listener and fleet-footed interpreter, collaborating in the realisation of other people's unpolished visions.' For me now, it is among these amateurs, dreamers, pragmatists, bodgers and – perhaps most importantly, trees – that I thrive, in the knowledge that all of my own work will, one day, revert to the woodland matter from where it came.

Discovering the Spinney

SPINNEY WOOD, CAMBRIDGESHIRE

Deb Wilenski

It is early morning in the second week of June. In the middle of the deep, green woods, something is missing. The lake with its crocodiles, monsters, battles and secret passageways, has disappeared.

The water level rises and falls in the Spinney right through the year. Each week I go to check the woods before we come in with the teachers and children, and it's often a time of surprises. Once a fox held my gaze: still, blatant, brave. Often there is riotous birdsong that quietens when the children arrive.

But the lake has never been lost before.

I climb over the rope barrier to check the water has really gone and to see how muddy it is. I walk in a new and weird world: white bones of wood, unreadable ground. When was the lake last empty? Why does walking on ground once covered by water feel so uncanny? This word, 'uncanny', is used by Seamus Heaney in his translation of *Beowulf*, a text the older children brought into the woods. It was perfect for describing the mere in the 'frost-stiffened woods', and is perfect now for the missing water.

This is our first week working with Jackie Kay, and with what turns out to be characteristic strength and sensitivity she asks the seven and eight-year-olds where the water has gone, and to think about lost things and secrets. They rush to enter the new world of the dry lake, and some children spend most of the morning there. The mud monster's city expands. There are bubble monsters in the mud that make it stink, and treasures that rise to the surface; an old bicycle, a bottle with potion inside, a white staff, a huge piece of bark.

When we stop for a drink Jackie asks the children to write down three things that were lost in the woods and three things that were found. They place their words in the old collecting cabinet.

We first explored this small patch of woodland with children from The Spinney Primary School in January 2014. Before then, for more than ten years, the Spinney had been fenced off and behind the fence a tangled world was growing. Our first discussions with head teacher Rachel Snape and county grounds manager Richard Rice were about how 'wild' to keep the space. Should we clear pathways to make access easier? Would this affect the feeling of adventure and visual complexity? Should we introduce new structures – a bridge, a shelter? Who should begin the exploration?

Cambridge Curiosity and Imagination (CCI), a small creative organisation, has been working in rough and ready wildness for many years. We encouraged the school to remove only deadwood overhead, and enough brambles to clear a couple of paths. And we decided to let the children tell us whether other changes were necessary, by listening carefully to their languages of exploration – where they went, what they said, what they did, what they imagined.

In spring 2014, CCI invited the youngest children in the school to discover the Spinney. We knew from previous work that four and five-year olds are inexhaustible explorers of the wild and we wanted to call into question how a place becomes known. Most descriptions, maps and guides are made by adults; what if children's own voices were given more weight? What if the voices we heard first were the youngest ones, those least associated with 'authority'?

The Spinney sits right on the boundary of the school playing field, but the children recognised its 'otherness' from the beginning. Their list of animals that might be found in the woods was brilliant, a combination of everyday detail and adventurous fantasy: a giant lizard, a dinosaur, insects, rabbits, ants, a chameleon, a wild lion, an owl, a fox, crocodiles, a hedgehog in its house.

And just moments into our first visit, Adam looked up at one of the tall trees growing on the other side of the ditch and said: 'This tree is bigger than Earth!'

We were already in a land where impossible things might be true. It was immediately clear that the tangled qualities of the woods, exactly the parts we didn't cut back, were what fascinated the children. Most of my photographs from this first morning show children from the back, children disappearing into the undergrowth, children sinking into mud. They are literally immersed in the woods, searching for its hidden places as well as its obvious invitations. And they are imaginatively immersed; in the lake tracking crocodiles and sharks, looking into burrows for snakes, finding and occupying rockets and dungeons.

The decision to take children into woodland can have many motivations. Fresh air, physical activity, a connection with nature are clear benefits. Less often quoted as a reason for leaving the classroom is the imaginative ownership an unknown wild place can offer. But it is exactly this playful exploration of real and fantastical worlds in the wild that forms the strongest bonds between children and places. Freedom to explore the physical woodland is nothing without the freedom to make meaning from those explorations.

And so although I could tell you of the many actual places the children discovered – the huge muddy puddle, the fallen tree, the dry ditch, the paths through the nettles – I'm not going to. Instead we will stay in one place, by the lake, where real and imagined worlds slide around each other, where Pavel has just spotted another crocodile nose, and Andrei shouts: 'I can feel it with my stick, it just bit my stick!'

It's surprising to find water in any woodland in Cambridge, and the lake always draws children to it. It's a place where water, mud, roots and trees, the smell at certain times of year, are all very real. But the water's surface suggests something else; a strange reflected world where tree tops lie on the water and birds fly low across the land.

And beneath the shifting surface? Another world, a hundred

other possible worlds? Several weeks before we begin our project the older children come into the woods with their teacher Emily Garrill and read parts of *Beowulf*, including the underwater battle between Beowulf and Grendel's monstrous mother. The resemblance between the mere in this ancient poem, and the Spinney lake where a deer skull has been found, is eerily close. Perhaps the lake has always been here. Perhaps it has been rising and falling for a thousand years:

A few miles from here
a frost-stiffened wood waits and keeps watch
above a mere; the overhanging bank
is a maze of tree-roots mirrored in its surface.
At night there, something uncanny happens:
the water burns. And the mere bottom
has never been sounded by the sons of men.
On its bank, the heather-stepper halts:
the hart in flight from pursuing hounds
will turn to face them with firm-set horns
and die in the wood rather than dive
beneath its surface ...

translated by SEAMUS HEANEY

Back in the classroom after their first morning in the woods, we invite the older children to map the Spinney. We look at the work of sixteenth and seventeenth-century cartographers, at the relationship between mapped fact and fiction; we explore monsters and their place in the wild unknown, and we use Adam's words, 'This tree is bigger than Earth', as an invitation to play with scale.

All the children know precisely what they want to map. A huge collaborative drawing then extends across the floor, with landmarks, monsters and maps inside monsters. On a smaller piece of paper Michael draws a schematic plan of the Spinney, labelling the *grass, school meadow, neighbours, log pile, log circle* and *entrance*. You could navigate perfectly with it. Viren also includes the neighbouring houses, but they are about to be eaten by a massive underground snake.

Tavi begins his map by drawing the lake in bright blue on black paper, and then I watch something extraordinary happen. From the lake's deepest level a line extends, a walkway that turns into a tunnel, a

tunnel that leads to steps, then more walkways, more levels, and finally
a chamber of enormous spikes where a lone hero battles a monster. It's
extraordinary because in one map I read the old story of *Beowulf,* the
contemporary graphics of computer games, and every classic story in-
between of worlds within worlds.

Tavi's map of the world under the lake, and other maps from his
classmates, are offered to the younger children the following day in
the woods. Adam, Layl, Billy and Pavel triumphantly carry Tavi's map
straight to the farthest corner of the lake. Part of the rope barrier has
blown over in the wind – could this be the way down? Adam moves
a fallen tree trunk to see if it's hiding an entrance to the underworld.
Billy stands looking at the lake and says: 'But how can we get really
under the water? I really want to go down under the water.'
    I look at the leaning tree whose roots must be buried in the bottom
of the lake. I see it as if for the first time. I imagine murky water
swirling round its base, weeds caught in the mass of roots, maybe a
secret way through.
    In the afternoon, Tavi's map inspires more underground drawings
in the younger children's classroom. Thomas draws 'the ancient city of
the bats' deep under the earth's surface. Roland's underground land
has passageways and rooms to which there are secret entry codes. New
ideas are born, a Spinney mythology grows about the woods at night
and the unseen lands beneath our feet.

Five weeks into the project, before Jackie Kay comes to join the
children, there are already many voices in the Spinney. As Katie writes
later 'the green heart of the woods is bubbling'. So let's stand for a
little by the lake before it disappears, and listen ...
    There are the Old English voices telling the story of Beowulf, and
the voice of Seamus Heaney translating their words a thousand years
later; there are the voices of cartographers from centuries ago, and the
voices of the Spinney children as they make new maps; there is Adam
saying 'This tree is bigger than Earth', opening a world of enormous
possibility; there are the voices of the evil emperor, the mud monster,

the guards, the cook, the queen running by the lake refusing to get married; there are the voices of teachers and parents remembering when they used to play like this, and realising how deep such play goes; there are the voices of all the creatures the four and five-year olds imagined a year ago, even the giant lizard.

And then there are moments when thirty children in the Spinney fall silent, and there's only the sound of trees, water, sky and earth. As Kirsten tells Jackie Kay: 'I love the wild woods. It makes its own decorations in its own mind.'

In fact Jackie's voice is already in the woods too. Halfway through our first visit with the younger children I offer words and phrases from her poem 'The World of Trees', face down on pieces of torn paper. The children spend a long time finding just the right place for Jackie's words to live in their Spinney. Dreaming appears in a tangle of creepers. 'You go inside a dream there,' Sofia explains. 'Waiting for another tree lies patiently among old roots. Bony fingers sits provocatively by a pile of pale thin sticks.'

The children from the older class who find the words the next day are fascinated: 'It could be clues ... it might be a puzzle ... Maybe it's someone's dream and they left it in the woods'. Maybe it's a poem of a dream of the woods.

When Jackie begins to work with the children she is sometimes very direct: 'Think about what the tree feels like, what does it remind you of? What does it look like?' Sometimes she is playful and the children laugh uncontrollably, as the boundary disappears between invention and truth in stories of her own childhood. She plays with accents, picks up phrases from the children, reads the words they have left in the cabinet: 'A nest of nettles' from Yijin, 'The long piece of bark was treeless' from Tavi. Some appear later in her own poems, an exchange of words received and given back:

> Drink the magic potion
> And dream of what was lost

> Like the trees dream of saps and rings
> And nettles dream of nests

Dream of what became ash
Our loved ones, and what was returned to earth

Like the trees dream of saps and rings
And nettles dream of nests …
from 'SAPS AND RINGS AND THINGS TO SAY IN THE FOREST'

The lost lake is a fantastic gift on this first day with Jackie. It means the children are deeply immersed in the substance of the woods, and in important ideas of time and change, secrets and revelations. When Jackie asks the children to write down three things that were lost and three things that were found, their responses bring tangible and metaphorical worlds together:

Pulled out nettles have lost their sting. New-born trees have found their family of leaves. (GABE, AGED EIGHT)

When a plant dies it loses its life. When a plant lives it finds a new birth. (MICAH, AGED SEVEN)

A tree loses its leaves, roots and shape. (KIRSTEN, AGED SEVEN)

It finds its strength, imagination and style. (SUMMER, AGED SEVEN)

In the afternoon the children work ideas of lost and found into longer poems. Micah's cycles of life and death, as well as his morning excavations in the dry lake bed, become part of his poem 'The Lost Silver':

Beneath the fallen tree
Struck by lightning
There lies something silver
It was lost by me and found by me
Then its power turns the woods into winter
With deep white snow
As the swallow calls its final call
The silver returns to its place.

Jackie talks to the children about writing and drafts, and encourages them to make changes to their work if they want to. Words are important, and finding the right words matters, but at the same time, words are there to be played with. If a lake can come and go, then words can too. Jackie writes later in the foreword to the project publication:

> We made poems by mixing ingredients … Poems arrived out of spells … It was wonderful watching the poems being printed in the creative landscape of the woods and just as wonderful to watch them vanish with disappearing ink.

Things of importance can be said in the forest. Things can be said for pure riotous fun. You can borrow words someone else has used and make them your own. You can offer words to be taken in turn. Jackie invites the younger class to experiment with many voices, to write poems that bring words together from themselves, their friends, the animals in the woods, themselves when they are older. I wonder how these five and six-year-olds will imagine old age and am amazed:

> My tree would say he is afraid
> My tree is afraid because of the wind
> I would say to my tree, I am cold
> Animal is howling
> If I was an old lady I would say to this tree:
> 'Look how lovely this tree is
> It's lovely because of the bright leaves.'
>
> *by* ELIA, AGED SIX

The poems Jackie writes are full of voices too. An old woman remembers the woods and the children in 'Trunk'; 'Two Stanzas for the Spinney' finds in children's fantasy play timeless ideas of fate, change, good and ill; 'The Y Valley' is full of words the children call out in the woods when Jackie asks for names of places and things to take to new lands.

And this is what I come to understand by exchange: that it's not a 'my turn your turn' kind of conversation, but a desire to listen to each other's language, to find points of recognition and surprise, to explore words like we explore the wild, with daring adventure and quietness, alone and together. It's a balancing act, to find a clear voice of your own, and be in connection with other voices around you.

At the end of the project we invite illustrator Elena Arévalo Melville to make a new kind of map of the Spinney from our project documentation. It will have points of orientation, and fantastical references, words and images from the children, lines from Jackie's new poems. Elena also spends time in the woods exploring and sketching, and her final design has over fifty technical layers that catch perfectly the multiple voices in the Spinney.

When we design our anthology of poems and illustrations, Elena works with the children's intricate drawings of trees and monsters alongside her own fluid sketches in ink, and with paths leading off the page there are invitations for other voices to journey into and out of the Spinney.

All of the children's trees in the book are drawn from memory. I am moved by the detail and intimate knowledge each carries; how you can hear the voice of the trees, the bark, the leaves, even in the midst of the children's fast and dramatic play, as kingdoms fall in the woods and monsters rise from mud. And how in the middle of it all sits the lake. A quiet pool, a murky underworld, a reality and an illusion, rising and falling. A gathering of wild voices.

Rackham's Treasure

MERTHEN WOOD, CORNWALL

Philip Marsden

M erthen Woods are a remote strip of densely-packed trees that stretch for a mile or so along the northern slopes of Cornwall's Helford estuary. The woods are not very large and the trees are not very tall – but they represent one of the most remarkable pieces of woodland anywhere in the country.

Oak woods rarely meet the sea as they do here: at high-water springs, the crenellated lower leaves can be glimpsed, like strange fish, beneath as much as two feet of water. The woods are almost entirely sessile oak (*Quercus petraea*, sometimes known as the Cornish oak) rather than the pedunculate or English oak (*Quercus robur*). They are classified as 'temperate rainforest' for in the mild air the bark's fissures provide habitat for bryophytes, lichens and polypody fern (the existence of such epiphytes is what defines rainforest). But what really distinguishes Merthen Woods is their purity. Hidden away in private ownership for generations, they retain much of the complex ecology and diversity of a traditional coppice wood – intact soil structure, ground flora and understorey – that in most other coppice woods have been corrupted by the seed-bringing boots of visitors, or by intrusive planting and the good intentions of recent management. Merthen Woods' value lies in their very neglect and isolation. Oliver Rackham reckoned that they must be one of the least-visited woods in England.

Coppicing as a practice is thought to go back to the Neolithic. Where woods were not burned and cleared, they remained a sustainable source of fuel and timber. Each year, in rotation, a block was felled to leave stumps or 'stools' which would then readily sprout stems. After a couple of decades those stems would warrant felling again, and so on. In this way, the ground was periodically exposed to sunlight to allow a diverse flora, and the emergence of new trees. With no wildwood left in the country, old coppice woods like Merthen are precious examples of early woodland, of how man and trees can benefit each other.

The Helford River constituted one of Oliver Rackham's favourite spots in the world, 'one of the very few places where ancient woodland meets the sea'. He found its various shoreside woods 'astonishing … a place of wonder and delight'. In 1987, he wrote *The Helford River Woods*, a report on their history, ecology, and conservation. The report was commissioned by the local district council and remains little read; I dug out the only copy in the store of the Cornwall County Library – a photocopied typescript. Rackham was a botanist who never allowed science to get in the way of his sense of reverence, and the report begins with a lyrical evocation:

> To the few people who set foot in the woods are revealed hillsides of bluebells, jungles of holly, sudden headlong ravines, and bottomless swamps of golden saxifrage. Polypody fern grows far overhead in the crowns of giant corkscrew oaks 90 feet high. A few yards away … the oaks are so dwarf that a tall man looks out over their tops.

The body of the work is signature Rackham – that blend of archival historical research and botanical expertise that has so enriched our understanding of the natural landscape. The report came just a year after his pioneering *The History of the Countryside* and constitutes a diverse intellectual habitat of its own. The discussion of Anglo-Saxon charters fuses into Middle Cornish toponymy, the medieval practice of pannage, the exact size of a Winchester quart and the formation of podzols.

What Kerrier District Council made of it all is not clear. The conservation recommendations revolve principally around Rackham's oft-repeated policy of *laissez-faire*: 'doing nothing has much to be said for it. Those owners who leave their woods alone should not be reproached nor urged to do something "positive".' By 'positive' he meant planting – and planting trees, for Rackham, was the greatest of sylvan sins. It encourages the traffic of root-stock and the consequent export of disease. It is intrusive – non-native trees often spread and out-compete locals. And it ignores the basic truth of arboreal ecology: woodlands – even managed or coppice woodlands – are not just groups of trees but a long-established, highly-evolved balance of soils, fungi, flora, invertebrates and fauna. The sorry state of our woodlands – lacking diversity, more and more prone to disease – might have been avoided if our policymakers had listened to Rackham several decades ago.

I live with my family on the tidal inland reaches of the Fal, just ten miles by sea from the Helford River. Similar in topography to the Helford, the upper reaches of the Fal is one of the few other places where oak woods meet the tide. Immediately around us are woods that are largely put over to the industrial rearing and slaughter of pheasants. Beyond them are pockets of woodland that are at least as unvisited as Merthen, if less studied.

A couple of years ago, we put part of our single, creekside field into a Forestry Commission Woodland Creation Scheme. Obliged to follow the Commission's rules, we planted 1,500 broadleaved trees, but also won a concession to set aside over half the ground – about three acres – as more Rackham-friendly 'natural regeneration' (already here I have deer-guarded about 300 sessile-oak seedlings that have sprung out of the grass).

The whole exercise has made me much more aware of the intricacy of woodland. I have also found that tending trees, keeping the grass at bay by mulch-matting, bark-mulching and hand-weeding each tree, spending hours in the presence of trees, is a wonderful thing – and the perfect antidote to long mornings sitting at a desk, trying to write. Another is a boat. Last summer I bought an old wooden boat whose oak frames give me a frisson of connectivity when I look down into the bilges and see them converging in an ogee at the keel, or back among the seedlings I gently press down the mulch mats around their matchstick stalks.

One afternoon in late September, with Rackham's report on board, I sailed over to the Helford. I wanted to see what had happened to Merthen Woods in the three decades since he examined them. I spent the night moored in the pool known as Abraham's Bosom and in the morning rowed up-river.

There was little other activity on the water that morning; I put up a curlew from the shore and watched it bank away, crying its lonely cry and following its scimitar beak away downstream.

The estuary is a couple of hundred yards wide at this point, and soon divides into two at Groyne Point, with the start of Merthen Woods covering the wedge of land between the creeks. Paddling in close, I looked for somewhere to land. The low cliff was a continuous overhang of soil and dense roots and boughs, and below that a layer of shaley rock that shelved into the water. Nowhere to leave a dinghy, nor reach the woods above. I rowed back to the point, and found a little strip of shingle beneath the trees.

Jumping ashore, I hauled up the boat. I clipped the painter to a low branch. The oaks here grow out over the water, with their lower branches *below* the cliff-gripping roots. Searching for a way up, I was pulled up short by an extraordinary sight. Resting on the rocks was what looked like an outsize oak burr. About a metre in diameter, it had rising from it a tangle of more than half-a-dozen limbs. The whole thing looked like an upside-down octopus. I stood there for some moments trying to work out what had happened. Three of the limbs were branches, woody tentacles that tapered out towards the low-down canopy. The others grew into the cliffs; they had started life as roots, pressing through the eternal darkness of the soil. But the cliff had collapsed, exposing them not just to the light but, twice a day, to the sea. They had shed their capillaries, grown bark and become branches. But what about this burr-like hub? What was it exactly?

Animated by the strangeness of it all, I scrambled up a series of boughs and into the wood proper. Ahead was a pathless wall of plant life. A calf-high tangle of bilberry, heather and fern gave way to an understorey of holly and honeysuckle. The oaks themselves were short and twisted. Straight lines appeared anathema. Every section of new branch looked as though as it had been made in reaction to the last. I recalled the reports of shipwrights coming into the Helford Woods with set-squares: to achieve the curves of a ship's hull, timbers usually need to be steam-bent, but here was a source of naturally-curved timber that would provide the knees and grown-oak frames for the best sea-going craft.

Cobwebs brushed at my face. Nobody had been here for months, for years. I stood there unable to see my feet, listening. A fencepost hammering in the distance, a faint herring gull from downstream – but from inside the wood, nothing. All around me was growth and movement, cells dividing, microbes multiplying, moisture being sucked up stems, sugars flowing down, mycorrhizae advancing, carapaces wriggling through leaf-litter. Yet none could I see or hear. The wood was doing its woody thing all around me, but invisibly.

I felt suddenly an imposter, a barbarous heathen who'd barged into this arboreal sanctum. Retreating the few yards to the cliff, I climbed down and rowed away.

It was winter before I returned. I took the land route, and drove down from the village of Constantine.

Above Merthen Woods stands Merthen Manor, a sixteenth-century house with small windows and a dipping and curving scantle roof. In a nearby field are the earthworks of an Iron Age fort. The earliest known spelling of Merthen is 'Meredin' where '-din' is the Cornish for 'fort' (the 'mere-' possibly meaning 'great'). The entire site, down half a mile of private road, is rich with a sense of timelessness.

Getting out of the car I glimpsed, some three miles to the east, the blue of the open water and the tiny gunsight-V at the mouth of the Helford. It is easy to understand Merthen's early significance. For hundreds of years – particularly during the pre-Roman and post-Roman periods – the Atlantic seaboard was a busy conduit of power, trade and ideas. The archaeologist Barry Cunliffe speaks of the early Christian centuries and the 'vital importance of the Atlantic seaways to the development of Europe'. Control of estuaries like the Fal and the Helford, gateways to a source of alluvial tin, provided considerable leverage. The records of ownership bear it out: Merthen first appears as the property of Saxon kings, probably appropriated from earlier Cornish kings. Edward the Confessor owned it. William the Conqueror owned it. In the thirteenth century, it was in the hands of Richard, Earl of Cornwall, powerful brother of Henry III who swapped it for the bleak site of Tintagel (hugely significant since Geoffrey of Monmouth identified it as the site of King Arthur's conception). Ancient Merthen was the trade-off.

In the converted piggery of Merthen Manor now lives Paul Knight, a tree manager at Cornwall Council. His day job involves maintaining the county's park and street-side trees (a lot of his time is currently spent trying to purge public woodlands of Sudden Oak Death). But clearly he was delighted to be able to live within walking distance of such a place as Merthen Woods. As we strode down through stubbly fields towards the trees, he spoke of the value of such wildwood, its local rarities like the service tree and he recalled with some longing the springtime bloom of bluebells, dog's mercury and golden saxifrage. From this side, the woods present a very different face to that at Groyne Point where I'd landed months earlier. A perimeter of tall beeches, planted some 200 years ago, give way to the shadowy interior of more familiar woodland. A 60-foot sycamore, ivy-trunked and robust, swayed its leafless crown far above us. The floor underfoot was soft with leaf-mould, with none of the thick cover that helps prevent access to the other end of the wood. Single brambles arced out of the ground and there were a few scattered holly and wiry saplings – but little else.

Paul stopped beside one of the saplings. It was a beech, with last year's leaves still on it. 'This is the problem. Beech and sycamore, both brought in from elsewhere. When they're mature, their canopy is much denser than oak. This one will eventually shade out anything trying to grow underneath it.'

No coppicing has taken place here for half a century and a number of oaks lay on the ground, like the toppled warriors from some ancient battle. We reached one still standing, with its six or so coppice stems each 50 feet high. The circumference we measured at 15 feet – several centuries old. I bent in close and smelt its pore-filled smell and saw a tiny trickle of water seeping down through the stool's mossy crevices. It looked like the waterfall in a micro-jungle.

Over a small stream, the path pushed out towards the estuary. The soil thinned and the trees reverted to sessile oak. Salt-stunted at about 20 or 30 feet, they were actually a similar age to the giant we'd just seen. Beneath them grew holly and heather, bilberry, alder buckthorn and honeysuckle. There was bramble too and madder and bracken and it gave the sense that nothing was about to take over, nothing was rampant, that each species had found its space, fitted to the slot of light and soil it occupied.

But then we spotted something else – the shrivelled rust-red leaves of young beech trees. None was yet higher than the oak. At fifteen or twenty years old, they would not have been here when Rackham wrote his report. The more we looked the more we saw. There was something horribly confident and enticing about them, spreading into that rare and isolated place like the pioneering outlets of a fast-food chain.

'Are the woods destroying themselves or falling to pieces through neglect?' For all his gloomy pronouncements elsewhere about disease, Oliver Rackham's response to his own question in the Helford River report was upbeat:

> I have searched for evidence that they are, and can find none …
> What happens in the long run cannot be predicted with certainty,
> because no woods have remained unmanaged for more than 200
> years. An informed guess is that nothing much will change until
> at least the twenty-second century.

No. It appears to be happening now, in just three decades. Project the beech growth another thirty years and these arm-thick trunks will be mature trees. They will have broken through the low canopy to spread their leafy parasols out over the oak. Then for the old coppice trees the summer light will grow dimmer year by year; they will start to struggle, while at their base the under-shrubs and flora will thin and any young oaks that do appear, pressing up through the soil as a two-leaf shoot, will not live long in the shadows. As one of the preserved ancient woodlands in the country, Merthen will cease to exist.

A narrow path led on towards the west. We followed it single-file, in silence. Through a grille of bare branches the sun was sliding into a cloud-bank that sat heavy on the horizon; below us the waters of the estuary were already black. From across the creek came the sound of the wind rising in the trees – a chill, distant sound that made me think of a hundred other wintery dusks.

We came to a hut. It was boarded up now, but in the summer the woods' owners use it to camp in. The hut stood on a small jut of land and just beyond it, the slopes faced west. They dropped steeply to the cliff. The bare oaks showed bone-white in the last of the sun, rising from a bed of orange fern.

The trees here were markedly squatter, more marginal. A mile or so up-river the Helford estuary narrowed to a stream – but just a few miles beyond that was the Lizard's Atlantic coast. When the storm-swells broke there, they filled the air with spray which was driven inland on the back of the gales to nip out any west-facing buds. That is why the hedges of coastal Cornwall so often appear to be leaning away from the wind, and why here the shape of the trees follows the steep angle of the slope, why they look like the bristles of a well-used brush.

Among the weathered oak was a young beech. Its bole, too, was scarred and knobbly, and its canopy had fused in at the same angle of the oak. There was something furtive about its disguise, something spy-like and threatening.

Woodlands are a dynamic system, but one whose pace of change should be measured in centuries. Like landscape, they are in a state of constant flux – advance and retreat, advance, retreat – but much too slow for our own impatient vision to comprehend. We see trees take root, grow and die. In recent centuries, we have used that process to our advantage, planting trees where we want them, felling them where we do not.

It is this misunderstanding that Oliver Rackham made his mission to correct. Trees are not a crop, grown from seed and cut down when required. 'Trees are wildlife just as deer and primrose are wildlife.' During his career he witnessed the spread of plantations and the growth of a forestry industry whose aim was to maximise timber yields, which trumpeted its success in learning to plant boggy moorland with conifers. Rackham knew the damage that was being done – but without evidence nobody listened. Now we have it in spades – Horsechestnut Bleed, Box Blight, Alder Disease, Acute Oak Decline, Sudden Oak Death, Ash Disease. Even when there is no disease there is the extinction of ancient woodland by dominant species.

In 2006, introducing his *Woodlands*, Rackham outlined the simple principle behind effective woodland management:

> It does not pretend that trees are merely part of the theatre of landscape ... It deals with trees as actors in the play, and with the mulitiple interactions between trees and the environment, trees and other trees, trees and other plants, trees and fungi, trees and animals, and trees and people.

Merthen Woods are one place these 'multiple interactions' can still be seen, just. From the weevil *Achonidium unguiculare* found nowhere else in the UK, to the rare slug *Limax cinereoniger*, from the scarce holly blue butterfly and wild service tree and the areas of hazel wood deemed as examples of pre-Neolithic Cornish wildwood, to the ancient coppice stools, Merthen is a living museum.

It was now dark in the woods. Overhead, the branches were silhouetted against a deep-blue night sky. In places, polypody ferns could be seen marching up the side of an oak trunk. Paul said he came out here sometimes, on nights like this, or when it was cold and windless. 'The astonishing thing then is the absolute quiet – the whole wood is absolutely still.'

We came again to the first piece of woodland we saw, with its spreading beech and sycamore. 'It wouldn't take much to stop them. You wouldn't need to fell them, just ring-bark the larger ones. You could then prune out the saplings – even slowly start the oak coppice again.'

Still Lives

BERKHAMSTED COMMON, HERTFORDSHIRE

Richard Mabey

I keep it on my desk as a memento of where I grew up, and as a constant warning against hubris. A turner had cut a section from a beech trunk and opened it up into a bowl, and in the process unwittingly created a frozen picture, a still-life, of a woodland ecosystem. It isn't that the bowl itself is anything less than a striking cultural object. It's massy, about 18 inches across and finished with the lustre of silk. A slight cracking in the wood has been tracked with a gilt inlay. But the form of the bowl is overshadowed by what is happening in the wood. Even the hollow that defines its function seems part of another narrative, its gently curving surfaces acting like a lens on the real business of this piece. Running across the pale surface of the beech and diving into the pit is an extraordinary lacework of dark lines. It has the look of a contour map of rocky terrain, or maybe an exercise in woody tie-dye. The lines meander, fork, run close together for a few inches. They outline ridges and plateaux and small, abrupt bluffs.

The patterning is called spalting, and is caused by what foresters would call a disease. The organism responsible, the fungus *Ustulina deasta*, is a serious rotter, of beech especially. But it's an impeccably native species with its own status in the variety of life, and is only malign from the tree's or forester's point of view. The negotiation it performs with the beech, and with other individuals of its own kind, is more fairly seen as a complex dance of advance and retreat and territorial compromise. The fungus grows membranes of tissue between the woody cells of the tree, and attempts to expand along its water-conducting vessels. The tree responds by producing tannin and other fungus-repelling chemicals, and dark zones form in the marrow of the wood. The fungus argues back, building its own barriers of hard tissue as a defence against the tree's antibiotics. These make up some of the lines that edge the dark zones. More result when individual colonies of the fungus drift like fluids through the solid wood, come up against each other, and create mutually defensive barriers, often running in parallel. The tree becomes occupied by the fungus. If areas begin to rot, the tree attempts to isolate them. If the fungi are frustrated they probe other vessels and fault-lines. The end result isn't often a clear 'victory' for either side, but a kind of dynamic equilibrium, of which the interior of the trunk provides a cryptic fossil record. But the trunk was felled, stopping this process in its tracks, and the turner opened it up, revealing a three-dimensional chart of its history that is profoundly beautiful and meaningful to human eyes, but which has no visual function whatever for the participants.

I ponder my bowl endlessly, but can take no simple lesson from it. It's both a literal and metaphorical representation of the dialogue between pattern and process that is at the heart of all living systems. The cutting of the tree and the turning of the wood, like all acts of 'management', has frozen a natural process and unfolded a map of a single moment in its development. Yet there is another side to the story. Life proceeds by alternations between free-form evolution and periods of consolidation. Meandering cells join forces to become organised animals. The solitary mutation becomes the self-perpetuating species. One kind of tree becomes dominant and settled in a wood for centuries until soil and weather conditions no longer suit it and it's succeeded – if humans permit – by another species. What happens when the dynamic phase of this cycle is shut down indefinitely?

Given its inherent invisibility – buried deep in the interior of trunks – I never thought I would see spalting 'in the wild'. But in June 2014 a huge beech pollard in a wood on Berkhamsted Common that I'd known since I was a child was blown down, and on part of the newly prostrate trunk the bark had been ripped off, revealing a patch of bare wood covered with that characteristic mottle of hieroglyphs and enclosures. I'd paid my respects to the fallen veteran just a few days after its collapse, but wasn't sure if I'd found the right tree. The space it occupied had changed dramatically, not just because the beech was now cleaved down the middle and lying like two wooden cliffs on the forest floor, but because of the light, reflected off gashed wood and tree surfaces that hadn't seen the sun for a hundred years. Much of the arcane culture of the upper reaches of the tree had fallen into plain sight – birds' nests, the healed edges of ancient wounds, scores of old graffiti. One read 18.v.44. The characters were incised deeply enough to be Victorian, but I think this was 1944, when homesick US airmen were stationed nearby, and carved their memorials on the receptive bark of local beeches. And now I could get close, it was clear that though the *Usnea* fungus was responsible for the spalting, it wasn't the chief cause of the tree's demise. There were brackets of *Fomes fomentarius* along the trunk, as big as carthorse hooves. This is one of the most debilitating parasites of beech, turning the heartwood into something resembling crumbly cheese. In what is one of the least touched beech woods in Europe, the *réserve biologique* at Fontainebleau, its brackets mount the immensely tall and uncut trunks and crash to the ground like meteors as the trees decay. There is no management in this wood save the exclusion of the public.

The wood where the pollard had collapsed has a different history, and it helps make sense of what happened that June evening when a natural event echoed on a landscape scale the internal realignments in the spalted branches. There was an extensive open beech wood, a wood pasture, at Berkhamsted long before the Norman invasion. The local commoners put out pigs and lopped the trees for firewood. The invaders appropriated the entire area, put in their own pigs (Domesday lists it as 'wood for a thousand hogs') and in the mid-fourteenth century enclosed a large patch as a hunting park, to which they introduced a herd of fallow deer. Over the centuries that followed the wood, called 'Del Frith', shrank as patches were illegally enclosed and trees looted, first by the crown and then the Duchy of Cornwall. But it continued to be an assemblage of beech pollards in grazed heathland, a rich cultural landscape but biologically in a state of arrested development.

In 1866, the land-grabs reached a climax, when the landlord, the young Lord Brownlow, illegally enclosed 400 acres of the common, including Del Frith and its venerable pollards. The outcome was a historic moment in conservation. The recently formed Commons Preservation Society coordinated a brazen exercise in direct action which involved dismantling the three miles of iron fencing. They also sought a court injunction to prevent any further enclosures on the common, and clarification of what rights existed over it. The action dragged on for four years, confirmed grazing rights, and was a decisive step on the way to granting the public rights of 'air and exercise' on commonland.

But one ancient right for which no evidence was offered was 'estovers', the taking of the 'lop and top' of the trees. Perhaps the practice was already obsolete as a result of cheap coal. Whatever the reason, by the last quarter of the nineteenth century, pollarding had ceased in what was now called Frithsden Beeches. And a new destiny opened up for the wood. Without cutting, the beech branches grew thickly and elaborately, many progressing to the condition of secondary trunks. Large branches began to be shed, leaving rot-holes which sometimes became host to aerial tree-seedlings. Fungi, beetles, wood-nesting birds proliferated in the zones of dead wood. In places the high, outgrowing branches of adjacent trees fused, echoing the way the roots were linked by underground mycorrhizal fungi. By the last quarter of the twentieth century, the uncut pollards became increasingly top heavy and there were casualties in most major gales. As new light flooded in, natural succession was unlocked for the first time in centuries. Tree seedlings began to colonise the gaps – dense thickets of beech in places, but also birch and oak. Many were munched back by the descendants of the Normans' fallow deer, but a few always got away. By the late 1970s, Frithsden was an extraordinary, mercurial place. There were still large numbers of pollards, which were becoming increasingly gothic. Flared root buttresses, cankerous paunches, snags, bosses and burrs abounded. The volume of fallen and standing deadwood (or 'fallow wood' as the Rev Francis Kilvert usefully called it) was beginning to edge towards the 50 per cent that is the norm in the near-natural high forests of Eastern Europe. All kinds of natural cycles began to re-emerge – not just the replacement of pure beech wood by a tree population more varied in age and species, but the constant metamorphosis of live wood into humus. Over the course of a decade or so I was lucky to witness one particular tree go through this entire cycle. I called it the 'Praying Beech' from the way two branch stubs had fused like a pair of clasped hands. One summer it was split open by a lightning strike. Bees nested in the hollow gash. A while later it was toppled in a storm. For the next few years it was host to a legion of wood-decaying fungi, a kaleidoscope of coral spots, dead-men's fingers, porcelain tufts. Then, one autumn, I was caught in a ferocious rainstorm nearby, and watched the trunk start to liquefy in front of my eyes. I wrote down what I saw, conscious of being a privileged spectator at something wondrous: 'The rain was hammering drills of water at the already rotting trunk. Flakes of bark fell off, then threads of fungi and sooty dregs from the lightning-charred heartwood, and essence of beech dripped onto the woodland floor like the oil from an alchemist's still.'

It hardly needs saying that this theatre of transformation with its craggy wooden cast was not to everyone's taste. I once tagged along behind a party of foresters and landowners on a tour of the Beeches. They were outraged that what they called a collection of 'mutilated freaks' had been given living space for so long. The consensus was that they should be cleared away and replaced with proper, productive trees. This became a serious suggestion to the current owners, the National Trust, accompanied by dark hints about the dangers to the public of derelict trees. The Trust, well aware of the local public's affection for the beeches, warts and all, put up notices instead: 'These very old pollarded trees and associated deadwood in this area are being managed for their nature conservation and historic interest. They are liable to shed branches and the public is advised to keep to the waymarked rights of way.' In fact, beyond a little clearing of fallen branches from pathways, these notices were the limit of the Trust's 'management'. After the catastrophic mismanagement of woods across England following Great Storm of October 1987, non-intervention became Trust policy on wooded commons.

The epicentre of the whole wood was a tree known as the Queen Beech. It was an immense pollard, maybe 400 years old, with low-slung main branches that skirted the ground and gave the whole organism the air of a giant squid. It was the matriarch of the wood, and had such a low centre of gravity that I always imagined it indomitable. But this was the tree that split open in June 2014. And looking at the panorama of its levelling, it seems to me a still-life analogous to my spalted bowl, a snapshot of a moment in woodland evolution, evocative of past history and suggestive of possible futures. I find it hard to feel much sorrow for the fallen Queen, so *present* does it still seem to be. The surrounding trees show hollows in their crowns where they had been shaded out, which will become the templates for new growth. The great wedges of fallen wood, the spalted trunk, the graffiti, will endure for decades. Even the National Trust seems to view the change positively. It has put up another notice a short distance from the wreckage saying: 'This famous tree has entered the next stage of its existence', a sentiment that would have been unthinkable on public display even a decade previously. In the shadows I can make out burgeoning clumps of young birch, beech and holly around the dark hulks of earlier tree-falls. They show the irrelevance of deliberate planting here, and the likely future of this sunlit space. In front of them the Queen's roots are hard and rippled, and remind me of stromatolites, the compacted clumps of silt and cyanobacteria that were some of the first living communities to form on dry land more than three billion years ago. Below ground their symbiotic fungi will already be linked with the new trees, trading nutrients and information about soil conditions in what has been called 'the wood-wide-web'.

For a moment everything is perfectly poised. What should we do?

Green Man
OUT OF THE WOOD, 1989
by Peter Freeman

Peter Freeman's neon Green Man was included in an exhibition **Out of the Wood,**
*a collaboration between Common Ground and the Crafts Council which – through
glass, ceramics, sculpture, jewellery, wood-turning, photography, metalwork
and neon – explored the vitality of wood as a material and the historic cultural
relationship between craft and the natural world. The show opened at London's
South Bank in August 1989 and travelled to Barnsley, Middlesborough, Stoke
on Trent, Leicester, Birmingham, Derby, Kendal, Eastbourne and finally,
Aberystwyth, where it closed in 1991.*

Contributors

Simon Armitage is a poet, translator, playwright and novelist. His many works include *The Dead Sea Poems*, *Killing Time*, a version of *Sir Gawain and the Green Knight*, *Seeing Stars*, *Little Green Man*, *The Poetry of Birds*, *Walking Home* and *Walking Away*. In 2015, he was elected Oxford Professor of Poetry.

Will Ashon is a novelist, former music journalist and founder of the Big Dada, an imprint of Ninja Tune records.

Kathleen Basford (1916–1998) was a British botanist but was also known for her research into the cultural significance of the Green Man in the British Isles and around the world.

William Boyd is a writer whose short stories and novels include *A Good Man in Africa*, *An Ice Cream War*, *Any Human Heart* and *Restless*. His work has been adapted for stage and screen, and translated into over thirty languages.

Madeleine Bunting was for many years a columnist for the *Guardian*. Her books include *The Model Occupation*, *Willing Slaves*, *Love of the Country* and *The Plot: A Biography of an English Acre* which won the Portico Prize.

Sue Clifford is a writer and co-founder of Common Ground, which she directed with Angela King for thirty years. In 1994, she was awarded an MBE for services to the environment.

Jim Crumley writes mostly on the landscape and wildlife of Scotland. He has published many books, including *Nature's Architect*, *The Eagle's Way* and *The Last Wolf*. He is also a columnist and radio presenter.

Ellie Davis is a British landscape photographer whose work has focused on UK forests, particularly her native New Forest, examining the complex interrelationship between the landscape and the individual.

Tim Dee is the author of *Four Fields* and *The Running Sky*. He is writing a book about the spring and also *Landfill*, a book about people and gulls. He has worked as a BBC Radio producer for more than twenty-five years.

Helen Dunmore is the author of fourteen novels, including *Zennor in Darkness*, *A Spell of Winter*, which won the Orange Prize, and *The Siege*, which was shortlisted for both the Whitbread Novel of the Year and the Orange Prize. She is a Fellow of the Royal Society of Literature.

Paul Evans spent years as a gardener working in rose nurseries, graveyards, historic gardens in Wales and a botanical garden in New York. He is a writer, broadcaster and a playwright, best-known for his contributions to 'Country Diary' in the *Guardian* and his books *Herbaceous* and *Notes from the Edge*.

Alec Finlay is an artist, poet and publisher whose work crosses a range of media and forms. Much of his work reflects on our interaction with nature.

Alan Garner is a novelist whose many books include *Strandloper*, *Thursbitch*, *The Weirdstone of Brisingamen*, *Elidor*, *The Moon of Gomrath*, *The Owl Service* and *The Stone Book Quartet*, all of which are rooted in the landscape and folklore of his native county of Cheshire.

Andy Goldsworthy is a British sculptor, photographer and environmentalist producing site-specific sculpture and land art situated in natural and urban settings. He lives and works in Scotland.

Germaine Greer is the author of *The Female Eunuch*, which took the world by storm in 1969 and remains one of the most influential texts of the feminist movement. She has also had a distinguished academic career in Britain and the USA, and since 2001 she has been rehabilitating 60 hectares of subtropical rainforest in Queensland as founder of Friends of Gondwana Rainforest.

Jay Griffiths is author of *Pip Pip: A Sideways Look at Time*, *Wild: An Elemental Journey*, *Kith*, *A Love Letter from a Stray Moon* and *Tristimania*.

Jen Hadfield is a poet whose collections include *Byssus*, *Almanacs* and *Nigh-No-Place*, which was shortlisted for the Forward Poetry Prize and was winner of the 2008 T.S. Eliot Prize. Her work is inspired by Shetland, where she lives.

Gabriel Hemery is a forest scientist and author of *The New Sylva*. He is a fellow of the Institute of Chartered Foresters and a co-founder of the Sylva Foundation, a charity working to revive Britain's wood culture.

Philip Hoare is author of several works of non-fiction, including *Spike Island*, *Lost Eden*, *The Sea Inside* and *Leviathan*, which won the Baillie Gifford Prize (formerly known as the Samuel Johnson) for non-fiction.

Kathleen Jamie is a poet, essayist and travel writer. She became Professor of Creative Writing at the University of Stirling in 2011. Over the last decade, while raising her family, she has worked on shorter non-fiction and poetry, and has published two books of essays: *Findings* and *Sightlines*.

Tobias Jones is the author of *A Place of Refuge* and the co-founder of Windsor Hill Wood.

Jackie Kay was born in Edinburgh and grew up in Glasgow. She is a multi-award winning poet and novelist who was appointed MBE in 2006 and made a Fellow of the Royal Society of Literature in 2002. She was named the new Makar, National Poet for Scotland, in 2016.

Paul Kingsnorth is a novelist, environmentalist and co-founder of the Dark Mountain Project. His books include *Real England, The Wake* and *Beast.*

Zaffar Kunial was born in Birmingham and lives in Hebden Bridge. His debut pamphlet, 'Hill Speak', was published by Faber & Faber in 2014.

Simon Leatherdale worked for the Forestry Commission in the ancient woods of the east of England, most recently in the Sandlings. Now retired, he works his own small, ancient wood near where he lives with his wife Mary in Suffolk.

Nina Lyon is the author of *Uprooted: On the trail of the Green Man* and helps run the HowTheLightGetsIn philosophy festival in Hay-on-Wye.

Seán Lysaght was born in 1957 and grew up in Limerick. His poetry collections include *Noah's Irish Ark, The Clare Island Survey, Scarecrow* and *Carnival Masks.*

Richard Mabey has written some forty books, including *Food for Free*, the groundbreaking *Flora Britannica* and *The Unofficial Countryside, Beechcombings, The Cabaret of Plants*, and his memoir, *Nature Cure*. He is an Honorary Trustee of Common Ground, Vice-President of the Open Spaces Society and Fellow of the Royal Society of Literature.

Sara Maitland is the author of numerous works of fiction, including the Somerset Maugham Award-winning *Daughters of Jerusalem* and several non-fiction books, including *Gossip from the Forest* and *The Book of Silence.*

Peter Marren is a wildlife writer, journalist and authority on invertebrate folklore and names. His books include *Rainbow Dust, The New Naturalists*, which won the Society for the History of Natural History's Thackray Medal, *Britain's Rare Flowers* and *Bugs Britannica*, for which he was awarded a Leverhulme Research Fellowship.

Philip Marsden is the author of a number of award-winning books including *The Bronski House, The Crossing Place, The Levelling Sea* and *Rising Ground*. His work has been translated into fifteen languages and he is a Fellow of the Royal Society of Literature.

David Nash is a sculptor and draughtsman, well-known around the world for his land-based works, especially in wood.

George Peterken is a Londoner whose interest in wildlife and landscape was stimulated by childhood holidays in the New Forest. He specialised in woodland ecology and conservation for the Nature Conservancy and its various successor bodies. Since 1992 he has worked independently for the Forestry Commission and others while living in the Lower Wye Valley. He is president of the Gwent Wildlife Trust and an associate professor of Nottingham University. He was awarded an OBE for services to forestry in 1994.

James Ravilious (1939–1990) was a photographer of rural life in Devon and the west of England, contributing work to the Beaford Archive, intended as a photographic record of life in a largely unspoilt but vulnerable rural area.

Fiona Reynolds became the first female Master of Emmanuel College, Cambridge, in 2012. She has been Director-General of the National Trust, Director of the Women's Unit in the Cabinet Office and Director of the Council for the Protection of Rural England (now Campaign to Protect Rural England), and the Secretary to the Council for National Parks.

Neil Sinden is based at Ruskin Land, the Wyre Forest, working with the Wyre Community Land Trust to restore and promote the cultural landscape. He is a trustee of Civic Voice, the umbrella group for local civic societies, and was Director of Policy and Campaigns at the CPRE until September 2015.

Richard Skelton is a musician and artist from Lancashire. Over the past decade he has produced a diverse body of work, including films, exhibitions, pamphlets, books and albums of music. All his work is informed by landscape.

Ali Smith was born in Inverness and lives in Cambridge. Her recent books include *There But For The*, winner of the Hawthornden Prize, *Artful*, winner of the Foyles / Bristol Festival of Ideas Best Book, and *Autumn*.

Fiona Stafford is a Professor of English Language and Literature at the University of Oxford. She recently broadcast *The Meaning of Trees* on BBC Radio 3, on which her book *The Long, Long Life of Trees* is based.

Piers Taylor has designed a number of seminal buildings, including the RIBA Award Winning 'Room 13'. He has founded two architectural practices and is a former Design Fellow at the University of Cambridge and a Studio Master at London's Architectural Association.

Adam Thorpe has published collections of poetry, short stories, an acclaimed memoir, *On Silbury Hill*, and ten novels including *Ulverton*, considered a modern classic. He lives in France with his family and teaches at the Ecole Supérieure des Beaux Arts de Nîmes and at the University of Nîmes.

Robin Walter began his work with trees by picking up sticks for a tree surgeon. He has since worked as an arboricultural climber in London, 'on the saws' in Dorset and as a woodland officer for the Woodland Trust. Since 2010 he has been working independently as a forester.

Deb Wilenski is an early childhood education consultant and writer with an interest in landscape, language and the imagination.

Evie Wyld was born in London and grew up in Australia and south London. Her first novel, *After the Fire, a Still Small Voice*, won the John Llewellyn Rhys Prize and a Betty Trask Award. In 2013, she was included on the *Granta* Best of Young British Novelists list.

50 Trees
WATERLOO BRIDGE, 1989
by Martin Mayer

Common Ground is an arts and environmental charity working both locally and nationally to seek new, imaginative ways to engage people with their local environment and celebrate the intimate connections communities have with the wildlife and landscape that surrounds them. A catalyst for change, not a pressure group or membership organisation, the charity is open to collaborations and always needs help spreading ideas. Get in touch if you would like to be involved with a project or have something to say about the land, wildlife, history or culture of your area.

Common Ground fundraises independently to enable collaborators and to commission new work, but relies on sales from its website and donations to its Seed Bank to develop projects and cover daily costs. Please do explore its website **commonground.org.uk** *and support current and future work in whatever way you can.*

Little Toller Books

We publish old and new writing attuned to nature and the landscape, working with a wide range of the very best writers and artists. We pride ourselves on publishing affordable books of the highest quality. If you have enjoyed this book, you will also like exploring our other titles.

Field Notes

MY HOME IS THE SKY: THE LIFE OF J.A. BAKER *Hetty Saunders*
DEER ISLAND *Neil Ansell*
ORISON FOR A CURLEW *Horatio Clare*
LOVE, MADNESS, FISHING *Dexter Petley*
WATER AND SKY *Neil Sentance*
THE TREE *John Fowles*

Monographs

HERBACEOUS *Paul Evans*
ON SILBURY HILL *Adam Thorpe*
SEA SOUNDS *Cheryl Tipp*
THE ASH TREE *Oliver Rackham*
MERMAIDS *Sophia Kingshill*
BLACK APPLES OF GOWER *Iain Sinclair*
BEYOND THE FELL WALL *Richard Skelton*
LIMESTONE COUNTRY *Fiona Sampson*
HAVERGEY *John Burnside*
SNOW *Marcus Sedgwick*
LANDFILL *Tim Dee*

Nature Classics Library

THROUGH THE WOODS *H.E. Bates*
MEN AND THE FIELDS *Adrian Bell*
THE MIRROR OF THE SEA *Joseph Conrad*
ISLAND YEARS, ISLAND FARM *Frank Fraser Darling*
THE MAKING OF THE ENGLISH LANDSCAPE *W.G. Hoskins*
BROTHER TO THE OX *Fred Kitchen*
FOUR HEDGES *Clare Leighton*
DREAM ISLAND *R.M. Lockley*
THE UNOFFICIAL COUNTRYSIDE *Richard Mabey*
RING OF BRIGHT WATER *Gavin Maxwell*
EARTH MEMORIES *Llewelyn Powys*
IN PURSUIT OF SPRING *Edward Thomas*
THE NATURAL HISTORY OF SELBORNE *Gilbert White*

A postcard sent to Little Toller will ensure you are put on our mailing list and be among the first to discover our latest publications. You can also subscribe online at **littletoller.co.uk** where we publish new writing, short films and much more.

LITTLE TOLLER BOOKS
Lower Dairy, Toller Fratrum, Dorset DT2 0EL
W. littletoller.co.uk **E.** books@littletoller.co.uk